Still More Adventures

Still More Adventures

by Robert F. Marx

 MASON / CHARTER   NEW YORK 1976

Library of Congress Cataloging in Publication Data

Marx, Robert F   1933–
   Still more adventures.

   Includes index.
   1. Treasure-trove. I. Title.
G530.M352   910'.453   76–25126
ISBN 0–88405–359–8

For my good friend, Wilson A. Knott

Contents

Still More Adventures

Introduction
Background for Adventure

For me, adventure is a way of life and I wouldn't change it for anything in this world. Risk and chance are words which excite and challenge me. My restless, lifelong search for new adventures no doubt grew out of the circumstances of my childhood. I was born in Pittsburgh, Pennsylvania on December 8, 1935, the oldest of three children. My father, an Austrian immigrant, was a truck driver, and my mother was of Yugoslav parentage.

Like many Europeans, my father was fascinated by stories of buried treasure. As far back as I can remember, he used to spin fanciful tales about vast hoards of gold and fabulous treasures that were hidden all over the world. These tales sank deep into my young mind and I was certain that one day I would search for and find numerous treasures. After learning to swim at an early age, I used to dive with goggles in the murky lakes and rivers near my home. Probing through the mud and twisted branches of long-dead trees that lay strewn along the bottom, it was easy to imagine the faint outlines of a twisted hulk and to probe deeper, deeper, deeper into the strong room of a treasure galleon. From the age of six I was reading everything concerning sunken and buried treasure that I could get my hands on.

My parents were divorced when I was eight, and about this time I developed an insatiable curiosity about the outside world. I would disappear from home for weeks, wandering alone and penniless to points seven or eight hundred miles away. Once at the age of nine, I rode my bicycle all the way from Pittsburgh to Chicago. When I returned from these unauthorized expeditions, I was a hero among the neighborhood kids. My mother, relieved to see me again, would smother me with affection. Then, in a few weeks, I would be off again. So unusual was my wanderlust that legions of teachers, child psychologists, and priests were called in to curb it. Pittsburgh was the end of the world as far as I was concerned, especially since it was so far from the sea where I knew my destiny lay.

Finally, at the age of 13, I left home for good. Hitchhiking until I reached Atlantic City, New Jersey, I established a temporary home beneath a pier on the beach until a deep-sea diver named Joe Novak found me and took me in. I started my career as a boat hand on Novak's salvage vessel. As I watched him go down and come up in his hard-hat rig, working on pier pilings and other mundane underwater projects, I was thrilled beyond words—and I vividly recalled my father's tales of sunken treasure. After much begging on my part, Novak relunctantly taught me how to dive. It was an experience so absorbing that I was convinced that my future was inextricably intertwined with the sea and the unknown treasures and adventures it held.

Soon I became restless and moved on. I went first to Bridgeport, Connecticut where, because I looked the 18 I claimed to be, I was able to obtain employment as a hard-hat diver with a small salvage firm. Then I headed west to Los Angeles to live with a great-aunt. I reentered school and managed to graduate from Hollywood High School, although it was not school but the sea that held me in its grip. I spent every possible moment on and beneath it.

Within a few days of reaching California I made contact with some divers in the Los Angeles area and sampled the sport of skin diving. What a contrast! With fins I could reach the bottom twice as fast and with half the effort. Face masks in those days were primitive things made of hard rubber which had to be sandpapered down to fit the contours of one's face, and snorkels were usually nothing more than a length of garden hose. But primitive or not, both these pieces of equipment made a tremendous difference: one could dive deeper, see better, and never really have to surface completely. Soon I was initiated into the use of the recently developed Cousteau-Gagnan "aqualung," or SCUBA gear, which made the complicated helmet rig Joe Novak had taught me to use seem prehistoric by comparison. A whole new world now waited for me to explore it.

I feel almost antiquated when I think how far skin diving has come since those days. The skin-diving club I joined, the Los Angeles Neptunes, was one of the few in the world and the second one to be formed in the United States. Most of the members were men in their forties who had pioneered the sport in the late 1930s and 1940s, inventing or developing much of the equipment in use today. Skin divers were such a rare breed when I started diving that people would gather on the shore as we came out of the water in our weird equipment, half expecting one of us to say, "Take me to your leader."

Most of my early dives were devoted to exploring and spearfishing, but I soon discovered that diving was a good means of supporting myself as well. On weekends I could average between $50 and $100 a day merely by recovering lost outboards, anchors, fishing tackle, and even golf balls. This led to bigger and better jobs such as collecting marine specimens for universities and government agencies, and underwater photography which was a new and highly profitable field.

It was on one of my first underwater photography assignments that I had my first brush with death. I was diving from a rocky stretch of coast near the Palos Verdes cliffs, taking still photographs of some small fish, when I spotted a group of sea lions playing around some nearby rocks. As I approached, they suddenly started to screech and swim around frantically, some trying to scramble onto the offshore rocks and others trying to reach shore. At first I thought they were afraid of *me,* but then I saw the real cause of their panic (a sight I'll never forget): four killer whales, each about 20 feet long, among the most deadly creatures in the sea, as vicious and powerful as the Great White Shark, but much more intelligent, since they are mammals. I was, if possible, more panic-stricken than the sea lions. I didn't even try to swim to safety, not that I could have outdistanced those monsters anyway. I just froze, sinking like a stone to the seafloor about 30 feet down. This was probably my salvation (luckily I had plenty of air left in my tank), for, as I looked up, the killer whales closed in, expertly cutting off their victims' line of retreat to the shore. Seconds later the surface was a churning cauldron of blood. Smaller sea lions were cut in half with one crunch from those massive jaws, while the larger ones, some weighing up to 500 pounds, were finished off in three or four bites. In two minutes there was nothing left of the twenty-odd sea lions but gory bits and pieces that filtered down on top of me. Fearing that the killer whales might notice the tidbits they had missed—and me in the bargain—I quickly set out for shore, hugging the bottom like a snake. I was so rattled by the horrifying scene I had just witnessed that I left my underwater camera and case, which had taken me a month to build, on the bottom and was never able to locate it again.

Never far from my thoughts were my father's tales of lost treasures. I devoured every book, magazine article, and pamplet written on the subject, taking notes assiduously, until my records filled over 11 footlockers. I never seemed to tire of collecting these records or probing deeper and deeper for facts, these being difficult to sort out of all the fanciful fiction masquerading as fact which has been published about sunken treasure. I wrote to the authors and established correspondence with a worldwide network of those interested in this somewhat singular subject. Since stories of sunken treasure stretch from remote antiquity to the present, I inevitably became a history buff and something of an expert on ships, sailing routes, and related subjects. After graduating from high school I enrolled in day courses at Los Angeles City College and night courses at UCLA, majoring in the earth sciences, with my interest focused on history and archaeology.

During the Korean War I joined the U.S. Marine Corps and after boot camp was assigned to the Marine Corps base at Camp Lejeune, North Carolina where I was in charge of salvage operations. This improbable place turned out to be a treasure hunter's paradise. Only a stone's throw away was treacherous Cape Hatteras, known to seamen as the "graveyard of the Atlantic." No one can say with certainty how many hulks lie scattered in this area—the estimates range from 600 to 3,000. The notes in my footlocker, which I had shipped from California, indicated such wrecks as Spanish galleons, German submarines, copper-laden Victory ships, and sailing vessels with rich cargoes of gold dust inbound from California via Panama.

During my year at Camp Lejeune, I probably spent more time chasing after old shipwrecks than actually working for the Marine Corps. I was then transferred to Vieques Island, located between Puerto Rico and the Virgin Islands, to run a diving school. Between classes, I usually had several weeks of spare time. I made good use of them by visiting many of the other Caribbean islands in search of sunken and buried treasures. My three-year stint in the Marines temporarily satisfied my wanderlust; I managed to see a great deal of the world: Hawaii, Wake, Guam, Okinawa, Japan, Korea, Greenland, Iceland, most of the countries touching on the Mediterranean, and the greater part of the Caribbean.

While in the Marines I had completed a number of correspondence courses from the universities of Maryland and Illinois. Combined with the college credits I already had from UCLA and Los Angeles City College, these brought me within one semester of a bachelor's degree. So I resumed my studies at UCLA but found it very hard going. Sometimes I had the feeling that I knew more about the subjects I was taking than the professors teaching them and that the best way to learn was out in the field, supplemented with research in libraries, and not in a stuffy classroom. I never finished the semester. At this time I was keenly interested in the ancient Mayan civilization of Yucatán and Central America, and I learned that a small movie-production unit was going to Mexico's Yucatán peninsula to film the ancient, majestic pyramids and temples of the Maya. I couldn't resist the lure and joined them, offering to work in exchange for my transportation, lodging, and food.

As it turned out, I spent three fascinating years in the undeveloped Yucatán. The whole time was an extended adventure, sometimes rough but never boring. When the movie was completed, the production team returned to the States, but I stayed on to explore the ruins that dotted the land. I trekked into the dense jungles, staying a couple of weeks at a time. I descended into the sacrificial wells, recovering many Mayan artifacts, and even hunted jaguar and wild boar in the dense jungles of Quintana Roo.

In time I settled on the island of Cozumel, which in 1956 was an out-of-the-way paradise. I helped a local entrepreneur start the island's first tourist hotel and operated a fishing business. The people were simpatico, the island lovely, and the water as clear as gin, and the beautiful fish on the coral reefs were large, plentiful, and unhunted. Most of my daylight hours were spent underwater on the magnificent, multicolored reefs surrounding the island. At night I talked to the local fishermen, who often knew the locations of wrecks. This research led me to a half-dozen ancient hulks which lay on the nearby reefs. The wreck that fascinated me most was a large vessel with some twenty iron cannon which lay on a dangerous reef off the Yucatán mainland opposite Cozumel. Local legend had the wreck filled with an immense treasure in gold and jewels. With several American friends, I mounted three well-planned expeditions to the wreck, and we brought up thousands of artifacts but very little treasure, only a gold pocket watch, several pieces of jewelry, and a few coins.

For over three years I worked hard to determine the origin of the mysterious ship. I had many clues, but none of them was definite. In time the identification of this wreck became an obsession. I gave up my life and work on the island and moved to Washington, D.C., to be close to the libraries there, as well as the National Archives, where I labored feverishly for three months. A final crucial piece completed the puzzle. The ship was a Spanish merchantman, *El Matanzero,* which sank in 1741 while sailing from Spain to Veracruz, Mexico.

The adventure with that wreck made me a confirmed treasure-hunter. In the next year I explored every island in the Caribbean, noting the locations of the wrecks I found and recording local legends of lost treasures. My purpose in this grand exploration was simple: to find the most likely treasure wreck and settle near it until I had worked it clean. From the secondary sources I had researched, I selected a hundred sunken ships as the targets I would hit during this expedition. Of these, I managed to locate only two, and neither yielded anything of interest. This was not surprising. I was to learn later, in the course of intensive research in various European archives and libraries, that almost every one of the hundred wrecks was merely the imaginative figment of a romantic author. However, the time spent roaming those sunstruck islands was worth it: I had located more than 75 other shipwrecks and gained a great deal of knowledge and experience.

Back in Washington, I took stock. Pursuing my career as a treasure hunter meant having access to reliable information, and the only way to get that was to do research myself from primary sources. Most of the documents relating to Spanish galleons are housed in the great palace of the Archivo de las Indias in Seville. The archives contain more than 14 million handwritten documents of the Spanish colonial period.

Spain, then, was the logical place to go. I spoke and read contemporary Spanish, but the documents were written in the archaic Spanish of the sixteenth and seventeenth centuries. To prepare myself for the challenge of research in the Seville archives, I holed up in a lonely cabin in the Canadian wilderness for several months. I studied old Spanish as if my life depended on it, with a bit of time off for diving in the icy lakes and some romps with curious bears. I emerged from the woods bearded and scrawny but able to decipher old Spanish, something experts had warned me would take a couple of years.

My days in Seville, in that treasure house of galleon history, were enchanted. I was transported back in time, living in a world not many men have thought about and fewer still have studied. I pored over hundreds and hundreds of first-person accounts of transatlantic voyages by passengers, seamen, soldiers, captains, and admirals of the treasure fleets, written in fading, elaborate cursive on crumbling parchment. My mind boggled at the millions and millions of dollars in gold and silver that came from the mines in the New World to Spain. There was enough precise information on wrecks to keep a dozen historians working for a lifetime. It was all there in infinite detail, but one had only to be careful not to drown, as many historians have, in the sea of documents. Occasionally on weekends, when my mind was saturated and numb, I drove to the seacoasts of Spain and Portugal to dive on sunken ships and ancient, drowned cities. I kept up this frantic pace for two long years. Then, feeling confident and much wiser than the eager, naive lad who had first climbed the great marble stairway to the hushed, dim archives, I knew it was time for a great adventure.

While in Seville, I had conceived the idea of building a replica of a Spanish galleon and sailing her to America along the same routes the Spaniards plied during the sixteenth, seventeenth, and eighteenth centuries. Investigating the possibility of constructing such a vessel, I learned that a Spaniard named Carlos Etayo was building a replica of the *Niña,* the smallest of the three ships used by Columbus on his first voyage of discovery to the New World. Etayo had planned to sail her only around the coasts of Spain, but without much trouble I convinced him to trace the route Columbus took in 1492. To gain the maximum value out of such a voyage, we decided to do it as authentically as possible. This meant eating the same kind of food and wearing the same kind of clothes, using the same type of primitive navigation equipment and gear, and sailing with no lifesaving equipment. Our only concession to modernity was carrying still and motion picture photographic equipment.

After months of preparation we set sail on what turned out to be a five-month-long voyage. We had a crew of nine, with Etayo as captain and myself as navigator. The first leg of the voyage was from Pasajes, a port on the northern coast of Spain, to the southern port of Palos. The second leg took us to the Canary Islands, and the final one carried the tiny ship across the Atlantic to San Salvador in the Bahamas where we finally arrived on Christmas Day 1962.

The voyage was the greatest adventure of my life, despite the dangers and hardships we faced throughout most of it. All of the food and water spoiled rapidly, we suffered constantly from hunger and thirst, and we fought through countless frightening storms, including three hurricanes. The voyage received worldwide publicity. The Spaniards in the crew became national heros in Spain, and Etayo and I were made Knight Commanders in the Order of Isabella the Catholic by the Spanish government.

The complete story of this fascinating voyage is covered in my book, *The Voyage of the Niña II*, published by the World Publishing Company in 1963. Another of my books—*Always Another Adventure,* published by World in 1967—covers many of my adventures up until the period of the *Niña II* voyage in 1962. This book takes up where *Always Another Adventure* ended.

1: Operation Save-the-World

I had been off the *Niña II* barely long enough to get my land legs when I was embarking on a new venture, one that was as far removed from the fifteenth-century world of the *Niña II* as the launching of a space-ship to Mars.

I had actually been planning another project even further back in history than Columbus. Far from being fed up with primitive sailing conditions, I decided to build a replica of a Phoenician or Greek ship and sail to America and back to test my theory of pre-Columbian voyages. But one evening after stepping ashore on San Salvador, as I was explaining these plans to Clay Blair, the conversation somehow switched to Cuba, Castro, Communism, and other related topics. I had for years been messing around the Yucatán jungle, diving off some Caribbean island or burying myself in the archives, besides not being particularly interested in politics or international affairs anyway, and knew next to nothing about what was going on in the world. I wasn't even sure exactly what the Cuban missile crisis of October 1962 was all about, since I had been aboard the *Niña II* the whole time.

Clay, as editor-in-chief of the *Saturday Evening Post* and a longtime journalist, naturally was better informed about current events and, like many people at the time, was very concerned about the danger pre-sented to the United States and the Latin American republics by the activities of the Castro regime in Cuba. Shocked to discover my igno-rance of these matters, he kept me up all night trying to bring me up-to-date on Castroite subversion in Venezuela, Russian missiles in Cuba, and other aspects of the "Cuban situation."

Just when I thought he had talked himself out and I could get back to planning my next voyage, Clay exclaimed: "You probably think I'm exaggerating some of these things. Well, I'm going to give you a chance to see for yourself how screwed up things are." A few days earlier, he explained, one of the directors of the Curtis Publishing Company had phoned to say that a close friend of his, an American businessman living in Mexico City, could provide the *Post* with a lot of secret information about Castro and Communism in Latin America. The director vouched for the man, assuring Clay that he had already cooperated closely with U.S. intelligence agencies, so Clay had contacted him. The man was to arrive the next day, which by that time was already "today," and Clay wanted me to sit in on the conversation.

The conversation—or more accurately, monologue—took place in Clay's midtown Manhattan office. Clay and I sat in amazement while our guest—we shall call him Robert Brenan—poured out a stream of information, pausing occasionally to light one cigarette from the end of another. Of all the information he gave us, two items particularly interested Clay as potential material for the *Post.* The first was that Castro's 26th of July movement to overthrow Batista had from the beginning been masterminded and financed from Moscow solely for the purpose of gaining a fortified base close to the U.S.; the second was that hundreds of Russian medium- and long-range intercontinental ballistic missiles remained behind in Cuba, hidden in caves. Now, neither of these two allegations was novel in itself. A number of people had already voiced suspicions about Castro's early Communist affiliations, as well as his reluctance to permit a United Nations inspection team to enter Cuba and verify that all the missiles had, in fact, been removed. What fired Clay's interest was Brenan's claim that he could obtain irrefutable proof of both allegations. He said that he would be leaving that same day for Europe but would return in a few weeks, bringing a man who could enter Cuba freely, who was on friendly terms with high-ranking Cuban officials, including Castro himself, and who could travel all over the country and take photographs of the missiles. The question of proving Russian aid to Castro in his overthrow of Batista would be even easier, he said, since the work could be done right in Mexico where Castro had set up his revolutionary headquarters and trained his guerrilla forces before going to Cuba, and Brenan suggested that Clay assign a good bilingual reporter to work in Mexico under Brenan's direction.

Up to then we had simply listened. Then Clay, like a good reporter, started to probe for cracks in Brenan's story. How did he know so much about Castro's early activities? Brenan claimed he had known him in Mexico. Pulling out some photographs showing himself arm in arm with Fidel, Raul Castro, and Che Guevara, among others, he hastily added: "That was before, when I thought they were good guys." Asked why he had not contacted the United States government, he said he had offered his help to the State Department on several occasions, both through the U.S. embassy in Mexico City and on a personal trip to Washington, but they had refused it, either because they knew the missiles were there themselves or because they could do nothing about it. Finally Clay asked just why Brennan was offering his help to the *Saturday Evening Post.* "Because I'm a patriotic gringo like you," Brenan answered. "And besides, I know I'll be well paid for my efforts."

After Brenan left, Clay and I spent several hours discussing his story. It might be pure fiction—all of the missiles might have been removed —but then again, they might still be there, concealed from any aerial photographs, as Brenan had alleged. Clay and I had to agree that it was worth trying to find out. Then Clay said: "Bob, you are the only guy I can think of that I can depend on to handle this. I would do it myself, but I'm running five magazines, one of which is close to folding, and, besides, I don't speak Spanish."

I argued with him for awhile, protesting that my plans for a pre-Columbian voyage were already underway, that spy stuff wasn't in my line, that almost anyone else would be better qualified for the job. In short, I used every kind of argument I could think of. But in the end, as so often happens in any debate with Clay, he convinced me. First he reminded me that it wasn't members of the CIA or any other U.S. intelligence agency who had discovered that the missiles were in Cuba in the first place, but a group of exiled Cuban university students instead. Then, getting into high gear, he spoke of the invaluable service I would be performing for world peace and national security, not to mention the *Saturday Evening Post* which, at that point, was in serious financial difficulties. The upshot of it was that I was named "Adventure Editor" of the *Post* as a cover and went to work immediately.

After about a week on a crash program, reading every article and book I could find on Castro, Cuba, and Latin American politics in general, I went to Washington to see an ex-girl friend of mine who conveniently happened to work in the Latin American section of the State Department. Officially, of course, she was no help but unofficially, after spending the first evening calling me every bad name she could think of for jilting her a few years back, she provided me with a wealth of information. She herself couldn't say one way or the other if she thought there were still missiles in Cuba, but she did say that reports reached the State Department daily— from the anti-Castro underground, Cuban exiles in Miami, and the foreign diplomatic corps in Havana, among many sources—indicating that there *were* missiles in Cuba still and that more were arriving every month by both submarine and freighter. And she produced a big file on Brenan, containing quite a lot of interesting data. For one thing, he had been a friend not only of the Castro brothers, but of the Cuban dictator, Batista. In 1958, when Castro and his *barbudos* were holed up in the Camagüey mountains, Brenan had acted as an intermediary, offering Castro $10 million from Batista if he would call off his revolution and get out of Cuba. Castro refused the bribe. Brenan had consistently put himself on record as an ardent anti-Communist, even going so far as to appear before a Senate subcommittee in the early 1950s to denounce a number of people in the State Department as active Communists. Whether he was right or not, some of those he denounced were either forced to retire or were fired soon afterwards. In addition, at the time I was investigating him, Brenan was publishing a strongly anti-Communist, Spanish-language newspaper that was being circulated throughout Latin America. He was either overzealous or unscrupulous, however, for he constantly denounced people who never had been or who were no longer Communists. The person who seemed to receive the worst treatment in Brenan's paper was Romulo Betancourt, then president of Venezuela. I suspect in this case, at least, that there were personal motives, for Brenan claimed to me sometime later that Betancourt had welched on some business deals with him and had had him thrown out of Venezuela. Whatever the truth of these allegations, Brenan certainly bore the man a grudge.

From Washington I moved on to Miami where I made contact with many Cuban exile leaders who knew Brenan. Although most of them labeled him as either a "crackpot" or a "crook" or both, they all agreed that there were still many Russian ICBMs with nuclear warheads in Cuba, as well as secret submarine bases. I was skeptical about everything that was told me (something that infuriates me when I'm on the receiving end, but Clay had been working hard to try to turn me into a good reporter), so everyone did his utmost to provide what evidence was available. I had interviews with more than twenty exiles who had recently escaped from Cuba, and all had either seen missiles themselves or had someone in their immediate families who had. Three of the men had actually worked as laborers in constructing subterranean silos for missiles. As further proof, the exiles produced six American skin divers (two of whom I knew personally) who had been shipwrecked off Cuba on their way to Haiti for a treasure hunt two months before and had been held in a Cuban prison until sent back to the U.S. All of them claimed they had also seen missiles, but I am sure that if they saw any missiles at all, they were only the ground-to-air types everyone knew were there anyway. Castro himself had admitted downing an American U-2 plane with a missile and had threatened to do so again if there were any more reconnaissance flights.

Brenan arrived back in New York on February 10, bringing the man he had assured us could get into Cuba and obtain authentic photographs of missiles. The man, who called himself Bermúdez, claimed to be the representative for Mexico and Central America of the Italian weapons firm of Beretta. He produced letterheads, business cards, and a stack of catalogues, showing everything from small pistols to machine guns as proof. Like Brenan, he had a series of snapshots (although they were supposedly more recent) of himself and the Castro brothers. His frequent trips to Cuba, he explained, were to negotiate the sale of vast amounts of weapons his firm was exporting to Cuba, mainly for reshipment to Castro-supported guerrillas in other Latin American countries. Bermúdez, like Brenan, professed violent anti-Communist sympathies, but, of course, he too would need a great deal of money for his help, since both of them planned to "disappear" afterwards to some unspecified country until the heat was off.

Clay agreed to pay him $50,000 plus expenses for a group of photographs showing the missiles concealed in Cuban caves and a detailed report containing the necessary background information for the article that would accompany the photographs. To insure that the photographs had been taken recently, Clay gave Bermúdez a copy of that day's *New York Times* which had to appear in some of the photos as part of the deal.

Brenan, if anything, was even more interested in his idea that the Cuban revolution had been a "Kremlin plot" from the beginning (his main obsession seemed to be that the U.S. State Department and the CIA were either incompetent, subversives, or both; by showing that the U.S. had indirectly supported what was in reality a Communist revolution, he hoped to prove it), and since our previous conference he had come up with another allegation: that Mexico was about to be taken over and turned into another Cuba by Communists within the government itself. Claiming to be a member of the Mexican Secret Police (which we later verified, as well as finding out that Brenan held five different passports, among them Mexico's), he said he had made contact with several high-ranking members who were willing to turn over hundreds of highly secret documents to verify both of these allegations. His plan was for me to go to Mexico and work with him in amassing the data.

Bermúdez was supplied with photographic equipment and a $10,000 advance on expenses, which he insisted he would need in Havana to throw parties for the Castro brothers and other officials. Then he and Brenan flew to Mexico the next day. I was to follow as soon as Bermúdez had left for Havana, so that he would in no way be associated with me.

While waiting for the coded telegram from Brenan reporting Bermúdez's departure, I decided to make further investigations on my own into the missile subject and flew to Miami again. This time I went directly to Dr. José Miro Cardona, president of the Cuban Revolutionary Council and the spokesman for the thousands of Cuban exiles in the United States. He showed little surprise when I explained my mission, merely stating that since his organization was subsidized by the State Department at the time, he and his people were being forced to hush-hush the missile business; but he had been wondering how long it would take before someone had the courage to open the eyes of the American public and force the government to take action. He explained that he had made many trips to Washington to pass on the intelligence reports on missile activity in Cuba, which his organization received almost daily from the Cuban underground, giving the reports primarily to a number of senators since no one in the Administration seemed interested. Then his face got red with anger and he went on to tell how only the week before, during his most recent trip to Washington, he had been notified by a top official in the State Department that if he or any member of his organization gave further information on the missile question to those senators or anyone else, the large annual subsidy the Revolutionary Council received would be cut off. He went on for an hour, wondering loudly how the U.S. government could possibly be so blind to its own interests. Then he finally lowered his voice and said: "However, Mr. Marx, if that is really your name and you really work for the *Saturday Evening Post,* I will take a chance and help you anyway."

He turned me over to one of his trusted assistants, whom we shall call Hector. Hector, who was a graduate of Harvard University, was without doubt one of the most brilliant Cuban exiles I was ever to meet in Miami. Ever since the spring of 1962, when the Miami-based Cuban Student Directorate, with which he was also associated, had announced the presence of Russian missiles in Cuba, Hector had devoted all his energy to proving this report. Then, when reports started arriving that the Russians had not, in fact, removed all the missiles, he continued his intelligence work with even greater zeal. He too had made countless trips to Washington, all of which ended the same way as Dr. Cardona's —with some State Department official saying, "Interesting, but we don't think it's true."

I had barely finished introducing myself to Hector when he pulled a cord drawing away a set of drapes I thought had been covering some windows; instead there was a huge map of Cuba that spread across the entire wall. Like a geography teacher with me as a pupil, he took a long pointer and systematically covered every square mile of the island. He showed me the locations of 24 underground ICBM sites, two underground submarine sites, 15 caves serving as secret hangers for Russian-built MIG fighter planes, and a large number of subterranean supply depots.

For the next 10 days I worked almost around the clock with Hector, stopping only every so often to catch a few hours sleep or grab a bite to eat. He allowed me complete access to his vast files on the missile question, which showed beyond doubt that he had established the authenticity of everything on his map of Cuba, not by one fragmentary piece of information from some Cuban who had fled his homeland and reached Florida in a small boat, but by painstaking investigation of a huge amount of reports from a variety of sources. He also put me in contact with people who had firsthand information on the missiles, in addition to those I had met on my previous trip to Miami. One of the men I met had been an official in the Castro government before defecting. In 1959, immediately after the Cuban revolution had triumphed, Fidel Castro himself had given him the job of making a thorough survey of every cave and cavern in Cuba. To speed the task along, even Boy Scouts were used. After his report of over 10,000 pages was turned in, both Castro and Che Guevara, along with men of some east European nationality (he did not know exactly which country), personally inspected many of the caves. Hundreds were selected, for what reason he was never told, and the government either bought or seized the land surrounding the caves for a great distance.

This information convinced me that I was on the track of something that was of vital importance to the security of the United States. But try as I might, I could not understand the attitude of the government concerning the missiles (and still don't today). Did they truly not believe any of the evidence? Or did they prefer to suppress it, and if so, why? I soon had reason to favor the second explanation, though what reason they had for suppressing the facts I still could not fathom. During my last night in Miami, someone entered my motel room without waking me and stole my bulging briefcase containing all the data I had amassed on missiles, as well as a copy of Hector's map showing all the missile sites and other secret locations. I phoned Hector who said he wasn't surprised. Two CIA agents had paid him a visit the evening before, demanding to know what I was up to, and just a few minutes before I called, he had received a phone call from Dr. Cardona who told him that the State Department demanded that all the missile files be turned over to them that very morning. Hector had no intention of letting up on his investigations, so to save Dr. Cardona and the Cuban Revolutionary Council further embarrassment, he resigned from the council that day. Dr. Cardona, because of this incident and several others, also resigned from his post as president of the council soon afterwards.

The theft of my files was a serious blow, but we still had our trump card, the on-the-spot photographs Bermúdez was to take in Cuba, plus the investigations to be made in Mexico. Clay had sent word the evening before that Brenan's coded telegram had arrived, reporting that Bermúdez was in Havana and that it was safe for me to come down. I myself had double-checked, arranging for a friend who lived in Mexico City to be at the airport when the weekly flight for Havana departed, and he also wired in code that Bermúdez was on the flight. Before leaving for Mexico City, I was able to have Hector put on a retainer by the *Post* so he could continue his investigations on the missile question and supply us with data.

As soon as I landed in Mexico City, Brenan, who wanted to show me how influential he was, had me taken off the plane before any of the other passengers and whisked right to his waiting limousine without having to clear immigration, customs, or health checkpoints. (This, no doubt, aroused a great deal of suspicion about me right from the start.) He deposited me at the Hotel Reforma where a room was already reserved under a fictitious name, and to play the spy bit to the hilt, he offered me a personal bodyguard as well as an automatic pistol, both of which I refused as being unnecessary.

Brenan left no stone unturned in his efforts to convince me that the Russians had engineered the takeover of Cuba and were about to do the same in Mexico. He felt so confident that I would get Clay to run the articles in the *Post* that he even began to amass a collection of photographs he thought we would need to illustrate both articles. By the end of my stay I found that the imminent Communist takeover of Mexico was a complete laugh, with only the scantiest evidence to back it up. About the only concrete facts Brenan could produce was that Mexico was one of the few Latin American countries that still maintained diplomatic relations with Cuba and that there was a weekly flight between Mexico City and Havana. All this proved was that Mexico had diplomatic relations with Cuba and weekly flights to Havana.

The question of Russian involvement in Castro's takeover of Cuba was something else again. There seemed to be a sound basis for this theory, but a little problem developed that forced the *Post* and me to forget about trying to prove it. Brenan had asked $50,000 to provide all the documentation straight from the files of the Mexican Secret Police, but when, through Brenan, I met several high-ranking members of the Secret Police, the price was upped to half a million dollars, and to whet my appetite, several juicy documents were shown to me which if not fakes were of immense value in proving this allegation. However, Clay was unable to persuade the Curtis board of directors to authorize the expenditure of such a large sum—not surprising, considering the financial state of the *Post*—and plans for the article were also dropped.

Meanwhile Brenan was taking me around Mexico City to meet people who could provide additional data. One of them was Castro's sister who was married to a Mexican doctor and lived in Mexico City. She could not say whether her brother had overthrown Batista with Russian help, but she did say that ever since his student days at the University of Havana, his best friends had been fanatical Marxists and that he had taken part in various Communist-led riots in Colombia, Mexico, and other Latin American republics. But most of this background information was already well known, and without documentation attesting to the presence of Russian advisors and to financial backing in Castro's guerrilla training camp, for example, there was no real story.

I had brushed aside Brenan's and Bermúdez's talk about the dangerous nature of this venture, regarding it merely as theatrics to raise the price of their services. But I had not been in Mexico City long before I began to think there was something to it after all. Thanks to Brenan, who had told dozens of people the purpose of my trip to Mexico, I was under constant surveillance from the very moment of my arrival. This didn't bother me much, although Brenan claimed that some of the men following me were Communist agents (the others he identified as members of various Mexican intelligence agencies). Then on my third day in Mexico we had a little scare. Brenan and I had just left the house of a Cuban diplomat who had recently defected and who had given us information on the missiles. As we were walking toward our car, which we had discreetly parked down the street, a black Mercedes-Benz, travelling very fast, came right up on the sidewalk behind us. Only by diving over a low wall into somebody's yard did we avoid being run over. All Brenan would say as he picked himself off the ground was: "Those boys are always pulling that trick."

That same evening, while I was having a cold beer in my hotel bar, an American walked in and, ignoring the entire row of empty bar stools, sat down next to me. I pegged him as an agent of some American intelligence outfit—probably the CIA, I thought after one look—and knew I was right after a few minutes of conversation. I'm not saying I could do much better at passing myself off as a tourist while trying to pump someone, but I could hardly do worse. He never really introduced himself, but I learned his name, or at least the one he went by, the following morning when I saw his face plastered all over the front pages of the Mexican newspapers. At first the press claimed he was a wealthy homosexual and had been murdered by one or more of his "boyfriends," but the afternoon editions reported that an anti-American slogan had been written on the wall of his room in the man's own blood and that his murder might have had a political motive. I paid a hasty visit to the press and political attaches at the U.S. embassy, hoping to get the truth. When they refused to talk about the matter, I became even more suspicious. Then, while waiting in the embassy lobby for a rain shower to end, I struck up a conversation with the U.S. Marine on duty and in a short while learned that the murdered man had worked right there in the embassy. The scuttlebutt was that the Reds had rubbed him out. I didn't think there was necessarily any connection between the man's murder and my investigations. It was enough to have an example of what could happen if you started to snoop around too much.

Two days later I got a phone call from a man with a pronounced Cuban accent who addressed me by my correct name and not the fictitious one on the hotel register. He claimed to have some very important information for sale, the nature of which he would not disclose over the phone. If I was interested, I should meet him the following morning at Teotihuacán, the ancient Toltec ruins located about an hour's drive from the city. I rented a car and without saying anything to Brenan drove out to the site, reaching it just about dawn, according to my instructions. It looked deserted. I got out, lit a cigar, and started pacing up and down, wondering what kind of information my anonymous caller had to offer. A few minutes later I heard a sudden screeching of tires and looked up to see another black Mercedes appear from behind one of the nearby pyramid temples and head right for me. Before I had time to think, the car made a 90-degree turn about twenty yards from me and someone began firing a pistol. I dove to the ground and as the car sped away, wrote the license number in the sand.

The Mercedes kept on going. Without waiting to see if it was coming back for a second try, I jumped into my car and drove off in the opposite direction, unaware that there was only one entrance to the archaeological site. I soon came to a dead end, but I had no intention of going back to where I had just come from. Smashing through a barbed-wire fence enclosing the site, I kept going across fields and over hills until I finally hit a secondary road which carried me back to the main road. Fearing that my friends in the Mercedes might make another appearance, I slipped in between two big trucks and stuck with them until we reached the city. I drove directly to Brenan's house where without any preliminaries I asked him for that pistol he had offered before. He gave me a .45 calibre automatic and a bulletproof vest, but I still refused the bodyguard, since I was doing quite a lot of research around town on my own that I didn't want him to know about.

After I calmed down and had some breakfast, which consisted mainly of Bloody Marys, I decided that the morning's episode had been intended only to scare the hell out of me (which it did). If they had really wanted to kill me, they could easily have stopped the car and shot me, since the area was deserted. Brenan disagreed, arguing that they had not stopped because they didn't know I was unarmed or that there was no one hiding in my car. Whatever their intentions, we soon knew who they were. Brenan made several phone calls and within an hour found out that the license number I had copied was from an automobile —no doubt the same one that had charged up on the sidewalk after us a few days before—that belonged to someone in the Cuban embassy. Brenan then arranged for the Mexican Secret Police to keep the Mercedes under constant surveillance, but he warned me not to count on not running into that car again—the next time probably under worse conditions.

After another busy day interviewing more leads, I went to bed early but was awakened around 2:00 A.M. by a knock at the door. Without opening it (by this time I had become just a little bit cautious), I asked who was there. A voice answered in Spanish: "A bellhop with a telegram." I thought this strange, since not even Clay knew I was staying in that hotel, so I told the bellhop—if that's what he was—to pass it under the door. The voice insisted that it had to be signed, so I said pass the receipt under the door, too. At this, the "bellhop" threw himself against the door after failing to open it with a pass key, since I had taken care to use the inside lock, too. I reached for my pistol, slipping a round in the chamber, and picked up the house phone and yelled to the operator to send up the police (I knew there were always a few stationed at the main entrance to the hotel). The intruder's efforts to break down the door continued. After pushing my bed against it, I sat down and waited to shoot as soon as he crashed through. In fact I was just ready to shoot through the door anyway when I heard shouts. Figuring the police had arrived, I removed the bed and gingerly opened the door, which was barely hanging on the hinges. Not one, but two men were running down the hall with two policemen in hot pursuit. About two minutes later the policemen returned, saying that the "thieves" had escaped. Having already hidden my automatic, I acted like the tourist I was supposed to be and agreed—yes, they must have been thieves.

After the police had taken down some information and left, I had my room changed, but just as I walked in, the phone rang and a voice said that if I wanted to stay alive I should plan to be out of the country within 12 hours. I decided that the bodyguard Brenan had offered wasn't such a bad idea after all, and I phoned him, intending to tell him to send one over. His phone was dead. I later learned that, after finding all five of his large watchdogs poisoned, he had called several friends to bring their pistols and spend the night at his home. Then dozens of threatening phone calls began coming in and, because his wife was pregnant at the time and becoming more upset by the minute, he had the phone disconnected.

I waited nervously in my room—ready to shoot anyone who came near the door—until a few minutes before nine, when the American embassy opened. I went down to the hotel door and offered two policemen there a fat sum if they would escort me down to the embassy a few blocks away, explaining that I needed their protection because the jealous husband of my current mistress was after me. They nodded in sympathetic understanding and fell in step beside me, all of us followed by three tails who had been dogging my footsteps all week. When we reached the embassy door, I paid off my bodyguards while the three tails stood across the street, glowering. Then I discovered that the embassy was closed. I had forgotten that it was Sunday. With one hand on the pistol hidden in my coat, I started banging frantically on the glass door with the other. After awhile a Marine guard came up to the door and pointed to the sign showing the hours the embassy was open, but when I drew my finger across my throat, he got the message and let me in. After pulling out my old Marine Corps identification card to let him know I was one of the boys, I explained that my life was in danger and that I would appreciate it if he could arrange for someone to escort me to the airport. For some reason he figured I must be some sort of U.S. intelligence agent, because when he telephoned an off-duty Marine, he said: "Boy, I have one of these Mike Hammer types over here, so get a few guys and come over to take him to the airport and kiss him goodbye."

I telephoned the airport, making a reservation on the next plane leaving for New York, which was in less than two hours. My three-man escort arrived—in civilian clothes but each carrying their service .45 automatics and itching for the opportunity to use them—and took me to the airport in an embassy car. They stayed right with me until I boarded the plane, thinking all along, I suppose, that I was a CIA agent. They talked constantly about the one who had been murdered, and I let on as if I knew him well, to keep up the farce which I really hadn't created.

As soon as I landed in New York, I telephoned Clay at his home in Connecticut and asked him to meet me at the *Post*'s offices in Manhattan. Arriving there before he did, I began going through the incoming mail tray on my desk and discovered a few interesting items that set me wondering just what kind of a crazy caper I had gotten myself into. A letter from the Berretta Arms Company in Italy, replying to my inquiry about Bermúdez, was only puzzling at first. They said he had been their representative but that he had recently resigned (he had told us he was going to Havana to make the final arrangements for a five-million-dollar arms sale to Castro). A letter from my old girl friend in the State Department—telling me that there had been secret violations of the U.S.-Italian agreement that no arms or munitions would be sold to Cuba—helped clarify this mystery. The Beretta people probably thought I had gotten wind of the arms deal and had claimed that Bermúdez no longer worked for them as a cover-up. They probably would have liked to claim they had never heard of him, except that he was listed among their representatives right on the company's letterhead. Then Bermúdez checked out as being on the level so far, but the letters and reports on Brenan, the other member of the team, were not so encouraging.

Before leaving for Miami and Mexico two weeks before, I had put my young Houston friend, Jon ("Momo") Kalb, to work digging up info on Brenan who had many business dealings in Texas, including the publication of his Spanish-language newspaper. Momo's report was an eye-opener. Brenan not only had recently swindled a wealthy Texas oilman out of a quarter of a million dollars, but was also wanted by the Internal Revenue Service for tax evasion. His newspaper had been closed down and he had "disappeared" from Texas shortly before his first conference with Clay and me. But this was only the beginning. There was a mound of interoffice memos from the two *Post* reporters I had put to work, which, along with verifying Momo's letter, reported that Brenan was wanted for various other offenses ranging from murder in Venezuela to fraud and extortion in several states in the U.S. I wondered how he could enter and leave the country so freely without being nabbed. Later I learned how, when he showed me his collection of five passports from five different countries and bearing five different names.

When Clay arrived, I filled him in on my exciting trip as well as what I had found in my mail. I suggested that we turn the whole matter over to the CIA, the State Department, or someone else, since we were unqualified to handle this type of work. Clay asked me if I was going soft and then went into one of his standard arguments about how important our project was and how insignificant my life was, "when you look at the overall picture and consider we might be saving the entire world." Come to think of it, Clay could have resolved the whole matter himself by getting appointed special U.S. envoy to Cuba. I've no doubt that he could have persuaded Castro to retire, join the Boy Scouts, and let the D.A.R. run Cuba.

By now—February 27—Bermúdez had been in Cuba over a week and was expected back in Mexico any day with the photographs. I agreed to make the pick-up in Mexico, as arranged earlier, but I swore that I would then get out of this cloak-and-dagger jazz and get back to my own line of work—regular sharks I could handle. But I was a sitting duck for the Brenan variety and the other bad guys I had been running into recently. Also, there was one big condition I insisted on if I did return to Mexico: I would not carry in the $50,000 to pay

Bermúdez, but instead leave it in New York where he or Brenan would have to come for it. Otherwise, I suspected, my life wouldn't be worth a plugged nickel. Clay didn't like this change of plans, but there was little he could do about it since it was *my* neck that was in the vise.

Brenan himself must have had quite an organized intelligence network in Mexico (probably the Mexican Secret Police). While I was still talking with Clay at the office, less than eight hours since I had left Mexico without even checking out of my hotel, Western Union phoned with a telegram from Mexico, saying, "Wife had baby boy." This was the code agreed upon earlier with Brenan if I should be out of Mexico when he heard from Bermúdez. It meant that Bermúdez was on his way with the photographs and that I should stand by and be ready to fly to Mexico at a moment's notice with the money.

Although, naturally, I was a bit uneasy about my own safety in this caper, that didn't bother me half as much as my uncertainty over the consequences of what I was doing, whether I was really doing my country a service or committing a howling blunder. This problem had been on my mind from the beginning, but now that the time had come when I would actually get the photographs—which I felt certain would prove the existence of the missiles in Cuba—I got into such a miserable state that neither the warm company of female friends nor unlimited amounts of Scotch would help. So the following morning, without saying a word to Clay or anyone else, I flew down to Washington and phoned CIA headquarters in McLean, Virginia for an appointment. After what seemed like ages, I was told that an agent would meet me in the airport terminal building.

The agent—for our purposes, he can be called Sam—arrived about an hour later, and after he had identified himself properly, we got down to business. I told him what I was up to, leaving out a few names and other information that I thought might get someone in trouble. But much to my surprise, when I finished, he filled in most of the names and other information that I had omitted—so much for my startling revelation to the CIA! Unwilling to tell me whether he believed there were missiles in Cuba or give me advice on whether I should go ahead with my work, he merely suggested that I keep in touch with him, and if I did get the photographs, to call him at any hour of the day or night at a number he gave me. I figured, though, that if the CIA really considered my project contrary to the interests of the U.S., they would not have hesitated to say so.

After suggesting that I carry a smaller pistol than the one bulging through my jacket, or I might get picked up in New York on the Sullivan Act and given a stiff prison sentence, we said our goodbyes. As we shook hands, Sam jokingly (or maybe he was serious—who knows?) said that I was living a more dangerous existence than most of the guys in his organization and if, when it was all over, I wanted a good job with little money in it, I should contact him and he would see what he could do about making me a properly trained spy.

Late the next day, Clay received another coded telegram from Brenan, instructing me to go to Mérida, Yucatán and wait there for the exchange of money and photographs. That suited me fine, since Mérida was almost like home ground to me. In fact, the desk clerk at the main hotel I checked into turned out to be a guy who had worked for me in Cozumel several years earlier. While I was unpacking, he came running into my room excitedly to tell me that a plainclothes policeman had posted himself in the small switchboard cubicle behind the desk to overhear all my phone conversations and that another was sitting in the lobby, pretending to read a newspaper, "just like in all the spy movies."

While waiting for further contact from Brenan and in order to avoid suspicion, I visited my old friends in the city as if that were the purpose of my trip. Several of them said they had heard rumors that the police suspected I had come back to smuggle some valuable Mayan artifacts out of the country. For once I hoped that they thought I was a "thief of Mexican antiquities" and that was why they were watching me so closely.

On the second evening of my stay I had a very brief phone call from a voice I recognized as belonging to Brenan's wife, merely suggesting that I go to Acapulco for some fishing. "But be sure to bring your tackle box," she added, which I interpreted to mean the money for the photographs. I was not exactly overjoyed at this switch in plans, for the only way to get to Acapulco was via Mexico City where I had so many unfriendly friends. From my agent, the desk clerk, I learned that there was a milk-run flight that night for Mexico City, which I caught, thinking at first that this was a brilliant move. With six intermediate stops, the flight arrived in the capital well after midnight when no international, and probably few national, flights would be coming in, and I figured I could outfox anyone watching the airport for me by arriving at such an unlikely hour on such an unlikely flight.

The Marx logic, as it had been so often in the past, was way off. While I was waiting to collect my baggage, I caught sight of two familiar faces —two of the tails who had been following me the week before. The next Acapulco flight was at 6:30 A.M., and I had decided that it would be safer and easier to wait in the terminal. But half an hour later, after all my fellow passengers had collected their bags and taken off in cars, taxis, and the airport bus, I discovered that I was completely alone in the vast terminal waiting room except for a few old women scrubbing the marble floor *and* the two tails. They looked even more menacing than usual, like a couple of demons in a Japanese play. To reassure myself that I wasn't worried a bit, I stuck my tongue out at them and gave them the well-known finger sign. I could almost see the smoke come out of their ears, but I wasn't very scared, since I had a pistol in my coat. But it was a different matter a moment later when they ascended a flight of stairs and disappeared. I got the queasy feeling that I was in the sights of a gun. Moments later I spotted the pilots and stewardesses from my flight come through the waiting room and climb into an airlines microbus. Grabbing my bags, I ran after them and asked for a lift into the city, explaining that my wife was about to have a baby and I couldn't get any other transportation at that late hour. As I climbed in, the two tails ran out of the terminal, shaking fists and yelling.

Someone said, "Probably some drunks."

"Yes," I agreed. "Drunks."

They dropped me off at the Continental Hilton in the center of town, and after checking in under another fictitious name, I phoned Brenan's house, telling his wife to let him know I couldn't go to Acapulco "for reasons of health" and that they should bring their "product" to my hotel room as quickly as possible. For the next 32 hours I did not leave my room, having all my meals sent up plus some paperbacks from the lobby, which, ironically enough, were spy thrillers, and waited nervously for some word from my not-so-trusted friends.

Finally, the next morning, I received a box of flowers containing a note from Brenan in which he said that all our lives were in great danger and telling me to sneak out of the hotel and meet him at a certain busy intersection on the other side of town. I followed his instructions, and after a short wait, a dark limousine with venetian blinds on all but the windshield pulled up. Inside were Brenan and five other men who, I assumed, were his bodyguards. After weaving around back streets for over an hour, during which time Brenan peeked constantly through the window blinds to make sure we weren't being followed, we suddenly turned into the garage of a large private house. The garage door was immediately closed, whereupon Brenan, wiping beads of perspiration from his face, said: "We're safe." The first words anyone had spoken since I climbed into the car.

He escorted me to a back bedroom where I shook hands with an even more nervous Bermúdez who repeated over and over that he was sorry he had ever embarked on this suicidal venture. Then both of them made a dive for my briefcase, demanding my key, which I gave to them, and opened it. I never saw two more surprised individuals in my life than when Brenan and Bermúdez found nothing inside but a few magazines and notepads instead of the packets of green bills they were expecting. Before their disappointment could turn to something more serious, I quickly explained that, because I was being watched so closely, I had left the money with a friend for safekeeping, but that they would have it as soon as I was given the authentic photographs. Bermúdez then pulled out three undeveloped rolls of 35 millimeter film, which immediately made me suspicious, since the two miniature "spy" cameras we had given him used a different type of film. When I asked him how the cameras had worked out and he said "perfectly," I knew something was drastically wrong. He told me about his trip to Cuba and handed me a long typewritten report containing a blow-by-blow account of everything he supposedly had done, seen, and found out during his sojourn in Cuba. Both of them suggested that we all go right then to my friend's house, or office, to get the money, but I refused. They would be paid only after I had seen the photographs. After making a few threats and seeing that these had no effect on me, they agreed to have the film processed; I was to meet them with the money at midnight, and if I was satisfied with the photos, I would pay them then.

While being driven back to my hotel by one of the bodyguards, I decided that if I ever had plans of becoming a grandfather, I had better get the hell out of Mexico before midnight; in fact, the quicker the better. After being dropped off at the hotel's rear service entrance, I walked straight through and out the front door, again without checking out of my room (the casualty rate on suits and shirts was becoming astronomical), jumped into a taxi and offered to triple the fare if the driver could make it to the airport in half the normal time. He did, but with about twice the normal number of near collisions. Without wasting time to see if my tails were around, I raced to buy a ticket for the next international flight, not caring whether it was to Madrid or Tokyo. Luckily there was one boarding for Houston. I didn't relax until we were airborne, and even then I glanced nervously around at my fellow passengers to make sure there were no familiar faces on board.

In Houston I wired Brenan to bring his friend and "fishing tackle" to New York, and then caught the next flight myself. Clay's first reaction was that I had acted a bit hastily, since I had no positive proof that they were not on the level. However, subsequent events not only justified my actions, but also convinced me that if I had been any less hasty, I would not be around to tell this tale.

I sent copies of Bermúdez's report to my friend at the State Department, to Sam, and to various contacts in Miami. But even before we received their comments, we knew it was a dud. I sat down with several of the best men on the *Post*'s editorial staff to analyze the report and in the very first sentence we found a lie. Bermúdez claimed that a certain important member of the Cuban Ministry of Foreign Affairs had met him at the plane, yet we knew that this man had not been in Havana during the entire time Bermúdez was supposedly in Cuba; instead the man had been in New York, attending a session of the United Nations. (I was also beginning to doubt that Bermúdez had ever been there at all; my Mexican friend had seen him go through the gates to board the plane, but who knows whether he actually got on?) On the night Bermúdez claimed to have thrown a big party for Castro in Havana and obtained a great deal of top-secret information from him, Castro was on an inspection tour of the eastern provinces of Cuba. Of the four locations Bermúdez gave for secret Russian submarine bases, none corresponded to the two I already had substantial information on, and one was in an area where the water was so shallow that a rowboat could barely navigate, let alone a large submarine submerged for purposes of concealment. In short, the report was worth less than the paper it was written on.

Two days after I arrived in New York, Brenan and Bermúdez walked into my office, both of them the picture of brash confidence. I immediately took them to Clay's office which he had had rigged with a hidden microphone and tape recorder. The door was locked and we sat back to see how far these two frauds would carry their game. Instead of the stack of photographs that three rolls of 35 millimeter film would have produced, they pulled out only four black-and-white snapshots. One was of a missile which Bermúdez claimed was concealed in a cave near a certain village on the northern coast of Cuba, and the other three were different scenes of a triple-silo, missile-launching site, the first with no camouflage, the second partially, and the third completely camouflaged. Clay looked at me as if to say, "Maybe you goofed and these guys aren't frauds after all." I quickly called in Hank Walker, the *Post*'s photo editor, and gave him the four photographs, asking him to make a thorough analysis to determine their authenticity.

Brenan and Bermúdez, still as cocky as ever, demanded the immediate payment of the $50,000. We told them we were not obliged to pay them anything for only four photos that had no indication of when or where they had been taken (no copy of the *New York Times* or anything), but said the amount paid would depend on Hank Walker's report. The protests and counterarguments were cut short an hour later when Hank walked in with four huge blow-ups of the photos and a triumphant grin on his face. He first demolished the missile photo. It was nothing else but a U.S. Nike missile slightly out of focus (no doubt deliberately), so that in the small original it could be taken for almost anything. Next came the three photos of the underground missile-launching site which, Hank announced, were so amateurish that he had to laugh. They had probably been taken in a sandbox, and the silo doors were children's building blocks. Placing the three blow-ups side by side, he pointed out that they had all been taken from the same angle and elevation. The chances of doing this from a plane or helicopter were a million to one. The only way to get this effect would be from a camera set up on a tripod. The shadows, he continued, which went in many directions, could have been produced only by artificial lighting close to the objects. But the clincher was a huge Coca-Cola bottle top half buried in the sand, fully one quarter the size of the silo doors!

Even before Hank had finished his report, obviously relishing the deepening tinge of green on the faces of our two guests, both con men had recovered from the shock and done some quick thinking. The photos, they protested, had been bought from a Cuban Air Force major who had obviously swindled Bermúdez. But that didn't matter, since they still had the three rolls of film, which they had left hidden in Mexico for safekeeping and would send up shortly by a trusted courier.

Leaving Walker—who is big enough and rough enough to handle any situation, in charge of our two guests, just in case they might decide to leave without saying goodbye—Clay and I excused ourselves to go to the men's room, and held a hasty conference in my office. Clay wanted to phone the FBI and have both Brenan and Bermúdez arrested on charges of extortion and fraud (they had already received $15,000 from the *Post*), but I convinced Clay that we ought to phone Sam first—after telling him about my secret trip to Washington a little over a week before. Sam suggested that we do absolutely nothing, simply let them go. As usual, he gave no reason for his advice.

Reluctantly we followed his suggestion, figuring that that was the end of the matter. But Brenan, instead of considering himself lucky to have gotten off scot-free, sent Clay a letter about two weeks later, claiming that his trusted courier had disappeared with the goods and that he was having the Mexican Secret Police investigate. He also included a large expense account and a bill for his services, which naturally ended up in the wastepaper basket. Then about a week later, he had the audacity to return to New York, barging into Clay's office unannounced and threatening Clay's life if he wasn't paid within twenty-four hours. I was in Miami at the time, but Clay's secretary had instructions, that if Brenan ever showed up again she was to phone the sheriff's office in New York and notify Sam in Washington. Clay and I had decided that we wanted to teach Brenan a lesson, no matter what Sam advised and to put him behind bars for some of his other swindles as well. Clay's secretary acted quickly, phoning while Brenan was still raising hell in Clay's office, and he was nabbed on the way out of the building. But he was released on bail, which he jumped, and once again he fled the country.

Just for our own satisfaction, Clay and I did some further research into the missile incident, but we were never able to determine whether the whole thing had been planned as a con job from the start or whether it had turned into one only after Bermúdez failed to get the photographs in Cuba. As for the team's future activities, Bermúdez dropped out of ~ht, but Brenan, at last report, was back in Mexico City, looking for backers for a new intelligence swindle involving the imminent Communist takeover of France.

It was the middle of March when we had that conclusive meeting in Clay's office, and already more than two months of my time had been consumed in the Brenan-Bermúdez fiasco. But unless all the data I had gathered from other more reliable sources was pure fiction, there was still good reason to believe that there were missiles concealed in Cuba, and I was more determined than ever to find out for sure. To my great surprise, my CIA friend, Sam, advised me to continue my work. Could it be that the all-knowing U.S. government intelligence agencies had failed to obtain conclusive proof of the presence of the missiles and were willing to accept a helping hand from a bungling amateur like me? Or was Sam a smart enough cookie to realize that no matter what advice he gave me, I would go ahead anyway, that by telling me that the CIA was interested in my findings, he could insure that I would keep him informed and save him the trouble of keeping tabs on me? Whatever the reason, I was glad to have Sam's approval.

My first plan was to enter Cuba and obtain the photographs myself, but my Cuban exile contacts dissuaded me of this folly, pointing out that I could not hope to last a day as a spy in Cuba with my looks and heavily accented Yankee brand of Spanish. Instead they presented two alternate plans: the first was to smuggle in photographic equipment to various underground groups in Cuba and let them try to get the photos; and the second was to send in our own men and have them do the job. I favored this second plan, since we could insure the clear photographs that were so essential by using men in Miami who already had some knowledge of photography and teaching them to use the complicated equipment we had, such as infrared film for night photography, and powerful telescopic lenses that would obtain a close-up from as far away as a mile.

A wealthy Cuban exile living in New York donated a large amount of money to buy all the photographic gear and cover the expenses of the entire undertaking. It was even arranged for the film to be brought out of Cuba in diplomatic pouches, if our men or the underground people could get it to one of the three foreign embassies in Havana that agreed to help us. But smuggling the men and equipment into Cuba was not to be such a simple matter. Actually the problem was getting them out of the United States. In December 1962 the U.S. government had already started to clamp down on the activities of the Cuban exile groups, but the bomb really went off (both literally and figuratively) in March 1963 when one exile group made two lightning raids against Russian ships anchored in Cuban ports. They caused only minor damage to the ships but created very bad publicity for the United States, which had to promise to put an end to raids into Cuba or risk another showdown with Russia.

The Administration acted quickly and efficiently. Swarms of U.S. intelligence agents descended on Miami, infiltrating the exile groups and hiring informants—estimates went as high as one in every four exiles. All boats belonging to Cubans were restricted; the most militant exile leaders were confined to Dade County, and intensive air and sea patrols were set up. After that, any raiding party that managed to elude the watchdogs on land (the CIA, the FBI, the Border Patrol, the Security Division of the State Department, and the immigration authorities, as well as every deputy sheriff and game warden in the state of Florida) and reach the open sea still had to run the gauntlet of U.S. Coast Guard patrol planes and vessels, plus the two naval blockades between Florida and Cuba, before tackling Castro's own security forces in Cuban waters.

Although I sympathized with my many Cuban exile friends who bitterly resented these restrictions, I believed that the hit-and-run commando raids really did more harm than good. But the missile-photo project was something else. This was pure intelligence work which hopefully would go undetected, and I felt no compunctions about going ahead with my plans. Of course, I could not expect the official watchdogs to see things my way, so I had to proceed very carefully. Realizing how heavily infiltrated the exile organizations were, I contacted four different groups without telling any of them about the others. Each group was to provide a two-man photographic team which would be assigned different sites in Cuba and enter by different routes. The teams were provided with some of the counterfeit Cuban money being printed in Miami (the equivalent of $100,000 could be bought for only $500) with which to bribe workers at the missile sites to take photos with miniature cameras, in addition to the ones that would be taken by the teams themselves with telescopic lenses.

The first team was to fly to Yucatán and contact a friend of mine there who had offered to carry them to Cape San Antonio on the western tip of Cuba and put them ashore at night. However, unknown to me, this particular exile group was in the pay of the FBI. Two hours after I had given the men a last-minute briefing, as well as the photographic gear, the bogus Cuban money, and a good-sized stack of legitimate American dollars, the travel agency where I had bought their tickets telephoned me to say that the two men, who I thought were on their way to Mérida, Yucatán, were at the agency trying to cash in their tickets. So much for Team One. Team Two was to leave the next day, and this time I went to the airport and made sure that they caught their plane to Nassau, from which they would fly to one of the Bahamian cays where a fast boat was waiting to take them to Cuba. The morning after they left, as I was briefing Team Three for departure, a news flash came over the radio, reporting that a force of British marines had landed on this same cay, which Cuban exiles had been using as a training camp and base for raiding parties, and had rounded up all the raiders and taken them to jail in Nassau. Later that day I learned that our two men had been nabbed along with the others.

Team Three was to take the direct route, that is, sneak out from the Florida Keys in a fast boat, try to get past the naval blockade, and land on the Cuban coast somewhere in the province of Matanzas. (I wish I hadn't promised myself to keep everyone connected with this project anonymous, for the two men on this team deserve to be named as the traitors they are.) Leaving shortly after nightfall and supposedly headed for Cuba, they changed course and went to Key West where they sold the boat and photographic gear, using the proceeds, plus the cash they had been given, to go on a three-day drunk. They would have remained undiscovered for some time if they hadn't gotten in a barroom brawl in which one was cut up a bit, which made the Miami newspapers. So I soon learned that Team Three had failed, too.

Team Four, which was being held in reserve for a week after Team Three had left, was scheduled to land on the southern coast of Cuba via the Cayman Islands. But I changed this plan at the last minute when I learned of Team Three's treachery, deciding instead that I would not only see to it that they left for Cuba but personally put them ashore on Cuban soil. A friend of mine had a boat capable of doing over 50 knots (it had been one of the top performers in the previous year's Miami–Nassau powerboat race), which he agreed to loan me. To prevent its being picked up on radar, I had the windscreen, the railings—in fact, everything that cleared the water by more than two feet—removed and the hull and decks painted sea blue. This low silhouette and seawater color made the boat nearly impossible to see on radar. With both men lying on deck under a canvas cover, I left right from the Miami municipal pier at ten one night, hugged the coast down to the keys, and then cut across the 90-mile Florida Strait to the Cuban mainland which we reached at 1:35 A.M. Both men were put ashore at a deserted spot, and I was back at the pier in Miami at 6:45, without having sighted so much as a fishing boat either going or coming. Such an uneventful trip was probably due to the heavy rain that had lasted all night, keeping visibility down to a minimum. A boat carrying a Cuban exile raiding party that left from somewhere in the Bahamas the following night was sighted by one of the fast, Russian-built "Komar" boats of which the Cubans had about a hundred patrolling their coasts. The Komar gave chase, running the exile boat aground on Sal Cay in the Florida Strait where every one of the eleven raiders was either captured or shot.

Three days after I had put Team Four ashore in Cuba, Radio Havana announced the capture of two "CIA agents" (the poor CIA; they get blamed for everything), naming my two men, and said that they had been shot as spies. This news really struck me hard, since I felt personally responsible for their deaths. My Cuban friends tried to console me, saying that every day, dozens of guerrilla fighters were being captured in Cuba and shot, so that two more lives made little difference; but I was not so sure the families of the two men would share this attitude. I paid their wives a visit and found that both women did feel much the same way, assuring me that their husbands had been planning to go into Cuba to join a guerrilla outfit anyway and had fully expected to get killed sooner or later. I still felt bad about it and arranged for both families to be given some money, at least enough to see them along for a few years until the children were older and the women could go out to work.

Once again, I started to think of entering Cuba and getting the photographs myself. I met a young Cuban priest who was known as the "Padre Paracaidista" (parachuting priest), because he had parachuted into Cuba from small planes on six occasions since he had been deported shortly after the Castro takeover. He had made the jumps to contact guerrilla fighters and the underground and encourage them to continue their struggle and had been back from his last trip to Cuba only a week when I met him. The "parachuting priest" was very enthusiastic about my project and offered to go back with me, but only if we did it his way—by parachute. I agreed, although I was not very happy about the idea, never having parachuted in my life. I was even less happy about it when I was given a practice jump and ended up almost drowned in some Florida swamp before being rescued by a fisherman who saw me come down.

The plan was that the plane—a World War II surplus B-25—would take off from a deserted airstrip in central Florida and, after dropping us over the mountains, would make a leaflet raid over Havana, approaching at treetop level to avoid radar contact. Final arrangements were made to leave at midnight on April 1, but somewhere there was a leak in our plans (what else could I expect, considering the date?). While the priest and I were already driving north to the pick-up place, the FBI seized the plane at Miami International Airport where the pilot was gassing up. We waited beside the deserted airstrip until dawn, when we decided that something other than the usual Cuban concept of punctuality had gone wrong, and then drove back to Miami.

Having already made one successful boat trip to Cuba, I decided I could do it again. The main problem was how to get back, since I would either have to sink the boat or have someone come along who could take it back to Florida; but I decided to worry about that when the time came to leave Cuba. The few people I mentioned this last-ditch plan to all said it was doomed to failure, again for the reason that I would be betrayed by my looks and accent. I argued that I was planning to land on a deserted part of the coast and would hide out in the hills and try to get the photographs on my own. But my closest Cuban friends thought I was being so rash that they refused even to help me make contact with the guerrilla units operating in the area I had chosen (being unfamiliar with the terrain, I did not have a hope of success without a guide). When I think back, I am probably very lucky that I was distracted from this plan by another, which looked like it had more possibilities for success.

Through my friend, the "parachuting priest," I was put into touch with a very intelligent Cuban exile, probably the most dedicated person I was to meet during my association with the exiled colony. Here again, I shall perserve anonymity by calling him Felipe, not for his sake, since he is now dead, but for the sake of his relatives still living in Cuba. Felipe was an intimate friend of Fidel Castro and had served in his diplomatic corps until, like many others, he realized that Castro was simply replacing the Batista dictatorship with his own brand of dictatorship, and defected to the United States. Since his arrival in Miami he had been active "sticking pins in Fidel's fanny," as he put it. Instead of making flea-bite raids like most of the other action groups, which accomplished very little except to gain publicity for the raiders involved, Felipe and a small group of men who worked with him had been making almost weekly trips to Cuba to supply different underground and guerrilla units with radio equipment, arms, munitions, and other material they needed to harass Castro internally, where it really hurt.

Felipe and I took an immediate liking to each other even though some of his close aides were willing to "stake their mothers' honor" on my being a CIA agent, a belief that was shared by many other exiles in Miami at the time. Shortly after meeting Felipe, I learned some interesting news which confirmed vague rumors I had been hearing for some time. Preparations for an invasion of Cuba on the order of the Bay of Pigs expedition, but much more ambitious, had been well underway when suddenly around the end of March the invasion was called off. All the secret training camps that had been set up in the United States and several Latin American countries were closed down and the exiles brought back to Miami. Felipe confirmed this news and confided that a secret exile organization had recently been formed in Miami (by then it had been three weeks since Washington had cancelled the preparations) which planned to go ahead with the invasion anyway. The new plan called for a small invasion force to enter Cuba, set up a provisional government in the mountains, and foment popular uprisings. In fact, it would be more or less a duplication of Castro's strategy against Batista. They hoped that once they had succeeded to that extent, the United States and many Latin American governments would send in troops to help them overthrow the Castro regime.

Felipe was in charge of getting the original invasion force into Cuba, and his motive for telling me all these highly secret plans was to entice me to join him. He knew I had influence with several wealthy Cuban exiles in New York who had followed my advice in the past about which ventures to back financially and that through my connection with the *Post,* I could see to it that the invasion received sympathetic publicity. (What neither Felipe nor I knew at the time was that the leaders of the secret organization had another reason for wanting me along, one that came as quite a shock when I eventually found out.) At first I was reluctant to join the venture, since I was still obsessed with the missile photographs; but then I decided that I still had a good chance of getting ashore and obtaining the photographs on my own.

Felipe's biggest worry, besides maintaining absolute secrecy, was how to get his invasion force—which numbered nearly 200 men, including the members of the newly elected provisional government—safely out of Florida. Here I was able to offer some help. I convinced Clay Blair that the *Post* should run a story on the recent restrictions placed on the Cuban exiles, how they were still trying to make raids into Cuba, and what our government was doing about it. Clay sent down a staff reporter, and in order to gather material for the story, we went around to the different government agencies in Miami, demanding to know "just what measures were being taken to prevent the exiles from making further raids and possibly triggering off a serious international crisis."

The answers we got were very enlightening. At the CIA office we were told that one out of every 50 Cuban exiles in Miami was directly or indirectly feeding information to one or more U.S. intelligence organizations and that the chances of a raiding boat getting away from Florida to Cuba were one in a million. This boast almost made me burst out laughing right then and there, since I had taken a boat out only two weeks before and personally knew of at least five other boats that had gotten through in the past week. The immigration people also swore that it was impossible for a boat to get away from Florida, because they had patrols stationed along the entire southern Florida coastline. The Coast Guard was the most helpful. Not only did they show us exactly where all the vessels of the naval blockade were stationed, they told us when and where the twice-daily reconnaissance flights were made in search of raiding parties and bases. This last was a stroke of luck because it meant we could plot our departure time and course with a good chance of getting through undetected.

Seven boats and a large amount of money were donated by both Cuban and American sympathizers, but the money ran out before the expedition was fully prepared and many of the 200 men selected to take part (most of whom had no idea what the plans were other than that they were going on a "raid") sold their blood to a blood bank to raise money. Several of the most dedicated men, like Felipe, even sold their cars, houses, furniture, and personal belongings to help finance the venture. Then when everything seemed just about ready and all the expeditioners had been put on twenty-four-hour standby, Felipe told me that the departure date had to be delayed about a week. A large supply of explosives one of his aides was supposed to have lined up did not materialize. (I had felt uneasy about this aide—an American—ever since my first meeting with him, but Felipe had insisted that he was invaluable, buying all sorts of equipment such as boats and weapons which no Cuban in southern Florida could hope to obtain.) The explosives were absolutely essential, since plans called for the demolition of several bridges and long segments of railroad tracks to prevent Castro from throwing a great number of troops against the small invasion force before reinforcements could be brought in. Felipe said that he himself had arranged for another supply when he found out the first deal had fallen through, but it was in California and would take a while to reach us.

That same day I was reading a Miami newspaper and noticed that a large ship carrying a cargo of explosives had been wrecked off Great Inagua Island in the Bahamas. I phoned the U.S. Coast Guard to verify the report, then rushed to find Felipe and tell him that I might be able to salvage a good part of the cargo. He agreed that I should give it a try and arranged for one of the boats in his invasion armada, which was then in the Bahamas loaded with men and supplies, to meet me at Great Exuma Island and carry me to the wreck. If the salvage attempt was successful, I was to stay with the boat and meet the rest of the invasion force at sea en route to Cuba.

While waiting at Nassau International Airport for another plane that would take me to Great Exuma, I ran into an old diving acquaintance, who had just come down from New York and was also waiting for a plane. We had a few drinks together and exchanged queries as to what the other was doing down in the Bahamas. I said I was on a secret treasure hunt. My friend's mission was also secret, he said, a job for the State Department about which he had been contacted only that morning. He was reluctant to add any details, but a few more drinks loosened his tongue with startling results: he was on his way to Great Inagua to meet a U.S. Coast Guard cutter which would take him to a wreck with a cargo of explosives. He was supposed to blow up the wreck, "to keep some radical Cubans in Miami from getting at the stuff and blowing up Havana or something." At this revelation I discreetly excused myself and caught the next flight back to Miami, surprising the Bahamian immigration official who had just checked me into the country an hour before.

Neither Felipe nor any of his aides would believe that there was a Judas in his group, claiming that only a dozen people knew I was going after the explosives, and every one of them was completely trustworthy. They argued that it was just a coincidence, that I happened to go after the explosives at the same time the U.S. government decided to destroy the wreck, probably because it was a hazard to navigation. But I knew better, and the following day, when we learned that the boat I was supposed to have met at Great Exuma had been seized by the British Royal Navy, Felipe and the others began to think twice about this "coincidence."

Soon after I returned from Nassau, Felipe announced that the explosives had arrived from California and that the expedition would get underway the night of April 24, two days away. I began to think that perhaps I had been wrong about the security leak and that everything would go off smoothly after all. But once again, I had last-minute misgivings about my participation in a venture that might possibly have disastrous consequences for my country. All this time I had been working on my own, and all that either Clay or anyone else at the *Post* knew about my activities was that "Marx is down in Miami and promises us the story of the century." I finally decided to contact the CIA, as I had done before, but this time playing the role of *Saturday Evening Post* reporter. I would say that I had heard rumors that a large-scale raid was in the offing and as though interested in material for an article, would sound them out about the possible consequences. If their objections were merely based on the government's reluctance to give any official encouragement to the Cuban exiles, I would go ahead; but if they believed that an invasion would really provoke another crisis between Russia and the United States, I would have to drop out whether I agreed with their prognosis or not.

I never got around to asking any of my carefully rehearsed questions. Just as I was walking into the Miami CIA office, out came the American member of Felipe's staff, the one I had suspected of being a Judas all along. He spotted me at the same time, and turning white, he kept on walking as if he did not know me. I turned around, not to follow him, but to get to the nearest pay phone and warn Felipe. He was able, in turn, to warn many of the other leaders who quickly went into hiding. By dawn the next day, all six of the remaining invasion boats, as well as most of the weapons and supplies, all the communications equipment, and several leaders, had been seized or arrested by the FBI and other law-enforcement agencies.

On the night of April 24, when we were supposed to have been leaving for Cuba, Felipe and about 20 other Cubans—most of whom I had never seen before and who, I learned, were the remaining top leaders of the secret organization—met in a dingy motel room I had rented in a small town south of Miami. I was looked upon as a minor hero because of my discovery, and they felt safe with me. Before the meeting started, I drew Felipe aside and suggested that they call off the whole deal, since they had no boats or equipment anyway, and wait for a more opportune moment to try again. That was the only time I ever saw Felipe lose his temper. "Every single day those murderers remain in Cuba," he shouted, "hundreds of innocent people are killed, and you and your damned government expect us to do nothing about it?"

He quickly calmed down and the meeting got underway. Someone started off with the suggestion that all the members of the organization flee the United States before they were arrested and make new preparations in another country with a more sympathetic government. But before he could finish, Felipe broke in. To everyone's astonishment, he told us that he had feared some leak in the original plans all along (but admitted that he had never suspected it would be his American friend) and had accordingly taken special, secret precautions. He announced that he had three other boats loaded with supplies and weapons, ready to leave. They could not carry the entire 200-man force, only about 50, but reinforcements could be rushed in within a few days if the advance group established a beachhead. The only thing lacking was a radio transmitter and power generator, both essential to the operation, since otherwise they could not keep in contact with the outside world and call for aid. But he assured them that these items would be obtained the following day.

The next item of business was to select a new provisional government, since most of the members of the previous one were in Miami jails. It was a real free-for-all. I was afraid the rest of us would end up in jail, too, for disturbing the peace. Finally, after hours of arguing, an ex-senator was elected provisional president and others were elected to the vice-presidency and seven ministerial posts. These nine men, along with aides they selected, were to accompany the invasion force which Felipe said would leave the following night. He refused to say from where, merely telling those who were going to be at certain places for pick-up. He was determined that there would be no security leak this time.

After the others had left, I told Felipe flatly that I thought this venture was suicidal, pointing out, among other things, that almost a third of his 50-man invasion force consisted of noncombatant politicians. Nothing would swerve him, but he admitted that it was a pretty risky business, to say the least, and assured me that he would not hold it against me if I backed out. I said I would still go, but only as a press representative, since it was obvious from recent events that my government was seriously opposed to the whole scheme.

The following evening, Felipe picked me up as planned and after two hours of fast driving we reached the little fishing village of Flamingo at the tip of the Florida peninsula, near Cape Sable. The "command boat" turned out to be a 24-foot cabin cruiser sitting so low in the water from the vast amount of weapons, munitions, and people on it that there were only a few inches of freeboard left. Felipe then took me to see one of the other boats in his three-boat flotilla. It was actually half sunk and had to be abandoned and the five men on it transferred to the command boat, thus bringing the number of people on board to 24.

While we waited in the pouring rain for the newly elected provisional president of Cuba and his cabinet to arrive, Felipe filled me in on his plans. The command boat would be used only to carry us 50 miles to sea, where we would transfer to a large fishing trawler that would take us to Cuba. He said the trawler was carrying enough arms and supplies to make us self-sufficient in the mountains for months. Little did we know that the trawler, making its way down the Miami River toward our rendezvous at sea, was at that very moment being boarded by dozens of FBI agents who, after throwing tons of ice overboard, discovered that there was a false lower deck bottom and under that a vast arsenal of weapons.

Overhearing several of the men say they were hungry (all the food was on the trawler), I decided to spend what money I had left on food, since I knew the money wouldn't do me any good in Cuba—that is, if we ever got there. At the end of the pier was a combination fishing tackle and grocery store, which remained open around the clock to cater to the fishing fraternity. As I entered, the man behind the counter greeted me with, "Boy, are you one of those crazy Cuban raiders, too?" I asked him what he was talking about. "Hell, there's two boatloads out there," he answered, "and I thought you was with them. Guess I was wrong." When I began buying up all the bread, lunchmeat, cheese, and other food in store, he said: "Boy, you ain't much of a liar." With nothing to gain by continuing the game, I admitted that I was going and then asked if he had notified the authorities. He said he hadn't, because we were sure to get caught anyway and also because he did not want the Cubans coming around and giving him a hard time—possibly breaking up his store—in retaliation.

Finally, around 4:00 A.M. the provisional government arrived, accompanied by their aides, all dressed in suits and ties and carrying bulging briefcases, as if they were going to a cabinet meeting. Some invasion force: 38 people, including 14 politicians, three women (supposed to be nurses), and one press representative! Castro should have been quaking in his boots. We cast off and started paddling away from the pier, hoping to get away without attracting any attention, but when the man from the store came out and shouted, "Good luck, you crazy bastards," Felipe knew we weren't fooling anyone. He started the motor and we headed out to sea.

From there on, the venture was pure farce. Although it was still raining hard, the sea was flat and calm. Nearly everyone on board became seasick, moaning and vomiting all over the place. Then I learned that except for Felipe, who was busy fiddling around with the motor which didn't sound too healthy, I was the only person on board who knew anything about boats. So I was elected to take the wheel and steer the boat which, because of the great weight of people and equipment on it, was barely moving. After awhile, when things seemed to calm down a bit, I asked Felipe where and when we were supposed to meet the "mother ship," and we all got into a panic—he couldn't remember if it was 10 miles *southwest* or 10 miles *northwest* of the Dry Tortuga Lighthouse! Besides that, we had no charts, and the compass was off at least 30 degrees because of all the metal (rifles, cartridges, et cetera) stored below deck. We were supposed to reach the rendezvous point—wherever that was—the following night. During the day we would hug the coast as though we were on a pleasure cruise. To avoid suspicion, it was agreed that only the three women, Felipe, and I would remain in the open, which meant that the rest, including our dignified provisional president and his cabinet, were stacked like cordwood inside the small cabin that was barely larger than a Ping-Pong table.

Shortly after leaving Flamingo, the boat sprang a leak. At first we were able to keep up with it by using the boat's automatic bailer, but it soon got so bad that we had to bail by hand. In order to reach the water—which was all in the cabin, since most of the weight was up forward—we had to throw all the food I had bought and many other things overboard. Then at precisely 8:25 A.M. the motor began to sputter and we discovered that we were out of gasoline. The fuel line had snapped and the tank had drained before we knew what was happening. We were adrift, surrounded by diving pelicans, about 10 miles from land. Everyone panicked again, only worse this time, shouting for someone to do something quick and scrambling all over the boat looking for life preservers (naturally, there were none), so that the leak got worse. In order to locate the leak we had to throw overboard several large recoilless rifles and several boxes of hand grenades, which to me was much less of a tragedy than the food. We finally found it, only to discover that the hull had come apart near the keelson. We stuffed in some canvas and rags, which checked the flow of water somewhat.

About an hour later we saw a vessel heading toward us, which everyone thought was a police launch, since it was travelling fast and coming from the direction of Flamingo. Third panic of the day. As it neared us, however, we saw that it was a large cabin cruiser. Several of the more militant members of the group demanded that Felipe let them take the boat by force and use it to reach the fishing trawler. I was against this move, and luckily for me, so were the leaders of the provisional government; Felipe agreed that we would only try to obtain fuel from them.

I hailed the yacht but found that it ran on diesel fuel and had no gasoline. Then we asked for a tow to a deserted cay about 12 miles off. After we had run our boat up on the beach to prevent it from sinking, the people on the yacht, instead of leaving, dropped anchor right there and sat down to eat lunch on deck. For a few minutes Felipe was able to contain his people, who were almost smothered in that small cabin, but they suddenly bolted out and started to jump ashore. The Americans on the yacht dropped their forks and stared in amazement at the sight, which was like one of those circus acts with people pouring out of a tiny car seemingly large enough to hold only one man; they, of course, had thought that the three women, Felipe, and I were the only people on board. The people aboard the yacht, not knowing what to make of the scene, apparently thought it was best to get away from there fast and started to pull up anchor. At Felipe's suggestion, I swam over and asked them to radio the Flamingo Yacht Club to send out a boat to pick us up. They did so, while eyeing me suspiciously the whole time, and left quickly.

The scene ashore was like a mass funeral. Half the people were weeping and all of them were milling around and wringing their hands. After awhile Felipe had them unload the boat and bury the weapons and munitions. About eight hours later our rescue boat arrived and we headed back to Flamingo where, we knew, the police would be waiting to welcome us. But Felipe had other plans. When we were about half a mile from Flamingo, but fairly close to shore, he suddenly dove overboard and headed for the beach. I followed him, and we both reached shore at about the same spot. Felipe suggested that we split up and each head for Miami on his own. I told him how sorry I was that things had turned out this way, and he replied: "Roberto, I'm sorry too, but in one way I'm glad. You see, the leaders had planned that somehow you would be one of our first casualties after landing, and your death would be used to arouse public sympathy for our cause in the U.S."

I sat stunned on the beach, scarcely able to take in what I had heard, as Felipe took off clad only in a pair of undershorts. That was the last I ever saw of him. He was arrested a few days later, as all the others had been as soon as they reached Flamingo, but was released on bond. Several months later Felipe managed to get to Cuba where he joined a guerrilla unit and soon afterward was captured and shot by government troops.

After Felipe took off down the beach, I made my way to the nearest phone booth (I was better off than Felipe; I at least had on a pair of swimming trunks) and made a collect call to Miami to a photographer who worked for the *Post*. He drove down to pick me up and hid me for the night at his house. The next morning, after the money the *Post* wired me had arrived, I went to the airport to catch a plane to New York, wearing some of the photographer's clothes and feeling slightly conspicuous, since the trousers were about four inches too short. As I walked up to an airlines ticket counter, I was greeted by the CIA spy who had messed up the original invasion scheme and another CIA agent and was taken to a small room in the terminal where I was questioned for several hours. I would not be arrested this time, they said, but if I participated in any further activities of that nature, I ran the risk of losing my American citizenship. I promised not to and even signed some kind of a declaration they produced.

That was the end of Operation Save-the-World. But I had not really needed this gentle prod from the CIA to convince me. Felipe's parting revelation had done the job for them. I still believed there were missiles in Cuba (and wonder what, if anything, the U.S. government has done to prove me and the many other people who shared this belief wrong), and I was willing to take my chances with Castro's security forces to get the photographs; but I drew the line at letting my so-called friends put a bullet through my head just to provide the "cause" with a Yankee martyr. I was glad to leave the Cuban exiles, missiles, and everything else Cuban (except Cuban rum and Cuban cigars) to the boys in the CIA and State Department and return to my old way of life which I was enjoying before Clay persuaded me that my services were indispensable to the security of the Western Hemisphere.

2: Serranilla Bank

After the Operation Save-the-World debacle I was ready for some excitement in the underwater world, where I felt far more at home than in the cloak-and-dagger world of playing at the spy business. I considered returning to Spain to continue my research in the archives, which had been interrupted when I sailed on the replica of Columbus' ship, the *Niña II.* Having spent almost two years as a landlubber, however, and nearly going blind in the dim and dusty reading rooms of the Spanish Archives, deciphering the spidery scrawl of thousands of faded documents relating to the Spanish treasure fleets, I was ready for what I was convinced would be "The Sure Thing." It was frustrating to sit in those archives day after day, month after month, reading about the tons of treasure lying on the sea floor, just waiting to be picked up. Each time I came across another wreck with a cargo of great wealth, a devil inside would tantalize me: "Marx, you fool, Go! Why waste your time sitting here and reading about it, when you can go find it and become a millionaire?" Then my guardian angel would counter: "Marx, be a good boy and keep studying; history is more important than corroded old treasure." The interior debate raged, but ultimately the "devil" prevailed, convincing me I should go after one good treasure, sort of a test to see if all the research was really worthwhile.

The area I selected was Serranilla Bank, a large barrier reef with several small barren cays dotted along the reef, located about 250 miles southwest of Jamaica. There, in 1665, the major part of a Spanish treasure fleet sank during a dreadful hurricane with almost total loss of life and more than $55,000,000 in treasure. The Spaniards made many attempts to salvage the treasure, but all ended in failure due to the inaccessibility of the wrecks that lay under huge breakers and pounded the barrier reef mercilessly year-round. Hell, I figured, with all that loot I could hire a large team of researchers to work in the archives and even make a donation so they would install lights. With the reams of historical data I had accumulated pertaining to this fleet, it seemed just a matter of picking a time when the seas were calm in the area of the wrecks and harvesting the treasure—like plucking fruit from a tree. I was soon to learn a bitter but valuable lesson. Even the best-planned treasure hunts can fail.

Determined that my "sure thing" would be completely successful, I worked to make it the best-organized and most scientific treasure hunt of all time. Weather is always a critical factor in deciding the success or failure of any expedition—especially one like this—so I spent several weeks talking with meteorological experts. But because the Serranilla Bank was so far away from any inhabited land area, no one really knew much about prevailing weather conditions. However, they all advised: "Try June and July; they're the best months throughout the Caribbean, and the seas will be flat calm."

Convinced that I had solved the weather problem, my next step was to get a vessel, divers, and the necessary operating capital. It was already the end of April, so what I needed was a superduper salesman who could get all of this accomplished while I spent a month in Scotland on assignment for the *Saturday Evening Post,* participating in an expedition to track down the ever-elusive Loch Ness monster. My old friend, Bruce Parker, was just the guy I needed. Parker was an entrepreneur who at various times in his life had operated water-skiing and skin-diving schools in Nassau, run a resort in the Adirondacks, and been bitten hard by the "treasure bug." At this time he was a consultant to Geraldines Laboratories, Inc., an underwater engineering firm in Annapolis, Maryland, which owned a two-man submarine and other equipment that I considered ideal for the venture.

Speaking with absolute certainty and admitting no margin of doubt or error, like an evangelist entranced with a vision of paradise, I easily talked Parker into joining me for the "sure thing." He was all eyes and ears as I pointed to a chart of Serranilla, which was covered with eight

Xs marking the locations of the lost galleons, and told him how we would all be millionaires in a few months' time. Before we had even finished the first bottle of whiskey, Parker said: "Partner, count me in. It's been my lifelong dream to sleep on a bed of gold bars." I put him in charge of logistics and gave him a long list of the essential items needed, never expecting him to obtain even half of them. Much to my astonishment, two days later, before I left for Scotland, Bruce phoned to announce: "Your worries are over, partner; I have every item on your list and a lot more, too." Less than an hour after I had left him in Annapolis, he had found two backers who would put up the funds to charter a vessel for two months and for other operating expenses, in return for a cut of the treasure. Parker chartered the *Sea Hunter*, a 65-foot research vessel that had belonged to Edwin Link, the noted inventor and undersea explorer. Parker got the use of the two-man submarine from the firm he was working for, plus mountains of diving gear from several manufacturing companies, two diving launches, four 80-horsepower outboard engines, two Japanese motor scooters, and an electric chain saw. The purpose of the last two items is still a mystery to me. A great promoter, he also managed the loan of two diving engineers to run the submarine.

On the way to Scotland I stopped off for a few days in Bermuda to see my old friend, Teddy Tucker. I invited him to join the venture because of his knowledge and uncanny ability to find treasure. He had become one of the leading experts in the field with his discovery in 1955 of a Spanish galleon, from which he recovered gold and jewelry valued at over $250,000. He claimed that he could look at a waterlogged timber or coral-encrusted iron cannon and tell not only its place of origin but its exact age. Of course, I knew he was overdoing it bit with these extravagant claims, but he was the right guy for the project. Teddy, who bore a strong resemblance to Sir Francis Drake, was witty and cheerful, but very supersitious. He was also in the habit of taking off his shoes in airplanes because a fortune-teller had predicted that he would die with them on. Tucker, who had the best spy system in the treasure-hunting business, was packed and ready to go when I arrived. Having heard of my project and convinced that I would be inviting him, he had already enlisted the aid of his two brothers-in-law, Robert and Donald Canton, both of whom had worked with him for the past ten years. Having also worked with them in the past, I respected them and knew they would be valuable assets to the venture. In contrast to Tucker, who never stopped talking, they were reticent men with lean faces and long beards which gave them the appearance of sorrowful monks.

After returning from Scotland without having had even a glimpse of "Nessie" (the Loch Ness monster), I had a lawyer draw up contracts for all of the participants to sign. The Tucker contingent would get one-third of the treasure we were sure to recover; the Parker contingent, which included his backers, would get one-third; and I would get one-third. I had planned on taking a few more divers, but both Parker and Tucker dissuaded me, claiming we would have to split the pot too many ways. Clay Blair insisted that I take a staff writer, since I would be too busy loading gleaming bars of gold aboard the salvage ship to take notes.

Phase one called for an aerial survey of the area, to determine the exact location of the wrecks. With constant heavy seas breaking over the wrecks, I was sure they would not be buried under sand or coral and that it would merely be a matter of sighting them from the air, dropping buoys, and then going down with my team of eager professionals on *Sea Hunter*. We planned to fill our vessel with tons of gold, jewelry, and precious stones, not bothering to pick up any of the silver because it was too bulky in relation to its value.

Tucker met me in New York and we flew to Fort Lauderdale, Florida where Parker, who claimed to have chartered a suitable plane for the survey, was busily preparing *Sea Hunter*. The plane was an amphibian, a Republic "Sea Bee," which has a small engine and propeller behind the cabin—commonly known as a "pusher plane." My plan was to use Jamaica as a base from which to work. Just to fly between Jamaica and Serranilla would require a cruising range of at least 500 miles, plus the flight time we would expend over the site. Upon questioning Parker about the performance and capabilities of this plane, he replied: "You treasure experts leave the flying to me and just concentrate on making me a millionaire."

Our first shock came when he announced that we couldn't carry any baggage at all because of a weight problem and that our departure would be delayed briefly while he learned how to fly this type of plane. After watching him make a few practice takeoffs and landings, Tucker said to me (using his nickname for me): "Father, we would have to be complete idiots to fly with such a nut." After the "nut" supervised the topping off of the fuel tanks, two somewhat apprehensive "idiots" climbed aboard. A Hollywood stunt man outdoing himself to perform the worst takeoff possible couldn't have equaled ours. After a dozen great lurching bounces, we ran out of runway and, though we got off the ground, we barely cleared a string of high-tension electrical cables. Once airborne, it wasn't so bad, but it did seem that we were going uncommonly slow. Parker assured us that this was due to strong head winds. I became a bit concerned when after two hours we hadn't even covered the distance between Fort Lauderdale and Key West, a mere 140 nautical miles. Then I noticed that the fuel gauge registered less than half full, and we weren't a quarter of the distance to Jamaica yet —all of which was over water, since we had to swing around Cuba. Parker claimed that the fuel gauge was wrong. He refused to land to check it until we informed him of the fate he would face if we had to ditch in the sea.

We had just passed Key West when Parker rather reluctantly turned the slow-moving plane around and landed there. Examination of the fuel tanks showed that the gauges were not defective. Checking with several pilots there, who knew the capabilities of this kind of plane for the task at hand, we learned that Parker had selected the wrong plane. Tucker was so angry that he refused to let Parker fly us back to Miami to charter another plane. We took a scheduled plane to Miami and from there chartered a twin-engine Cessna 310, along with a pilot who didn't need to be "checked out" on flying the plane before we departed.

From Kingston, Jamaica we made no less than six attempts to reach Serranilla, but each time were forced back after encountering severe thunderstorms. Finally, on the morning of the fourth day, we were successful. It was a wonderful day: we not only reached our objective but sighted no fewer than 15 shipwrecks on the reef—large ballast piles, with anchors and cannon strewn all over the place. Unfortunately, we had forgotten to bring the buoys along, so we marked the locations on a hastily drawn chart. The seas were flat calm, true to the predictions I had been given. It all seemed so beautiful then. We decided to facilitate the locating of the wrecks once we reached the site in the *Sea Hunter* by using an observer in a helium balloon, a method Tucker had had luck with in the waters around Bermuda. The balloon is towed behind a boat, and a man riding the balloon 200 to 300 feet up in the air spots wrecks and either drops buoys on them or directs a small boat to them.

Before setting sail from Key West, Parker and Tucker were constantly on my back, each demanding that I eliminate the other partner, for numerous reasons. But to me, both of them were essential at that stage; besides, the contracts had already been signed. One day before we left, Tucker said to me: "O.K., Father, since you're not going to get rid of Parker, I'm just coming along for the ride, and I'll be damned before I help that geek get rich from our joint efforts." Later I found out he really meant that. It appeared to be a personality conflict, but there turned out to be more to it than I had first realized. Each felt that the other would stoop to the lowest level of humanity to cheat everyone else out of his share of the treasure. I must admit, when Tucker and his brothers-in-law got into one of their frequent three-man huddles while still in Key West, they did resemble a bunch of cutthroats who would think nothing of cutting off your head and flinging you over the side. But I knew them well enough to know it was just an act they were indulging in to antagonize Parker.

Early in June we cleared Key West with the submarine lashed firmly to the afterdeck, a heavy four-man shark cage tied on the stern, the two launches secured to the cabin roof, and tons of equipment taking up every available inch of space below and above decks. Unlike many an expedition on which I had eaten the least appetizing victuals, this time we spent over $2,500 on food. A lot of it went for what I calculated to be a two-month supply of ice cream—my special brain food, which I like even for breakfast. Our cook was a Bahamian named Lionel Dean who had participated in various other unsuccessful treasure hunts over the years, always in the capacity of cook. A realist, he preferred this because he was at least assured of a salary whether or not any treasure was found.

My first task after leaving the dock was to search the vessel for booze. Liquor on boats means trouble, and I never have even beer on my treasure-hunting expeditions. A thorough search yielded a total of 75 bottles of whiskey and rum, eight cases of beer, and 12 gallons of wine —all of which, over the violent protests of the crew, I flung unceremoniously overboard. But, aware that I would pull this stunt, Tucker and his henchmen had already taken extraordinary measures. In the engine room I had stored several large boxes of chemicals and distilled water for cleaning and preserving the artifacts we expected to find on the wrecks. Several weeks passed before I discovered (and then only after I found the Bermuda trio totally zonked one night) that they had replaced the chemicals and distilled water with a healthy supply of gin, vodka, rum, and brandy—a total of 10 gallons of spirits.

In the Parker contingent were the two engineers, Hank Weinkap and George Bezak, and a new and unexpected addition: Commander Robert Thurman, master diver and senior salvage officer of the U.S. Navy. As a last-minute precaution, probably to insure that Parker wouldn't run away with their share, Parker's mysterious backers had insisted that we take Thurman as their personal representative. Then there was young Lewis Lapham, now editor of *Harper's* magazine, the chap Clay Blair had sent along as a staff writer. Poor Lapham wasn't a happy choice to send along on such a venture. He had been born with a silver spoon in his mouth and was accustomed to all the creature comforts. And he had never been to sea in his life.

From Key West we proceeded on a triangular course around the western end of Cuba—a place I wanted to avoid at all costs—to Georgetown, Grand Cayman Island, stopping there only long enough to refuel and replenish the ice cream supply, which much to my regret was ebbing at an alarming rate. After dragging some of the crew out of island bars, where they had already shared our "secret plans" with half of the inhabitants, we got under way again for Serranilla some 230 miles away. The first night out a heavy argument arose between the Tucker and Parker contingents, with me trying to act as peacemaker. Tucker discovered that Parker had locked up all four firearms belonging to the expedition in his own cabin. He accused Parker of planning to use the guns to rob all of the treasure from his group and me. Then, to make matters worse, it came out in the course of the ensuing battle that both Parker and Tucker had made special arrangements to dispose of their shares of the treasure. Parker had a DC-3 on standby in Miami, which would fly to Grand Cayman or Jamaica and pick him and his gold up and then fly to Switzerland. Tucker, equally prepared to do well for himself, had a large vessel en route from Bermuda, which would meet us on the high seas and carry the Bermuda trio and their share away to some undisclosed place.

Some of the author's nondiving team during the expedition to Serranilla Bank in 1964. They are inspecting a ballast stone. Left to right: Donald Canton, Bob Canton, Teddy Tucker, and Commander Thurman

All the following day *Sea Hunter* struggled against steadily rising head winds and seas. We were knocked about so violently that on one occasion Lionel was almost decapitated when his head smashed through one of the galley windows, and Thurman was thrown through the glass upper half of one of the wheelhouse doors. Luckily we stanched the wounds and avoided heading back to Grand Cayman for medical assistance. At noon we were forced to reduce speed to three knots. With a one-knot current setting against us, we were barely crawling along. At sunset the sky looked so sick that Tucker exclaimed: "Boys, if I saw such a sky in Bermuda, I'd go in the cellar and stay for a week!" Our ex-playboy-turned-journalist, Lapham, was unhappy. He turned as white as a ghost and wore his life jacket constantly. As each heavy sea hit us, he let out a yelp and begged us to turn about and take him to the nearest land.

At sunup the next morning the wind was blowing at over 50 knots and I was beginning to think we might be running right into a full-scale hurricane. To make matters worse, Thurman, who had insisted on being the navigator by virtue of his association with the backers, announced that he didn't have the foggiest notion where we were, other than "somewhere on the bloody high seas." Like the others on what soon resembled "a ship of fools," Thurman was quite a fascinating character in his own right. Physically reminiscent of Popeye, he had run away to sea at the age of 12 and had spent most of his life as a diver. Now almost 50 and within a few months of retiring from the navy, he had taken a leave to come with us. Besides the romance which appealed to him, he had the hope of "finding me a few quid and buying me a shack someplace."

According to the course we had set from Grand Cayman, we expected to reach Serranilla at dawn this day—even at our reduced speed. Fearing that we might end up as one more wreck on the reef, I told Thurman to try and get the LORAN set working, which he had been unable to do since leaving Key West. New at the job and peering fixedly into the glowing cathode-ray tube, adjusting the flickering signals, he finally got a reading and with a jubilant smile plotted a fix on the chart. It placed us in the mountains of Jamaica at least 250 miles to the east. Two more days were wasted in zig-zagging all over the sea, until we finally found Serranilla, and just when we were nearly on top of the barrier reef, it was rough as hell; the wind was blowing incessantly between 40 and 50 knots.

Expecting everyone to follow me, I donned my snorkeling gear and began searching the inside of the reef, because many of the lighter objects from wrecks are usually washed over the reef onto the inside. Since we would have to work without the balloon (we had been unable to obtain a supply of helium before leaving Key West), finding these goodies would help us locate the wrecks on the outside. After spending a few fruitless minutes in the water, I began to wonder what was keeping my "partners" from coming in, so I swam back to the boat to see what was holding them up. Letting everyone know of my indignation at having to dive alone, I still couldn't convince any of them to join me. Tucker said: "Entirely too boisterous, Father; not my sort of thing at all." The others all had excuses, too. Thurman claimed he had to erect the antenna for his ham radio set, and our diving engineers assured me they had to make some alterations on the submarine. Parker finally agreed to follow me around in our largest launch, since the area was swarming with large sharks—or "gobblers," as we called them—and I might have to make a quick exit from the water. I was even angrier when we pulled away: Tucker was up on the bow sunning himself, reading *Playboy,* and slurping away on a big bowl of ice cream. He waved and shouted: "Watch out something doesn't bite you, Father. There are some very nasty animals swimming about here."

By sundown I had been in the water more than six hours—bobbing around on the surface like a cork at the mercy of the heavy seas that cascaded across the barrier reef—and my only discovery was a rusty beer can. Yet I knew that only a few hundred yards on the outside of the reef, millions of dollars in treasure lay, just waiting to be recovered. If the 20- to 25-foot breakers had been a bit smaller, I might have even ventured out for a quick look. That night after a succulent meal—steak, chicken, and some lobsters I had grabbed that day—I gave them a rip-roaring pep talk that would have done credit to a field marshal.

The following morning I thought my team finally had the old fighting spirit when everyone except Lapham and the cook offered to dive with me. But what followed was enough to make a sane man laugh himself into lunacy. To start with, neither Tucker nor his two brothers-in-law had ever used swim fins or snorkels; their years of diving had all been with surface-supplied air sources. They would jump over the side of a boat, sink to the bottom, walk to where they had to work for the day, and sit there breathing the air pumped into their face masks through hoses connected to the surface. This was a different cup of tea! The water was still quite rough, and with a swift current running, they could barely make headway without the assistance of fins. After a few minutes they got out of the water for what I thought was a brief rest. But that turned out to be their first and only dive during the entire expedition. Our senior naval diving officer was loaded down with everything from three kinds of shark repellant to an abalone iron (abalone are found only in the Pacific Ocean), plus a large blue bag "for the gold" and a red one "for the jewels." After wallowing around in the water like a sick hippocampus (a type of sea monster) for a few seconds, he scrambled back aboard as if a Russian torpedo were chasing him. He announced that during 20 years of diving, he hadn't been able to master the use of the snorkel and wouldn't do any further diving until we got around to the "real" diving—either with SCUBA or helmet diving equipment. This was his only dive of the expedition. Engineer Weinkap developed a sudden "earache" even though he had been snorkeling only a few minutes and had barely had his head under water. It was his only dive, too.

When they had all jumped in there, at least six gobblers were cruising in the immediate area. No doubt these unwelcome guests helped convince them to leave the diving to Parker, Bezak, and me. At supper that evening, after another unproductive day, Lionel philosophically said to me: "Boss man, you've got the biggest pack of nondiving divers I ever didst see! If I didn't have to stay aboard to keep those hungry vultures from eating up all of your ice cream, I would come in and help you find that gold."

Within minutes of entering the water on the third day, we located ballast stones, iron spikes, ship's fittings, pottery shards, and other artifacts, all interesting and encouraging, but nothing that was really dateable. Around dusk, I was pulling a large lobster from a coral cave when I spotted the unmistakable gleam of gold farther back in the cave. Right next to what I saw was a gold coin, a large moray eel hovered, making menacing gestures at me. If I swam back to the launch for a spear gun to kill the moray, I might not find the right spot again; so

I took a chance and made a frantic lunge for the gold piece. The moray bolted out of the cave so fast that he knocked my face mask off. But with the coin secure in my hand, I surfaced, eyes burning from the salt water. I was elated! The coin bore the date 1664, which meant it was from one of the galleons I was after. I swam like a demon back to the *Sea Hunter,* rather than to our diving launch, to announce my discovery. But instead of the enthusiasm I had expected, I met only skepticism. Tucker even suggested that I had "planted" the coin on the bottom to fire up my useless team.

For the next three weeks each day was a repetition of the preceding day. At sunup Parker, Bezak, and I would take off in the launch and spend 10 to 12 hours searching for more signs of wreckage on the leeward side of the barrier reef. Not once during this time did the wind drop below 25 knots, which effectively prevented us from going on the outside where we knew the wrecks lay. On the inside of the reef we continued to find countless signs of wreckage and artifacts, most of them dating from the period of the 1665 disaster, plus some of more recent vintage. No more gold turned up, but we did find a silver snuff box, two silver buckles, and 28 badly corroded pieces of eight. At first, so all three of us could search together, Tucker helped us by running the launch, following close by and searching the bottom through a glass-bottom bucket. Then one day a big gobbler came out of nowhere and grabbed the bucket right out of his hand. This convinced him that he should be back on *Sea Hunter* playing cards with the others.

The gobblers were a constant problem. At times there were as many as twenty nearby. They were of all species and sizes; the worst were the smaller varieties about five to six feet long. The big grandaddies would usually just drop around for a few minutes to wish us a good day, but the smaller ones were feisty and would stick around for hours, making aggressive passes at irregular intervals. Consequently, we had to work out a system whereby only one of us actually searched the sea floor for signs of wreckage while the other two kept their eyes on the gobblers and drove them off when they came too close. I briefly entertained visions of the tranquil world of the archives.

One morning only moments after jumping in, we were surrounded by three very aggressive, five-foot makos. Within seconds these three were augmented by two larger lemon sharks and another mako. They began a coordinated attack, making quick passes at us and retreating only after being smashed on their snouts with crowbars or shark billies. This nerve-wracking encounter lasted almost three hours. Each time one of us tried to flip into the launch, at least two of the beasts would charge right at him, and only by frantic shouting, swinging of crowbars, and jabbing with shark billies did we drive them off again. In the end, our perseverance paid off. The sharks got tired of playing the game and meandered off en masse in quest of more willing prey. The number of "divers" now dropped to two, Bezak having decided that he had come along mainly as an engineer to run the submarine and not to make some gobbler a good meal.

Spearfishing to supplement our provisions was almost impossible because of the large number of sharks. We were getting tired of eating three-inch-thick steaks and lobsters every day and would have enjoyed a change of fare. Parker and I came up with a great plan to outwit the gobblers. We waited until the searching was done one day, then jumped aboard the launch and blasted away a full throttle, hoping to leave the sharks behind at the other end of the reef. We knew of a cave in the reef that housed a 50-pound grouper and anchored directly over it. Parker was to shoot it and I would ride shotgun. No sharks were about, so down we dived. Parker hit him with a beautiful shot right between the eyes and eased him out of the cave. Before we had reached the surface, no less than 15 sharks appeared in a feeding frenzy. Parker dropped the gun and fish, which probably saved us, because all of the gobblers went after the fish and each other while we shot out of the water like Polaris missiles and into the launch. One 12-foot grandaddy that had probably been too slow and missed out on the feed came up nearly as fast and hit the bottom of the launch with such force that we were sure the bottom would fall out of the boat. He began attacking the outboard engine, nearly twisting it off before we drove him away by beating on his hard head with our crowbars.

Aboard the *Sea Hunter,* life wasn't too bad if one could close his ears to the constant bickering and to Thurman's repetitious squawking into his ham radio. All day long he would drain the ship's batteries, talking to every joker who answered his call sign. "You lucky, lucky man," Thurman could be heard saying at all hours of the day and night . . . "You're the 167th person I've raised today from Serranilla Bank where we're on a top-secret treasure hunt. . . ."

Lionel announced one morning that he had dreamed there was treasure buried on the sandy cay nearest to the one where we were anchored. Our "nondiving" divers decided that it was the only sensible way to find treasure on Serranilla, so they took the second launch and went ashore. Although the only metal detector was in a waterproof container, one of them managed to get it wet, and thereafter it was sensitive to everything from sand to water, and of course they didn't find anything on Lionel's cay.

One evening when the tension level aboard *Sea Hunter* was dangerously high, I thought it would be a good idea to get the crew doing something less potentially dangerous than throwing threatening looks at one another and possibly plotting murder. I proposed that we all go ashore on one of the cays and catch a turtle that night, since spearfishing seemed out of the question. But the apathetic spirit that had characterized most of them throughout the expedition prevailed now, and I had no takers until someone suggested we should bet on exactly at which moment the first turtle crawled ashore. Then, because most of them were sure the others would cheat, everyone wanted to go ashore. We left Lionel aboard to keep an anchor watch, and I put Robert Canton in charge of running the shuttle service between the cay and the launch.

I don't know whether Tucker can secretly communicate with turtles or not, but shortly after dark and right to the exact minute he had bet the first turtle would appear, a 400-pounder came struggling ashore through the heavy breakers. It took all of us to flip her over on her back. With our prize thus immobilized, we began signaling with a flashlight for Robert to come pick us up. (It didn't do any good, because right after depositing us on the cay, he had returned to *Sea Hunter* and gone to sleep, not waking up until the next morning when his growling belly told him it was time to eat turtle eggs.) For nearly an hour we flashed our light, as well as cussed him out in every language we could muster. Finally we were faced with the unhappy choice of trying to swim the quarter mile through those gobbler-infested waters or roughing it for the night on the cay. After all of my craven comrades had tried and failed to convince me that it was my duty, as expedition leader, to swim back to the launch, we set about digging deep holes to crawl into for protection. All we had on were swimsuits, and the chilly wind was blowing at near gale force. With rather large and nasty crabs trying to bite chunks out of us, hundreds of booby birds screeching infernally, and the rain pelting down on our heads, we had still other hazards to face: the first turtle was followed by another and another and another. During the night no less than 187 huge turtles came ashore to lay their eggs. The cay was less than the size of a basketball court, and many of those turtles fell right into our holes, nearly crushing us to death. Finally I organized a "turtle watch," which amounted to one guy taking a turn at driving away all the turtles that came into our vicinity.

At sunup the maddest and sorriest-looking pack of derelicts went back on board *Sea Hunter,* all planning to murder old Robert. Suspecting this, he hid out in the hot engine room where he managed to stay for most of the day, with both doors securely locked, until all of us cooled down and wrote it off as merely another unique experience. Hell, watching all of those turtles digging their holes, seemingly weeping tears and depositing huge amounts of eggs, we had witnessed mother nature at work.

By this time we had completely searched all the sea floor inside the ever-pounding barrier reef. Now there wasn't much we could do but wait until it calmed down so we could get on the outside and pick up the damn treasure. The chart showed another cay on the same bank about 20 miles away, so Parker and I decided to take the big launch and check it out. We were surprised to find two Jamaican fishing boats and a fishing camp composed of a few thatch huts on the cay. Because the weather was so deplorable, most of the Jamaicans weren't fishing, and instead were busily stripping scrap metal from a small freighter that had run aground on the cay two years before during a hurricane.

They were as surprised to see us, as we were them, especially when we arrived in such a small boat. But they were very friendly and helpful. According to them, June and July are the worst two months to be on Serranilla. "It's the breeziest damn place in the whole Carribbean . . . just ain't no place like it any worse." Using our walky-talky, I radioed for the nondiving divers to move *Sea Hunter* to this anchorage, which was obviously much better than our old one.

That evening I invited the captain of one of the fishing boats aboard for a chat, and as most old salts do, he claimed to know of treasures in every corner of the bloody Caribbean. As we pushed one chart after another under his nose, he'd point and proclaim: "There! There you'll find a sunken iron chest with exactly 4,657 pieces of eight in it," or in another place he would tell us there was "a great old wreck just loaded with tons of gold; but one has to be careful when trying to enter it, since several of the people that drowned on it have been reincarnated into large sharks who guard it." Feeling that there just might be some truth in his fanciful tales, the next night I invited the captain of the other fishing boat aboard for a similar chat. I was hoping he would make his X's in the same spots the other captain had marked, which could mean there was at least some truth in all their bull. I can still hear him babbling away between big spoonfuls of ice cream: "Yea, mon, I swear to ye—there's great pigs of gold lying on this 'ere reef, and only because I like ye guys, I'm showing ye the exact locations." So much bull was coming from every mouth aboard *Sea Hunter* that we were knee-deep in the stuff. But by the time we got rid of the second great yarn spinner, it was over our heads.

We spent a few more days searching the inside reef area near the Jamaicans' cay, with little success. We were also waiting for the weather to improve. Meanwhile, I was confronted with a mini-mutiny in which about half of the men demanded that we head back to Grand Cayman where they could catch a plane for the States. I gave them the choice of joining one of the rat-infested Jamaican boats or sticking it out on *Sea Hunter,* and they elected to stay. Having done everything possible, given the conditions at Serranilla, I decided that the best way to wait out the bad weather was to go to Serrana Bank, 85 miles due south, where I knew of a number of valuable wrecks. I hoped that by some miraculous stroke of fortune, the weather would be better down there. One thing was for certain—it couldn't be any worse.

The voyage to Serrana was as fouled up as the one from Grand Cayman to Serranilla had been. We plowed into huge head seas at a nasty angle, so that every fifth or sixth sea broke over our port bow, each time causing the overloaded vessel to appear to be capsizing. Lapham was so sick that even the "Bermuda trio" felt sorry for him. We were supposed to make our landfall about sunup after a night crossing, but instead, we lost another day and a half searching for Serrana and might have taken even longer if Thurman hadn't discovered that inside an innocent-looking jersey set next to the compass, some villain had put a large metal tool to throw the compass off.

Serrana was forlorn, just as Serranilla had been—the same barren cays, the same sandbars and miles of reefs covered with churning white water—and the wind was still blowing, this time at a steady 40 knots. The shallow bank on the inside of the reef was, if anything, more difficult to navigate than on Serranilla. It was studded with shoals and small coral reefs, some of them hidden only a few feet under the surface. We ran aground repeatedly and once got stuck fast for four hours until Parker and I chopped away enough coral to get the boat off. We eventually anchored near an area where one of the Jamaican captains had sworn was a large pile of ballast stones covered with "guns of green metal"—which meant bronze cannon.

For the next three days Parker and I took turns dragging each other on a makeshift sea sled as close to the inside of the reef as possible. We could do this because there didn't appear to be many sharks around. Although we found debris from several modern wrecks, we couldn't get onto the reef where the bronze cannon were supposed to be because of the breakers.

On the fourth day the wind dropped to around 15 knots, the first time it had done so in the month since we left Key West. Compared to what we had been through, this was a calm day. By this time, I was ready to try anything! Though Tucker was the best small-boat handler in the crew, he declined the task, saying: "No, not me, Father, I'm strictly an inside man." And our naval hero refused with: "Damn young foolishness; only a stupid leatherneck would try anything so rash." Parker, who still had his DC-3 waiting in Miami, was as desperate as I was, so he offered to go along. We managed to con Bezak and Lapham into the deal by offering them the remaining quart of ice cream as a prize. They were to run the launch if both Parker and I dived at the same time.

Parker decided to try to get us out through the barrier reef rather than go about 20 miles to get around one of the outside corners and back to the same area. Finding a narrow break in the reef, he waited until a split second after a big wave broke; then he blasted through the gap at full throttle. Once outside, we saw that it hadn't improved as much as it had appeared through binoculars.

In a few minutes we sighted a large dark area close in to the barrier reef. It did indeed look like a large pile of ballast stones. Parker edged closer so I could check it out, and I was just climbing over the side to investigate when someone let out with a piercing scream. I looked up to see a 15-foot wall of water rushing down on us! It lifted the launch like a paper cup and dashed it on the reef, smashing it to pieces. The next thing I knew, I was crawling onto a high part of the reef, bleeding from coral cuts and stung by millions of sea urchin spines. I had also cracked some ribs but didn't realize it until I had an x-ray on Grand Cayman a few days later. No doubt, the four of us were blessed with the same luck that preserves other idiots who attempt such foolish things; though all of us were banged up, we were alive, and that's what counted.

Not only had our friends on *Sea Hunter* watched the giant wave wreck us, they had made bets on how long it would take to reach us. As Lionel later explained, everyone wanted to run the show and save us, and for the next two or three hours, it was like a madhouse on the boat. They managed to put the other, smaller launch in the water, but not before they had smashed a small hole in the side. Then they spent two hours unsuccessfully trying to start all three of the remaining outboard engines. Why? Simple: some character had filled the gas can with diesel oil, either deliberately or accidently.

Shortly after I had crawled up on the reef and was joined by the others, our walky-talky, which was in a plastic bag, drifted by and I grabbed it. Much to my surprise, it still seemed to be working. Not realizing that those on *Sea Hunter* knew of our plight, I tried in vain to reach them. They had neglected to turn their set on when we left. By a freakish chance, however, I reached a taxicab dispatcher in Kingston, Jamaica, who decided I was some kind of nut when I kept transmitting for help. The dispatcher, who was a woman with a large vocabulary of colorful curse words, kept responding to my call of distress with such messages as "Get your damn ass off this channel! What the hell is this bloody Mayday nonsense? I'm going to put your ass in jail! Cab 22, go to 340 Constant Spring Road."

As we waited and waited, Bezak said: "Last night I was reading one of those dirty books with nude pictures of Jayne Mansfield in them, and I had so many evil thoughts, I guess this serves me right." As the sun dropped lower and lower, there was still no sign of rescuers from *Sea Hunter.* Finally, when my second swim fin drifted up on the reef, I decided to swim the half mile out to the ship to see what the hell they were up to. Surely by this time, they had realized we were in trouble. It was like a scene out of a Hollywood buccaneer movie. There were more sharks around than we had seen in the last three days. They had probably been attracted by our bleeding wounds. Without a face mask, I nearly went blind trying to keep track of the gobblers "escorting" me back to *Sea Hunter*. Twice one of them brushed against my legs, which released a shot of adrenalin that enabled me to make the swim in something like record time. I climbed aboard and found a chaotic situation.

Using the small launch was out of the question, since they couldn't get the outboards working and there weren't any oars. To my horror, it looked like another swim back to the reef, pulling our two-man, cork life raft loaded with first-aid supplies, a jug of what I thought was fresh water, and a shark billy. After scrounging every piece of line we had aboard, the Cantons tied them together and attached one end to the raft so we could all climb aboard and be pulled back to *Sea Hunter*. Then, before jumping back in, Tucker applied some of his first-aid skills. One gash in my leg was quite deep, so, to arrest the bleeding, Tucker filled the gash with hot beeswax and taped it up.

Swimming back was one of the most grueling things I have ever done. The wind had picked up again to about 25 knots, and both it and current were against me, which made towing the raft, as well, a Herculean feat. I was so beat that I didn't even bother trying to keep track of the sharks that were keeping pace with me. Near sunset I reached the three men stranded on the reef. The jug of water, it turned out, contained gin—no doubt, a gift from the Bermuda Trio. At this stage of the fiasco, I didn't really care about finding out who had smuggled it aboard. Dazed but relieved, Lapham and Bezak joked about having earned the last quart of ice cream, only to discover when we got aboard that it had already been eaten by Tucker and his henchmen.

For the next two days I was nearly driven out of my mind by everyone insisting that we head directly for Grand Cayman. There were even threats of marooning me on one of the deserted cays if I continued to resist them. Up till now, most of the quarreling had been between the Parker and the Tucker groups, with me as the referee. Now the whole ship, including Lionel, was against me, and I knew I was fighting a losing battle. With no way to get near the reef, since *Sea Hunter* drew too much water, and in view of the fact that we still hadn't solved the mystery of why the outboards wouldn't start, things looked grim. It took a yarn by Tucker to make things look better.

After consuming the last of our steaks that night, Tucker became serious—a rare occurrence for him—and told us such a fantastic story that I was formulating new plans even before he had completed it. Earlier that year, he said, he had been in the Bahamas (which was true), that he had gone on a cruise with a close friend in Bahamian waters (which was also true), and that on the cruise, while diving for conch, he had accidently found a fabulous treasure wreck south of Bimini. Besides 26 brass cannon, there was a huge gold platter and numerous other gold objects, all of which he hid in a nearby coral cave. Had he brought it aboard at the time, he would have had to split it with about 20 other people, some of whom he didn't like. Although this tale seemed like something from Raw Guts magazine, we fell for it hook, line, and sinker. Tucker went on to say that he was telling us this only because he didn't want us to go back and become the "laughing stock of the treasure-hunting field."

The next morning, we were off for Grand Cayman. We had barely tied up to the racky dock when everyone except Parker and Lionel announced that they were leaving.

"What about the great treasure in the Bahamas, Teddy?" I asked.

"Ah, Father," he replied, "I'll meet you guys at Bimini."

It took Parker and me two days of hard drinking to convince Tucker to stick with us. Both the Cantons and Thurman had taken the first plane for Miami with a minimum of fanfare. In the case of Lapham, I phoned Clay Blair who threatened him with dire penalties if he deserted, so he was forced to stick it out a bit longer. We made a brief stop at Key West where we again had a devil of a time trying to keep Tucker with us. Finding his fabulous wreck was a cinch, since it was located only a hundred yards off a rocky cay. We set our course directly for the one he indicated on the chart. In contrast to what we had experienced in the past five weeks, we found the seas in the Bahamas as flat as a pancake; there wasn't a breath of wind, and the sharks were scarce. The only setback was that upon our arrival, Tucker announced that all those rocky cays looked alike, that he wasn't sure which was the right one. So for the next two weeks, Parker and I dived around every cay and rock south of Bimini, while Tucker searched from the small launch with a glass-bottom bucket. Bezak and Weinkap conducted a search from the submarine which we finally got to use for the first time.

Not until we had thoroughly searched every possibility, covering an area stretching some 20 miles, did Tucker come out cool as hell and admit that he had fabricated the whole story "to save us from the dangers of those treacherous banks," as he put it. He had convinced us so cunningly that not one of us had suspected that it was all bull. We were contemplating, again, murder, and it's only by some miracle that Tucker is still around to laugh about his hoax.

Sea Hunter still had a week left on her charter, but I had had enough. Parker dropped Tucker and me off in Bimini and then spent the next week searching for other wrecks on his own; but he was no more successful than we had been. Finally, rather than go back and face his backers empty-handed, he ran into another group of treasure-hunters and bought an iron cannon from them so he would have something to take back with him. Thus, the "sure thing" had failed. I should have listened to my guardian angel, after all, who was now chastising me with "there's no fool like a gold fool."

3: Serrana Bank

After spending an interesting month in Yugoslavia, working as a technical consultant on *The Long Ships,* an MGM movie starring Richard Widmark and Sidney Poitier, I returned to the hallowed, serene halls of the Archivo de las Indias in Seville. Once again I was living in the past, reading fascinating accounts of the men who braved unknown oceans in those cranky old ships between the Old and the New Worlds. On weekends, when the archives were closed, I explored the seas between Gibraltar and the Portuguese coast, and under the auspices of the Cádiz Archaeological Museum, recovered thousands of artifacts from the numerous wrecks that litter the coast, some dating back to the Phoenicians. Unlike the beautiful Caribbean, diving off the southern coast of Spain was more of a task than a joy. The water there is quite cold year-round, and the underwater visibility is seldom more than six feet—compared to the 100 to 200 feet I had seen in the Caribbean.

At first I wanted to forget all about the "sure thing" fiasco, but as the months of research wore on, I began giving more and more thought to returning to Serranilla and Serrana. I came to the conclusion that the only way to locate the wrecks was to do it on my own rather than try to cope with a large crew of crazies. To keep the project within my financial means, I determined to use the nearest point of civilization as a stepping-stone—either Grand Cayman or one of the Colombian-owned islands south of Serrana. I planned to stay as long as necessary and was determined not to let the weather win another round. To do this, I would need a boat large enough to carry me to one of the keys, set up a campsite, and operate out of a small launch. Two gems of historical facts gleaming among the hundreds of thousands I had gleaned convinced me that Serrana should be my main objective and that I should shelve the 1665 treasure fleet project until a later date.

In 1605 a Spanish fleet sailing between Cartagena, Colombia and Havana, Cuba was struck by a hurricane near Serrana, and six galleons carrying over $20,000,000 in treasure were dashed to pieces on the coral reefs, with a loss of all aboard. According to the hundreds of pages of documents relating to the disaster, nothing was recovered by contemporary salvors, because when they discovered a year later that Serrana was the site of the disaster, the ships' cargoes had been buried under shifting sands. What interested me was the fact that several of the ships had been swept over the barrier reef and their remains buried under the sands on the leeward, or calmer, side of the reef. This meant that it was possible to locate and salvage these wrecks, no matter how rough it was on the outside—barring a hurricane, of course.

But even more exciting to me, since I was fascinated with history, was an account written by a seaman named Pedro Serrano, from which Serrana Bank was named. Four centuries ago it was the setting for an almost unparalleled feat of human survival, one which many scholars believe Daniel Defoe may have based *Robinson Crusoe* on.

In 1528 Serrano was the master of a small ship that was wrecked during a storm on Serrana which at that time did not appear on any charts or maps. The ship quickly broke up in the storm, but Serrano and the others managed to reach a minuscule, treeless, waterless, deserted cay nearby. The rest of the unlucky survivors couldn't stand the rigors of life on the barren islet, so, except for Serrano, a young boy, and a man, they built a raft and took to the sea, never to be heard from again. Naked until he crafted a crude sealskin garment, Serrano survived on the cay for eight years. There was no water on the cay except for some brackish water he found by digging wells and that which he collected during occasional brief showers. Mostly, he sated his thirst with the blood of turtles, seals, and birds. During the first two months he ate his meat and fish raw, then one day he dived down to the wreck site and found a flint from which he was able to strike a spark.

During the third month two survivors from another ship wrecked nearby reached his cay. Soon after that, one of them, along with the boy who thought anything was preferable to captivity with no hope of rescue, left in a makeshift boat and were also never heard from again. With his remaining companion, Serrano erected two stone towers, and on top of one of them the two men carefully nurtured a sort of eternal flame, burning pieces of driftwood that the sea threw up, hoping to signal a passing ship. After seven years they were rescued and taken to Havana. The excitement must have been too great for Serrano's companion, for he died soon after arriving in Cuba. Serrano, however, went home to Spain where he became a celebrity. Wearing his exotic sealskin garb and with hair and a beard that reached almost to his knees, Serrano toured the courts of Europe, where the tale of his experiences aroused great interest. Pedro Serrano—unusually fortunate, as well as hardy—lived to a ripe old age and died a wealthy man.

Little did I realize after reading this intriguing account that I would one day find myself on the same barren cay and be forced to repeat Serrano's saga of survival.

My friend from Texas, "Momo" Kalb, was eager to join me on the venture. Momo had worked with me on several wrecks a few years before, off the coast of Yucatán, and I knew he had the endurance and temperament for such a project. We met in New York where we purchased the necessary equipment. While we were there, I heard rumors about treasure being found around Fort Pierce, Florida, so we decided to stop briefly there before heading for Serrana. I looked up an old diving companion, Carl Clausen, who was then working as the Florida State Underwater Archaeologist. Carl told us that a short time before, a young boy had been out catching lobsters one day. A small nurse shark was sleeping on the sandy bottom, and the boy grabbed it by the tail. The startled shark went berserk, kicking up clouds of sand. When it had settled and the water cleared, the boy saw that the bottom was paved with gleaming gold coins. Within an hour he had gathered over $100,000 in American double-eagle, twenty-dollar pieces.

Carl had not told us everything that was going on, however, as we discovered while enjoying a seafood dinner that evening. I noticed that our waitress was wearing a magnificent Spanish eight-escudo gold coin around her neck. A few discreet questions revealed that she had gotten it from none other than Mel Fisher, an old buddy from my early diving days in California. I decided to pay Mel a surprise visit, but I wasn't prepared for what I saw when we walked into his small apartment in Vero Beach. There was treasure-hunter Mel and another old friend, Rupe Gates, sitting on the living room floor with more than $1,000,000 worth of gold and silver treasure, inventoring the whole lot before turning it over to a bank. After more than a year of tedious salvage work on the 1715 Spanish treasure fleet that had been wrecked in that area, they had struck pay dirt the day before we arrived. After seeing all of this treasure, Momo and I were really primed for Serrana Bank.

Fisher and Gates mentioned that the National Park Service had recently bought six large bronze cannon that had been found on Serrana by a fisherman from Grand Cayman Island. This necessitated another detour before we headed for Serrana. We didn't have much trouble tracking down the fisherman. On the small island of Grand Cayman everyone knows everyone else, what they did yesterday and are doing today. The fisherman turned out to be a Captain Birdy who had been prowling the waters of Serranilla and Serrana for 50-odd years. For once, it looked like I had found an honest seadog, someone whose information would truly be helpful. He had quite a tale to tell. In 1932 he had found two large wooden barrels buried in the sand on the eastern end of Serrana. With the help of his two sons, the barrels were raised and opened. The men were disappointed to find that they were filled with tar. They began chopping the tar into small chunks so they could use it to coat the bottom of their boat. Disappointment fled and elation reigned when the lumps of tar proved to be gold! More than 2,500 Spanish gold coins and a number of small gold ingots had been hidden in the barrels. Not only did Birdy have a few of the coins as proof, but he showed us some newspaper articles and a receipt from the U.S. Mint in Philadelphia, which had bought the gold by the pound. Too bad, because the numismatic value was worth a hundred times the actual gold value; it was a shame to realize that the Spanish gold had gone into Uncle Sam's melting pot. In 1942 Captain Birdy was engaged in recovering iron cannon and anchors on Serrana Bank, to sell in the United States as scrap metal which, of course, was in great demand during the war. While searching, he found a large gold bell weighing over 50 pounds. As a result of these finds and others he made elsewhere in the western Caribbean, Captain Birdy owned a considerable portion of Grand Cayman Island. Asking nothing more than my word that I would give him credit, "if the Lord sees that you find a bonanza," as he put it, he marked on a chart of Serrana Bank the positions of all the wrecks that he remembered.

In studying the charts, I discovered that Serrana Bank is claimed by both the United States and Colombia. When I wrote the U.S. State Department, I was told (as I might have expected) that it was owned solely by the United States and that Colombia had no legal claim to it. (In 1972 the United States relinquished its claim, and it now belongs to Colombia, although Nicaragua and Honduras also claim it.) This cheered me because, under United States jurisdiction, everything I found would be mine, whereas if Colombia owned it, I would have had to obtain a permit from the Colombian government and split what I found with them. I had the State Department write to the Colombian governor on San Andrés, the nearest island to Serrana Bank, which I was going to use as my base. The letter was worded in such a way that the governor and others who read it interpreted it to mean I was working for the State Department, and even before Momo and I got there, the word was out that we were two gringo CIA agents. It created havoc, because, at the time, the island was not only one of the biggest centers of smuggling in the Caribbean but was also used by Castro agents as a base for fomanting subversion throughout Latin America.

When we arrived at San Andrés, Momo and I were unaware of this intrigue. Our only interest, after we had obtained supplies, was in hiring a boat to take us to Serrana. However, we quickly found out what the score was! Returning to the hotel from a bar, our first night on the island, we were attacked by five Cubans armed with knives and clubs. If it hadn't been for the intervention of two Colombian secret policemen who were trailing us, I doubt that I would be around to write this book. The next morning we were hustled in to see the governor who politely but firmly suggested that we leave the island as quickly as possible, since he did not want to be responsible for our lives. He was sure we were CIA agents, and nothing we said could shake this conviction. After the welcome we had had, I wasn't any too eager to stay either, so I hired a large coastal trading ship to carry us to Serrana, and we were off— or so I thought. We had barely cleared the harbor when I realized with a sinking heart that not only were several crew members the same guys who had attacked us the night before, but everyone was wearing a gun.

For awhile, nothing happened, but that night the crew broke out their bottles and urged us to drink with them. The captain, who had been one of the most hostile people on the ship during the day, soon mellowed from the effect of the rum. He said we had caused him a great deal of grief. He was engaged in gun-running activities with Castro's Cubans, and he knew we were CIA agents bent on disrupting his operation. He went on to say that he had been paid $2,000 to kill us, but since everyone on San Andrés knew we had left the island on his ship, he was having second thoughts about the deal.

About 4:00 the next morning, the ship's engine clanked to a stop. From inside our cabin, where we awaited our executioners with loaded spear guns, we heard the anchor drop. When the ship was dead still, we crept out of the cabin. About a mile away, I could see a faint light. Figuring it was either another boat or land, I decided to take my chances in the dark sea rather than wait until those drunks decided to finish us off. Leaving Momo and both spear guns in the locked cabin, I swam toward the light.

My objective turned out to be an American-owned lobster boat. It was on Quita Sueño Bank, about 50 miles west of Serrana. The captain and crew were eager to help us after hearing my story, but since the only weapon aboard was a pistol, an armed confrontation was out of the question. Then we came up with what I considered a brilliant strategy. I borrowed a skiff with an outboard motor and, unarmed, went back to the "pirate vessel." Everyone there was asleep by now, so I shouted until they appeared, waving their guns at me. Although my teeth were chattering from both cold and fear, I pointed to the lobster boat and as calmly as I could told the captain that I had given the other captain all the particulars about him and *his* ship, that if Momo and I were not permitted to transfer to the lobster boat, they would radio this information, and American planes would be there within an hour to blast his bucket out of the water. The bluff worked: the captain released us and our equipment, and we got out of there. The gun-runners quickly raised anchor and put to sea. We radioed the American authorities in the Canal Zone and told them what had happened, as well as giving them a description of the coastal trader. Then we set off for Serrana.

The captain of the lobster boat decided to spend a week lobstering on Serrana Bank. He deposited us on Southwest Cay, which is where I figured Pedro Serrano had lived four centuries earlier. The lobster boat moved off to the other end of the bank, leaving us on the cay, which was about a quarter of a mile long and several hundred yards wide, with the highest point not over 20 feet above sea level. At one end was an unmanned lighthouse run on butane gas and serviced twice a year by Americans from the Canal Zone. At the other were two coconut trees. There was little vegetation but a lot of guano and fine white sand so hot that our feet burned through the soles of our shoes. The only other inhabitants on the island were several thousand booby birds, millions of pesky crabs, and countless large loggerhead turtles that lumbered ashore at night during the summer to lay their eggs. Most interesting was the fact that the cay seemed to be covered with the vestiges of old shipwrecks and debris, left no doubt mostly by sailors who had lived on the cay after being shipwrecked. Although no beauty spot, it was a treasure-hunter's paradise.

From driftwood and other debris on the cay, we built a serviceable hut to sling our hammocks and stow our equipment in. We also had a 16-foot aluminum skiff with a 20-horsepower outboard motor, for searching the bank. In a way, it was like living on another planet, so cut off were we from the rest of the world. Momo, who was easy to get along with, worked like a demon—*when* I could entice him away from his favorite pastime of spearing the land crabs that sought shelter from the sun in our cool hut.

We had been on the island only about six hours when we accidentally found our first treasure—a piece of eight, dated 1624, from the Potosi (Bolivia) mint. We had brought two 55-gallon drums of fresh water for drinking, but decided to dig and see if we could find some water, even brackish, for cooking and washing. While digging the well behind our hut, Momo found the coin and began dancing a Texas-Irish jig.

Our immediate goal was to determine whether this was the cay on which Serrano had lived, and before the first day was over we had located the base of the two stone towers he had built for signaling passing ships. Nearby we found the site of his hut—or a hut, anyway. Possibly it had belonged to another sailor who had been forced to live there. Under a shallow layer of sand we discovered thousands of fish, turtle, and bird bones, as well as crude tools made from conch shells, fishhooks made from bones, a rusty piece of iron, and a flint stone— which may have been the very one Serrano mentioned finding on the wreck. It was a stirring feeling we had—one of kinship with a plucky man who died 400 years ago.

The next morning, using Serrano's narrative as our guide, we explored and found the remains of his shipwreck. The wreck was only about 300 yards offshore and was now almost completely covered by coral. Using sledgehammers, chisels, and crowbars, we recovered many artifacts: a big brass bell, dozens of brass door hinges and handles, and a large silver crucifix—all of which were intended for a new church on Isla Cubagua off the coast of Venezuela. We also found 11 cannon and hundreds of stone cannonballs which, according to the documents I had seen in the archives, were being transported to a fort on Isla de Margarita. In addition, there were hundreds of other miscellaneous artifacts of the type one normally finds on shipwrecks of this period. At the time, Serrano's wreck was the oldest ever found in the Western Hemisphere (four years later I was to discover two of Columbus' ships, which had been lost on the northern coast of Jamaica in 1504).

We were lucky with the weather. During the three days we spent exploring Serrano's ship, the seas were flat calm and we were able to climb on top of the barrier reef and over to the outside which, unfortunately, appeared to be the exclusive domain of some of the largest sharks I have ever seen. They averaged 12 to 15 feet in length, ranging from voracious tigers to docile bull sharks. Elated at our find and its historical importance, we began a systematic search for other wrecks on the 30-odd miles of barrier reef that encompassed the bank. As a safety precaution, one of us, using snorkeling gear, hugged the inside of the reef, while the other followed closely in the skiff. We covered about half a mile per day in this fashion. By the end of the first week, when the lobster boat that had brought us returned, we had located six other wrecks in addition to that of Pedro Serrano. Four appeared to be nineteenth century, which didn't interest me very much, but, judging from the artifacts we recovered, the other two were either late seventeenth- or early eighteenth-century Spanish merchant vessels. Since we had neither heavy excavation equipment nor a proper salvage vessel, my intention at this time was to pinpoint as many wreck sites as possible, select the most promising, and then come back equipped to salvage them.

The captain of the lobster boat brought bad news. He had received a message through the U.S. Coast Guard in Miami that Momo's father was very sick. Momo would have to return immediately to the States. He left with a promise to return as quickly as possible. The captain offered to leave one of his men behind with me, saying that he would be back in a month to check on us and bring fresh water and other supplies.

My new companion was a black chap about 25 years old, named Aldo, who professed to be a great cook and diver. (Actually, he had been useless on the lobster boat; the captain was just delighted to get rid of him.) About an hour after the fishing boat left, out from behind a sand dune walked another of the boat's crew. He was a boy of 17, nicknamed Bandido, and he was AWOL from the Colombian Army. Rather than face arrest when the lobster boat reached San Andrés, he had jumped ship to stay with us. If I had searched for years, I couldn't have found a crazier team. Not only could Aldo not cook, he couldn't dive either. The first time we went out in the skiff, I asked him to dive with me. He claimed he didn't need any diving equipment, but on his first (and last) dive, he jumped overboard head first, right on top of a coral head only a foot or so below the surface. But there was some compensation; I soon had Bandido diving like an expert.

After our first day together on the reefs, with Aldo running the skiff and Bandido and I snorkeling, I got out the metal detector and tried to find the buried treasure Captain Birdy had insisted was on the cay. A minute's walk from the hut, we stumbled on a human skull sticking out of the sand, which sent Aldo and Bandido into hysterics. They went running back to the hut, screaming at the top of their lungs. Actually the cay was littered with human bones from the countless victims who had seen their last days on this desolate bit of sand and coral. But Aldo and Bandido were convinced that the cay was haunted by ghosts. Each night they built large bonfires around the hut and played the portable radio full blast, singing lustily in an attempt to scare the spirits away.

Life on the cay was very pleasant. For instance, we ate quite well. Besides feasting on the great quantity of canned food I had brought, we had fresh fish, lobster, crab, and turtle. What I didn't realize at first was that both of my companions had an irrepressible sweet tooth. Within a week they had consumed the entire 10-pound supply of sugar. So I had to learn to drink my coffee unsweetened. All day long we would prowl along the reefs, searching for traces of shipwrecks. When the sun went down over the horizon, we would get in an hour or two of searching with the metal detector, and never failed to find interesting objects. Our best find was a beautiful gold pocket watch with a four-foot-long gold chain which we found among the bones of an intact skeleton lying under a foot of sand near the lighthouse.

By the end of our third week on the cay we had covered more than one-third of the barrier reef and had located 18 promising wrecks. I had also finally convinced Aldo and Bandido that there were no vengeful ghosts around. One night we heard on the radio that a hurricane was headed in our direction. At first I wasn't alarmed; I was sure the lobster boat would come for us before the hurricane got there, if it didn't change direction first anyway. But after a few days, as the storm got uncomfortably close and the boat still wasn't in sight, I really got worried. I could receive on my radio but not transmit. I thought the only way to get help was to put out the light on the lighthouse and hope that a passing ship would report its absence to the U.S. Coast Guard who, in turn, would investigate.

This worked in reverse. The lobster boat was within sight of the light when Aldo climbed the tower and placed an empty 55-gallon drum over it—and the boat got lost! When it finally reached us two days later, large hurricane swells were breaking across the lower parts of the cay, and we had to run for it. San Andrés and Providencia islands to the southwest were closer to the eye of the storm than we were, so the captain decided to head for Honduras. As we reached the vicinity of Quita Sueño Bank, Hurricane Cleo changed course at the last minute and appeared to be veering away from our refuge, so we waited there for three days until the massive seas calmed down. While anchored in the lee of the barrier reef, we kept our ears glued to the radio, in the event Cleo changed direction again—possibly toward us. During our first night I overheard the "U.S. naval ship *Mobile*" calling anyone who was receiving her transmission. I got to talking to them and soon learned that they had reached Serrana Bank just a few hours after we left. But instead of being a United States naval research vessel, as they had at first claimed, they were American treasure hunters from Miami. When I identified myself and told them that I had an exclusive lease to treasure hunt on the island, they suddenly went off the air.

Unfortunately, in our haste to get away, I had left behind nearly all of the hundreds of artifacts we had recovered from the sea and on the cay, and those unscrupulous guys scooped them up before setting sail for other parts. Before doing that, however, they left us a present that put Aldo and Bandido in a semipermanent state of shock. When we returned to the cay, we immediately noticed a crude wooden cross that had been erected on the highest sand dune. Painted on it was the name "Frank Holder." Digging only a few inches down, I unearthed the end of a human hand which crabs had already begun to eat. I tried to cover it over before my two helpers saw it but wasn't quick enough. Aldo announced that he was leaving with the lobster boat and departed three days later when it chugged off toward San Andrés. Bandido was of the same mind, but when I threatened to turn him over to the army if he deserted me, he had no choice but to remain. From that time on, though, Bandido never left the hut at night, not even to help me catch an occasional turtle.

Using the marine radio on the lobster boat, I notified the American embassy in Bogotá of what we had discovered, and two days later an amphibious plane from Miami landed and three FBI agents came ashore, wearing suits and ties, as if they were working on a case in New York City. I answered questions for several hours while furnishing them with fresh lobster and other fish. They dug up the body and put it in a large plastic bag; then they took off. The smell was incredible—they must have had a miserable flight back. Months later, I heard that Holder had been shot by a fellow treasure hunter during a quarrel. Eventually the man who shot him was apprehended in Miami, and the captain was arrested for impersonating a U.S. naval vessel.

Several days after Aldo left, we learned that another hurricane—this one named Dora—was heading our way. Although the hurricane eventually changed course, it rained incessantly for six days, and the seas around the cay were enormous, which kept us from diving. By wearing our rubber diving jackets, however, we were quite comfortable, using the metal detector and digging up the cay. Rather than jumping all over the place, checking out likely areas, as I had done in the past, we used pieces of driftwood as stakes and set up a proper grid system. Digging in wet sand is more difficult than in dry, but on balance, it is more pleasant than working under the relentless tropical sun or around sundown when the sand flies are out for blood.

Our spade work during those six wet days yielded more than we had taken out of the sea in the past month. After only a couple of hours the first day, we got a reading indicating metal near one of the coconut trees. We dug frantically and soon uncovered a chest. Bandido rushed to the hut for a hammer and chisel with which to knock the massive padlock off. As we swung open the heavy rusted lid, I was already visualizing the warm glint of gold and the sparkle of gems. Instead, the chest contained a mass of powdery dust which when later analyzed back in the States proved to be a type of parchment paper used in the seventeenth and eighteenth centuries. I decided to keep the chest, anyway. By tying a line to the chest and using planks and Coca-Cola bottles as rollers, we got the chest to the hut where it was used to store the most valuable items as we found them.

After a quick lunch of hot fish soup to take the chill off, we continued our search where we had left off. Less then 10 feet from the hole from which we had removed the chest, I got another strong reading. This time we had to go more than six feet down, which took almost four hours of steady shoveling—but it was worth it. The shiny metal was there this time. Lying in a three-legged copper kettle were 128 eight-escudo gold coins; 487 two-, four-, and eight-real silver coins; and 198 copper maravedi coins. All of the coins were dated between 1766 and 1780 and came from mints in South America.

The following day, working in the rain, we recovered intact from the same area over a hundred beautiful, pieces of Chinese porcelain cups, saucers, and bowls dating from the same period. Then we had three lean days in which our finds were a few iron nails and tacks, a small number of ceramic shards, and some broken, clay smoking pipes. On the sixth soggy day, when the rain had finally begun to slacken and we were working near the center of the island, I got another strong reading with the detector. Digging, we uncovered the springs from a modern bedstead, which Bandido soon found a use for: as a rack for drying surplus fish that he hoped to take back to civilization and sell.

An hour later fortune smiled on us again. I began getting numerous readings over an area about 20 by 20 feet. Bandido thought it was probably just more modern junk and refused to dig. He changed his mind when I promised him my two remaining candy bars, and we began digging in earnest. At a depth of five feet we found a marvelous silver sword with dozens of precious and semiprecious stones decorating the hilt. Minutes later Bandido found another sword with a solid ivory handle exquisitely carved with scenes of ships at anchor in a harbor. By nightfall we had an impressive display of fantastic items. Our driftwood hut was beginning to look a bit like the British Museum. In addition to the two ornate swords, we found 7 plain ones with wooden handles, 11 muskets, 3 pistols, 2 poinards, 2 silver tankards, 4 pewter tankards, 34 pewter plates, 44 pewter spoons and forks, hundreds of lead pistol and musket balls, more than a hundred intact ceramic objects (including a beautiful chamber pot decorated with multicolored birds), about 240 brass uniform buttons, 29 silver and pewter buckles, 173 silver coins, and 78 gold ones. From research done when I got back to civilization proved, the coins, as well as the other items, were of French origin and dated from around 1750.

While I photographed our treasure trove the next morning, Bandido was back in the same area, digging in the blazing-hot sun, wearing an empty potato sack over his head and back for protection. After unearthing a few pieces of broken pottery, he shouted that he had found what looked like a cannonball. I rushed out with my camera and told him to pick it up and brush the sand off. The cannonball was a human skull, and that was the end of the digging for Bandido. No matter what I offered him, he refused to dig another spadeful of sand for the remainder of his stay with me. After two more days of digging alone, I had found only a pewter snuffbox and a copper candlestick. By this time we had systematically covered about half of the cay.

We got back to our diving again, each day working farther and farther from the cay, which concerned me somewhat. I was afraid that if a boat appeared, its crew might go ashore and find our treasure. After several days of worrying about this, we dug a deep hole inside the hut and buried the most valuable items in it. With his half of the treasure, Bandido planned to head for the States and try to become a citizen, which I offered to help him with. Although he spoke both Spanish and English fluently, he could neither read nor write. I spent many evenings playing schoolteacher with him, and he demonstrated a remarkable ability to learn quickly and easily.

The vast amounts of sugar and other sweets he had consumed finally took their toll: poor Bandido was suffering from an excruciating toothache. After spending two days in the hammock, moaning and groaning, he let me extract the troublesome tooth with a pair of pliers. He was also accident-prone. On one occasion it almost cost him his life. Each day's diving brought new coral cuts which heal very slowly and can be quite painful. The best remedy was to clean them with urine and, despite his fierce protests, coat them with iodine. One evening while he was cleaning a fish for dinner in waistdeep water, a small barracuda darted in and bit the tip off one of his fingers. Another time he spilled a pot of boiling water on his left foot, and I had to force a fifth of rum down his gullet to calm him after which I applied a thick coat of grease to the burned area. But the clincher occurred one day when I was in the skiff and he shouted for the spear gun. I threw it to him, expecting him to surface with a small snapper or grouper for dinner. When several minutes passed and he didn't come up, I immediately dived and found him unconscious, tied around a coral head with a 400-pound jewfish next to him. In trying to force the jewfish to the surface, Bandido had foolishly speared it and snagged his leg in the line from the gun to the spear. The fish began swimming circles around the coral head, the result of which was that the gun caught under the ledge and Bandido got tied around the coral head with the line. Certain that he was dead I was really scared, but I quickly applied artificial respiration and in a matter of minutes was able to welcome Bandido back among the living —this time vowing never to shoot another fish. He blamed the accident on the fact that I had made him dive on Sunday which he referred to as "the day of the Lord."

We systematically worked our way up to area in which Captain Birdy had found the bronze cannon and, nearby, the two barrels of gold coins and ingots. We found our first bronze cannon within 200 yards of the spot where he had placed an "X" on my chart. This one, like the dozen or so others we had found, were buried on top of the barrier reef less than two feet underwater. When the seas were calm, which fortunately was often, we used various tools to dig them loose. The first one we uncovered bore the coat of arms of King Philip II of Spain, which indicated that it was very likely from one of the 1605 treasure-laden galleons. In this area the barrier reef was about 100 yards wide and at no place was it more than three feet deep. Huge ballast stones were scattered over the reef and held fast to it by coral growth. Each day we picked up several artifacts—tools, weapons, crockery, bottles, cannon-balls—but not a single piece of treasure. Finally, after a week of digging on the reef, I came to the conclusion that most of the wreck, including the treasure, must be buried in the sand on either side of the reef. Slipping over the deep end of the reef into 60 feet of water, I found a massive pile ballast with two huge iron anchors lying nearby. Digging into the ballast pile was difficult. I had only a few seconds on the bottom, since we were free diving without tanks. On one dive, after removing several heavy ballast stones, I grabbed what looked like a coral-encrusted cannonball and, lungs busting, fought my way to the surface with the burden. When I tapped the cannonball, I discovered that it was made up of silver pieces of eight, a total of 250, all dated 1604 and 1605, from the Potosi mint in Bolivia.

Bandido was in the water when I made this discovery, so I quickly wrapped the coins in a jersey and dove back down on the inside of the reef where I hid them in a small hole. It wasn't that I was trying to cheat him out of his share; it was just that I had been in this game long enough to know that you can trust very few people when treasure is involved, and that secrecy is the road to success. As it turned out, my caution was justified.

When Bandido came back for a rest, I suggested that we not do anything more on this wreck, since it appeared to have been salvaged. I was quietly elated, knowing that there were several million dollars out there beyond the reef, that it would only be a short time before I picked the treasure up. After a year of disaster, the sea was finally being kind to me.

During the next week we discovered traces of two of the other 1605 treasure galleons, but other than establishing their identity and locations, I didn't spend much time on them. What could be worse than to come back to Serrana and find that Bandido had revealed the locations to someone and that they had beat me to the treasure? Our only find in the area where the two barrels had been recovered was two modern anchors and a large brass propeller of a ship that must have run aground on the reef in recent years. After two months of combing the reefs of Serrana Bank, we had found 32 separate shipwrecks of which at least six were possible treasure galleons. Not bad for a shoestring operation: the expedition had cost me less than $2,000 and 20 pounds I was happy to part with.

The primary method we used to search the reefs was to tow one another by a line attached to the skiff. This is similar to trolling for big fish, only one time, *we* were the bait. Several sharks were always cruising around, but up till now, none seemed very aggressive except those on the outside of the reef. Then it happened! I was towing Bandido one beautiful, blue morning when suddenly I saw a massive shark fin cutting through the water straight for him. There wasn't enough time to stop the skiff and pull Bandido aboard, so I gunned the engine to full speed, made a quick U-turn, and headed for the shark, running across its back and cutting it with the propeller which broke off. Seeing what was happening, Bandido swam as fast as he could for a coral outcropping sticking above of the water, and climbed up. Meanwhile, the shark, which was about 16 feet long, charged the boat and tried to tip it over, while I pounded it on its head with an oar. The blood now pouring out of the shark's back attracted other sharks, and soon there were about 20 of them circling the boat and Bandido's minuscule coral refuge. At first they just circled, watching the one I had wounded attack the skiff. Then, as though on signal, they charged the wounded shark, which was some three times their size, and in a matter of minutes there was nothing left of it. When I was finally able to row over to pick up Bandido, he was almost in shock and screaming like a lunatic. We were in a fix. Our cay was more than 15 miles away (fortunately in the direction the wind was blowing), and I had broken one of the two oars on the shark's head. So, without a spare propeller—not that it would have helped, since the engine shaft was also broken—we took turns rowing back to the cay, a voyage that took us nearly 30 painful hours. Naturally, Bandido made another of his numerous vows, this time a doubleheader: he would never dive again, nor go out in a small boat on Serrana Bank. I myself soon regretted not having made the same vow regarding never going out in a small boat on Serrana Bank again.

Two days later, Bandido was still in such a state of nervous exhaustion that when the lobster boat came with our monthly ration of food and water, plus the first mail I had received since I arrived, I relented and agreed that he should return to civilization. The captain offered to drop him off on Providencia Island where he would have a better chance of eluding the Colombian authorities who were after him. Before leaving, Bandido promised to keep everything we had found a secret. As a safeguard, I was to keep all the items we had found until I left Serrana and joined him on Providencia. But Bandido was no fool either; to make sure our paths crossed again, he demanded my passport, airline ticket, and remaining traveler's checks—which I turned over to him.

Even though I offered to pay several of the crew four times what they normally made on the lobster boat to remain with me, all of them refused. Aldo had painted such a dismal picture of life on the cay that they were convinced I had to be crazy to not only stay there but actually enjoy it. I arranged for the boat to come back in a month's time to pick me up. As a parting gesture, Bandido slipped a beautiful gold ring with a large emerald on it into my hand, admitting that he had found it underwater at the site of the bronze cannon wreck. Why he suddenly turned honest, I will never know; maybe he was more religious than I had thought.

Although the weather took a turn for the worse, staying gray, windy, and wet most of the time, the 30 days I spent alone on Serrana Cay were some of the most peaceful and happiest I have ever spent. I got two good days of diving in around the bronze cannon site. Besides picking up the coins I had hidden, I found about 200 others scattered about in sand pockets on the reef. Then bad weather set in, and for two weeks it blew a bloody gale. The wind made it impossible to search and dig on the cay; the sand was being blown about as though by a powerful sandblasting machine, which cut my legs severely even though I was wearing a pair of Levi's. I amused myself by reading paperbacks, listening to my portable radio, and examining the treasure and artifacts Bandido and I had recovered. Toward the end of the month of foul weather, a dead whale over 30 feet long was washed up on the seaward side of the cay. The scavenger crabs quickly got to work on the carcass, and after a few days the smell was unbearable. Most of the time, the wind blew the stench right at the hut, so I slung my hammock on the lighthouse tower and slept there for several nights in order to get a decent sleep.

When the wind finally let up, I decided to try to complete my search of the last few miles of the barrier reef. It was slow going. I had to swim while towing the skiff with a line tied to my waist. My only find was a massive pile of railroad track, wheels, and axles which I later learned had been lost in 1922 en route to the Panama Canal Zone.

One morning I awoke to a sudden calm. I was jubilant at the chance to pull the skiff over the barrier reef and search outside where I had found the other 1605 galleons. All went well for the first hour or so. I came upon another large ballast pile, which contained more than 30 bronze cannon and six large iron anchors. One moment the sun was shining and the seas were beautiful and calm, and the next, it was incredibly dark. I surfaced—to face what looked like a huge black wall rushing down on me. As fast as I could, I jumped in the skiff and with an oar, began poling through the coral heads. About halfway across the reef, the squall struck with 60-mile-an-hour winds, and an enormous sea began pounding the reef, one of which flooded the skiff. Seconds later, a wave caught me abeam and I was thrown into the water, with the overturned skiff falling on top of me. Fighting for my life, I tried to push the skiff across the reef and with the aid of the heavy breakers, succeeded. Once on the inside of the reef, I discovered that the outboard motor, the gas tank, life jacket, and both oars were missing. I got the skiff righted and began bailing, using my fins and mask. The cold rain felt like needles piercing my skin, and the visibility was down to less than 50 feet. I was still more than 15 miles from the cay—chilled, tired, and nervous—and knew that I faced a grueling ordeal if I were to reach the cay, of which I could see only the very top of the two coconut trees when a swell carried me high in the air.

Tying the towline around my waist, I began swimming with a determined, relaxed stroke which I kept up for more than eight hours before taking a rest. When darkness fell, I realized that I couldn't continue, so I tied the skiff to a coral head and fell into an exhausted sleep. At first light, I was up again and swimming as though my life depended on it—which it did. By noon my entire body ached; my tongue was swollen from lack of water, and I had horrible blisters on my ankles from the rubber fins chaffing them. But I had covered about two-thirds of the distance home, and my spirits were up. After a brief rest I dived and brought up a conch shell but found it impossible to extract the nourishing mollusc with my diving knife. By sunset I was within a mile of the cay, but I was too exhausted to swim another stroke; so I tied up again for the night.

Around four in the morning, something woke me. A sixth sense was warning me that something was wrong. The lighthouse, which should have lay to the west, was now to the east. With a lurching feeling, I realized that the line had been cut by the sharp coral. I was adrift at sea! When the sun came up, I found myself about four miles west of the cay, with the current carrying me farther by the minute. I tried swimming against it, but could make no headway. Finally, my energy and resources gone, I gave up, resigned to whatever fate befell me.

Several hours later, the wind changed from the southeast to the west and began blowing me toward the island. I stood up in the skiff, using my body as a sail. About midnight, when I estimated that I was about a half-mile from the cay, I decided to gamble and start swimming in the dark even though it was feeding time for the sharks. If I didn't, the wind might change direction and I would be blown in the opposite direction again. It took me another five hours to reach the cay. When I got there, I was so exhausted that I fell asleep on the beach and didn't awaken until noon when several booby birds began pecking at me.

Crawling back to the hut, I didn't even mind the lingering smell of the rotted whale carcass; all I wanted was water and food. My throat was so swollen that I couldn't eat for several days, and I had considerable difficulty drinking liquids. I hadn't had the strength to pull the skiff very far up on the beach when I landed, and it had drifted away. Now I was without *any* boat, not that I needed one at this point, however.

On the third night after my return, I had just turned off the radio and was climbing into the hammock when I heard a boat engine. I went outside and several miles off saw a boat heading toward the cay. I figured it was the lobster boat coming a week early to pick me up. After my recent harrowing experience, I was all for returning to civilization. I had a mad craving for a large cool drink and a huge bowl of ice cream. Sometime later, when the boat finally dropped anchor a few hundred yards off the cay, I recognized it. It was the coastal trader Momo and I had fled from on Quita Sueño Bank. Minutes after anchoring, the men aboard it began lowering a skiff in the water. They were coming ashore to find *me.*

Grabbing fins, face mask, and knife, I ran for the far side of the cay, since there was no place on the leeward side of the cay that afforded concealment. When they reached shore, they started shouting my name, hurling oaths and broadcasting the fact that they had come to kill me. It was clear to me now that my only hope was to swim out to the barrier reef and hide in the dark. Fortunately, there was no moon that night, or they would have easily spotted me.

What a hell of a miserable night! There I was, clinging to the barrier reef in the dark, expecting some creature to take a bite out of me, while less than a quarter of a mile away, that pirate vessel was lit up like a Christmas tree, music blaring, while the bastards stripped the hut and set it afire. Then they rowed back out to their ship, raised anchor, and left. Hurrying back to my smoldering hut, I found that they had also dug up the treasure buried there. (Bandido was the biggest blabbermouth in the western Caribbean. Not only had he bragged about and exaggerated what we had found, he had even told them about *burying* it.)

I now found myself, more or less, in the same terrible situation that Pedro Serrano had been in 440 years before. My total possessions were a swimsuit, fins, mask, snorkel, knife, and a shovel I had left where I had last been digging. First I set about gathering all the driftwood and brush I could find. Then I built a small lean-to against one of the cay's two coconut trees. By midday I was so thirsty I felt dizzy. I decided to gather some coconuts. But both trees were over a hundred feet high. I couldn't climb higher than 20 feet before having to give up. Although I didn't like doing it, I dug up some fresh turtle eggs to quench my thirst. Unfortunately, they killed my hunger while increasing my thirst. I had no alternative but to chop down one of the coconut trees. With only my diving knife and the shovel as tools, it took me the rest of the day to complete the task, netting me 23 coconuts. I quickly opened four in succession and greedily drank the cool sweet water. Sleeping on the sand that night was far from comfortable, but compared to the previous night, it was like paradise.

The next 10 days (before I was picked up by the lobster boat) went smoothly. I even began to enjoy my Pedro Serrano existence—digging up turtle eggs, which could be eaten raw; diving for conch shells, the meat of which actually tastes better raw than cooked; and slaking my thirst with coconut water. On the fourth day of my new life-style, when the supply of coconuts ran out, I considered chopping down the other tree, on which I counted more than 30. But I decided not to. It was the highest feature on the cay (the lighthouse tower was only 20 feet high) that a boat could use in the daytime. This was the day I made the most important discovery of the expedition: water. I was willing to drink brackish water, the kind we had used to cook with and to clean our cooking and eating utensils. I began digging a new well because the old one had filled in with sand during the last gale. I knew from my experience on the *Niña II* voyage that salt water is not harmful when drunk in small amounts. Then to my great surprise, at a depth of only two feet, my new well turned out to have good water. Although not completely fresh, it tasted like champagne to me.

That morning I had found another striking flint on the cay (it *might* have been the one Pedro Serrano had used) and was in the process of making a fire to roast some lobsters I had caught, when the lobster boat appeared. After boarding it and answering their excited questions, I was a bit disappointed that I had been rescued so soon. My spirits improved somewhat, however, when the captain told me that only a few days before, the pirate vessel had been seized for smuggling and the whole crew was in a Nicaraguan prison. Also, before he left Providencia Island, Bandido had given him my passport, plane ticket, and traveler's checks.

Overall, the three months on Serrana Bank were more productive than I had dreamed they would be. Not only had I retraced Pedro Serrano's footsteps and found the ship he was wrecked on, I had found others that would eventually, albeit temporarily, make me a rich man. Most important, with ample time to reflect, I had learned a lot about myself.

4: *Providencia Island*

After leaving Serrana Bank in November 1964, I headed back to Europe where I spent a happy month diving to ancient shipwrecks along the coasts of Corsica, Sardinia, and France. Then I resumed my research in the Seville archives. But I wanted to get back to Serrana as soon as possible. According to the meteorologists, good weather would begin again in the Caribbean Sea around the middle of March, after the winter "northers" had stopped blowing. Shortly after Christmas I wrote to my main contact in the U.S. State Department and told him that I planned to return to Serrana. His reply almost drove me crazy with frustration. He said that the United States and Colombia were currently negotiating the ownership of Serrana and several other nearby banks and that although the United States had no objections to my going there, I would also have to get permission from the Colombian government, which had recently put a small garrison of soldiers on Southwest Cay and had a naval vessel patroling the area to keep everyone except Colombian nationals from fishing and lobstering in the area. At the time of this reply, I was doing research in London, so I went to see the Colombian ambassador there and applied for the necessary permission. In keeping with the Latin American mañana attitude and the slowness with which the wheels of bureaucracy grind, and despite the fact that I was hounding the ambassador almost daily, it wasn't until around the middle of April that permission was granted.

Nancy, then my wife, had just passed her exam for a Ph.D. in history at the University of London. An excellent diver, she was raring to go with me. I still needed one more diver, though, so I tried to contact Momo, only to learn that he was in Ethiopia, searching for King Solomon's lost gold mines. In his place I got Manolo Darnaude. He had sailed with me on the *Niña II* voyage and had done considerable underwater work with me off the coast of southern Spain. My plan was to use Providencia Island as a base. Several Americans had set up a freezing plant there and had a large shrimp vessel, *Lady Alice,* which they agreed to rent to me for six months. Another American, who lived in Bogotá, rented me a house on Providencia that he had recently purchased. After gathering more than $12,000 worth of equipment in Miami, problem number one arose. The next cargo vessel that could carry our equipment wasn't scheduled to sail for almost two months. Since there was no landing strip on Providencia, I had to charter a DC-3 in Miami to carry everything to San Andrés.

Arriving in Bogotá, where I was to pick up the permit to work on Serrana, I found the country under martial law because of an assassination attempt on the president the night before. It was a week before I could meet with the Minister of the Navy, the person who had to sign the permit. He was cordial but said he had to take the matter up with other government officials, and recommended that we wait on Providencia until the permit arrived. "On my honor as a naval officer," he said, "you will have your permission within two weeks."

Our equipment was waiting in San Andrés. Not only was the governor, who had been rather unfriendly the year before, helpful, but the customs officers turned over all of our stuff without charging any duties. (Things were a bit different six months later, however, when we were leaving and were accused by the same officials of having smuggled everything in to avoid paying the import duties. Everything we owned was confiscated, including our clothes. We didn't need a DC-3 to carry our gear back to the States; with just the clothes on our backs left, we could have hitched a ride on the back of a sea gull.)

The trip to Providencia was almost indescribable. I chartered a 30-foot motor-sailer called *Wave Crest.* We crammed her with two 16-foot aluminum skiffs, two large shark cages, and all the diving gear and supplies we had purchased locally. Nancy thought it looked dangerously overloaded, but when we boarded her the next morning for the 50-mile trip (which the captain said would take only five hours), we were in for a shock. *Wave Crest* looked like a cross between Noah's ark and a crowded Mexican bus. Besides the three of us and the boat's two-man crew, 28 people had hitched a ride! All of them had bundles and supplies, including several dozen live chickens and two small horses! Over the vehement protests of their owner, I was only able to persuade the captain to leave the horses behind. Our projected five-hour voyage took 26 hours. The engine broke down seven times, the mate had forgotten to bring the sails, the captain completely missed the island in a rain squall, and we narrowly missed being wrecked on the myriad barrier reefs that surround most of island.

Resembling one of the South Sea islands, Providencia is one of the most beautiful islands in the Caribbean. Its 1,190-foot summit, covered with bracken and tree ferns, rises above a jumble of lesser green peaks from which spurs radiate to the sea, terminating in precipitous cliffs. Idyllic beaches lapped by crystal water lie between the peaks. Most of the arable land is in the small valleys tucked into the folds of the spurs. With an annual rainfall of over 400 inches, the island is radiant and blooming, and more than 40 kinds of tropical fruits grow wild. Cool southeast trade winds blow throughout the year, the temperature hovers at a year-round 80 degrees Fahrenheit, and mosquitos and other pests are scarce. With Nicaragua, the nearest mainland, a hundred-odd miles to the west, it is a remote, blessed corner of the world that has been overlooked by the developers and tourist agents. The thousand or so inhabitants live scattered around this five-miles-in-diameter volcanic rock. They are the descendants of religious dissenters, runaway slaves, and pirates. English is the dominant language, and the literacy rate is high. Fishing is the leading industry, but it is not carried on at what one could call a frantic pace. Most of the islanders have already acquired a nest egg working in Colombia or the Canal Zone and have returned home to enjoy life. Consequently, activity is on the slow side. The main preoccupations seem to be gossiping, drinking, and having children, for which the marriage ceremony is not considered essential. One old man in his seventies boasted of having over a hundred children scattered about the island.

Providencia has nothing that resembles a store—no telephones, no movie theater, and, thank goodness, no television. One motorable road circles the island, but it is too bumpy for anything but the sturdiest trucks. The usual mode of transportation is horseback. We were surprised to find a few modern touches, though—a telegraph office and a generator that supplies electricity for several hours each night when diesel fuel is available. Most of the houses on the island have been constructed from items recovered from modern-day shipwrecks lost in the western Caribbean Sea.

The island was first settled in 1629 by English Puritans, but they were expelled in 1641 by the Spanish who, in turn, were forced out by the famous buccaneer, Mansveldt, in 1666. For the next two centuries it was one of the most important pirate strongholds in the Caribbean, the reason for which can easily be seen by a glance at a map of the Caribbean. The island lay on the direct route for Spanish treasure galleons plying between Porto Bello, Panama and Havana, the jumping-off point for the return voyage to Spain. Among the many cutthroats who stopped there, Henry Morgan is by far the most famous. His attack on Panama City in 1671 was launched from Providencia. Although the history books don't agree, the islanders will assure you that he came back after sacking Panama City and buried all of his plunder somewhere on the island. Apparently even high-ranking officials of the Colombian government believed in the Morgan buried treasure myth. Only two years before we arrived, they had sponsored a fruitless treasure-hunting expedition that lasted six months and cost over $100,000.

Separated from the main town on Providencia by a narrow tidal channel is a small rocky island known locally as Catalina. Its only prominent features are a fort built on the summit by Mansveldt and a headland called Morgan's Head which does resemble the old scoundrel. Supposedly the treasure is buried in a cave, and once, with explosives and heavy construction equipment, the Colombians nearly leveled the island, without success. Just a month before we arrived, the islanders told us, a privately owned amphibious airplane with several Americans from the Canal Zone arrived and anchored below the fort. For several days they used SCUBA equipment and allegedly entered a submerged cave where they found Morgan's treasure. Everyone on the island was convinced that they found "millions." The mayor, or alcalde, the only government representative on the island, and his four policemen went out to apprehend them, but the Americans quickly took off in their plane and were never heard from again.

Our first shock came when we entered the house we had rented from the American in Bogotá. It was being used as a brothel by some of the local belles catering to American shrimpers who frequently stopped at the island for fresh water, fruits, and vegetables. Manolo and I inadvertently interrupted a couple in their pursuit of happiness. Instead of the furnished house we had been promised, we found only six filthy mattresses which we quickly burned. Over the next few weeks we scrounged enough of the basics to make it a decent place to live in while we were in Providencia.

The next shock wasn't long in coming. The chap whom we had refused permission to bring his two horses on our boat turned out to be the new alcalde, replacing one who had been shot to death in a quarrel over a girl several weeks earlier. During our first meeting he let me know in no uncertain terms that he was very anti-American. But in the course of several night-long drinking sessions we became good friends—at least, until the end, when he turned out to be a thief.

During our first afternoon on the island, as we were getting to work, preparing for a vegetable garden in the backyard, a wizened little fellow came trotting around the side of the house. Without even a greeting he launched into a story about having found a chest of gold coins buried under a bush. Manolo and I dropped our shovels. We had been on the island less than 24 hours and already it sounded like Treasure Island! I asked the man if we could see the coins. Yes, we were welcome to see them if we brought our shovels to dig them up. I felt the first twinge of skepticism.

"How," I asked, "do you know the coins are under the bush?"

With a perfectly straight face he replied that he had had a dream and in the dream Henry Morgan had led him to the chest.

We sighed, picked up our shovels, and went back to spading the garden. But that wasn't the end of it. For the next few days, visitors filed into the yard at about 20-minute intervals. After welcoming us to the island, each one would then launch into his or her story of buried treasure. The treasures were sometimes buried under a bush, sometimes under a tree, or sometimes in a cave. Morgan himself was usually the guide, but occasionally it was Simón Bolívar, and once it was Micky Mantle. Manolo and I got so used to this that we didn't even interrupt our digging and planting when the latest "dreamer" showed up.

There was one dream, however, that we did not ignore, perhaps because it was told to us by a woman who didn't smell of rotgut rum, as did most of our visitors. She was a commanding figure—tall, gaunt, her white hair pulled tightly into a knot on top of her head. In a zombie-like voice without inflection, she told us that on the night of the next full moon we were to follow the path that led up the hill behind the alcalde's house. On the other side of the hill we would meet a rooster that would speak to us in Spanish. If we gave it some corn, it would guide us to a thicket. There we were to chop away the brush and dig. If we did this, we would find a cannon made of solid gold.

There happened to be a full moon that very night. In spite of the bit about the Spanish-speaking rooster, Manolo and I followed the woman's instructions. We weren't doing it solely for laughs: I knew from having studied a chart I found in the British Museum that during the seventeenth century a plantation had stood in the area we were to explore, and I wanted to see if any traces of it still existed. We didn't see the rooster, but we did find the thicket and foundation of the plantation house. Returning the next morning with machetes and a metal detector, we found a cannon made of brass instead of gold, but the fact that it was dated 1688 and was in an excellent state of preservation made it priceless. Nancy also dug up four English silver coins dating from around 1700, and Manolo found a small, gold religious medallion. We were off to an auspicious start.

This set me to thinking about the woman's "dream." I suspected that it was no dream at all, that she had come across the cannon during her waking hours. But if she had, why hadn't she dug it out of the underbrush herself? I did some checking on the local superstitions and learned that the islanders believe buried treasure is cursed by the spirits of early settlers who showed visiting pirates good hiding places and were then murdered for their trouble and buried with the loot. The curse, they believe, will fall on anyone who finds the treasure, but if someone dreams of a treasure and then sends *someone else* to find it, there's nothing to prevent the dreamer from sharing the loot. A dreamer can't be held responsible for what he dreams, can he? It was all neatly worked out.

It didn't mean that every "dream" was a surefire treasure find, though. Most were pipe dreams, nothing more. About a week after the experience with the woman, we decided to investigate another "dream." This one concerned an open chest filled with gold which an incredibly old man claimed to have seen years before at the bottom of a well near the fort on Catalina Island. He hadn't touched it because it was cursed, he said; and he had dreamed of it only the night before. The old man—who appeared to be about 100—had brought along a bottle of something he claimed was guaranteed to provide immunity against evil spirits. Moved by such solicitude for our welfare, Manolo and I agreed to look for the gold. Besides, one never knew. There undoubtedly were some treasure hoards buried on the two islands. As proof, only a few months ago, a woman had found more than 50 Spanish pieces of eight dating from the seventeenth century in her backyard.

The old man guided us to a clearing near Mansveldt's fort where he pointed to a pile of rocks, and Manolo and I got to work. It took us most of the day to lift the rocks, but we found no sign of a well under them. We went over the clearing with a metal detector and got only one weak reading, too weak to be a treasure chest of gold. Nevertheless, we began digging and almost immediately uncovered a complete skeleton, at the sight of which the old man shrieked and took off. Continuing our digging, we found a couple of brass buttons and a buckle that I later identified as having been worn by Spanish soldiers in the seventeenth century. This episode was the last request by an islander to pursue his "dream."

The first two weeks flew by, with us involved in fixing up the house, planting a garden, and chasing after "dreams." Meanwhile, *Lady Alice,* which I had chartered for $5,000 a month, was just rocking at anchor in the harbor. The permit should have arrived by this time, so I cabled the minister of the navy in Bogotá. He didn't reply to this cable or any of the dozen others I sent during the next month. In desperation I went to Bogotá myself and again got the same treatment—having to wait days to see him, being cordially treated when I finally did, and again being promised that within "two weeks" I would have the permit. I had paid the charter on *Lady Alice* for three months in advance; this waiting around could damn well bankrupt me. While in Bogotá I called on the director of the Institute of Culture and asked him for help. He offered to put in a good word for me with the Minister of the Navy. As a return favor, he wanted me to make an archaeological survey of Providencia and Catalina. I accepted; it sounded like an interesting project and would keep us busy while we waited for the permit to work at Serrana.

When I returned and told Manolo, however, he wasn't too keen on the idea. He reminded me that we were divers, that we had come to get rich on sunken treasure. Nancy, who was much more interested in archaeology than in treasure, was thrilled with the project. We started on Catalina, first locating and mapping five cannon batteries around the island. Then with the help of six islanders I hired, we spent almost a week clearing the trees and brush that covered Mansveldt's fort. The cannon were gone. At first we assumed that they had long since been carried away, but when we dived beneath the fort, we not only found them but the entrance to a submerged cave, as well. The entrance was so small that petite Nancy got the job of going in. She reported that after swimming about 20 feet, she came up into a large dry room. Apparently this was the cave the Americans were thought to have found Morgan's treasure in.

With Nancy's report, our spirits improved considerably. In addition, on the ground we found a number of recently opened, empty cans of food, some cigarette butts, and a diver's weight belt. Painted in red on the wall was: GO TO HELL   WE GOT THE TREASURE. Had they really, or was it a hoax? Using the detector, we located a large assortment of artifacts in the vicinity of the fort—cannon and musket balls, weapons, tools, pottery, glass, as well as meat, fish, and fowl bones.

One evening none other than old Bandido walked in, grinning from ear to ear, minus about half a dozen teeth which he said had been knocked out by prison guards. He had just been released from a six-month prison term in Cartagena, Colombia. I offered him a job and expected to see him the following day, but a week went by, with no sign of him until I was summoned to the alcalde's office and informed that Bandido was suing me for his share of the treasure that we had found the year before on Serrana Bank. I explained to the alcalde, as I had to Bandido, that all of it had been taken by the men on the coastal trader; but an unsavory character who claimed to be a distant relative of Bandido's and who had studied law (or so he claimed) said I had invented that story and had smuggled out the treasure on another boat instead. Fortunately, Bandido or his lawyer-relative had no idea what the value of the treasure was; they were only asking for the equivalent of about $2,000 in U.S. currency. I refused to give in, and the alcalde said he had no choice but to refer the case to Bogotá.

This incident ruined any chance I had of getting back to Serrana that year. It made the newspapers in Bogotá and soon thereafter, I was notified that I would not be given the permit and that I might even be prosecuted for smuggling "national treasures" out of the country. When I appealed to the U.S. State Department, they refused to get involved or even to acknowledge that the letters I had from them, stating that I could hunt for treasure and keep anything I found on Serrana, were genuine. A month or so later, a judge arrived from Bogotá to try my case, as well as the one concerning the murder of the former alcalde. Although the judge neither spoke nor understood a word of English, the testimony in both cases was given in English. The murder trial was first. The defendant was sentenced to only six years in jail because it was a "crime of passion," as the judge put it. (The defendant left the island before he could be sent back to Cartagena.) For $1,000 the judge said he would throw the case in my favor before it was heard, but I refused to pay. Naturally, Bandido won—but not really. *He* had to pay the judge a $1,000 bribe and his council, $500. I even had to pay court costs of about $800, which included the judge's transportation costs and his salary for a week. Manolo and Nancy tried to convince me that we should throw in the sponge and leave the island, but being a stubborn cuss, I wouldn't hear of it. I left on the same boat as the judge and flew on the same plane with him from San Andrés to Bogotá. Except for the director of the Institute of Culture, who was sympathetic and offered to take the matter up with the president, I drew a blank. Not even the American ambassador would talk to me. Convinced that there would eventually be a reversal of the decision not to give me a permit to work on Serrana, I returned to Providencia to continue the archaeological survey.

Our next objective was the site of New Westminster, presently called Old Town by the locals, which had been leveled by the Spaniards in 1641. In the seventeenth century it was a settlement of over a hundred private dwellings, two sugar mills, a small fort of eight "long cannon," and over 500 English residents, not counting slaves. According to documents I had found in the Public Records Office in London, when the Spanish invasion fleet was sighted in 1641, the islanders buried their most valuable possessions—the majority of which was recovered by the Spaniards who used torture to make the English settlers reveal the hiding places. Yet more remains to be found today.

After surveying and mapping the foundations of the old buildings, we put our metal detectors to good use. In three weeks time we were able to cover only about one-tenth of the overall site, but we had recovered thousands of artifacts. These included everything from a gold toothpick with "Thomas Gilbey, Esq." on it, to hundreds of intact glass bottles, several with wine and brandy still in them. Besides the toothpick, the only other items that could be called treasure were four gold wedding bands, seven silver plates, two large silver candlestick holders, and about 200 silver coins of Spanish, Portuguese, French, and English origin—all dating from before 1640. Although I knew we would have to turn these items over to the government, it was exciting work, and I planned to complete the site even if it took another six months, which it looked like it would, judging by the progress we had made so far. But that wasn't to be.

From the beginning of our work on the site, rumors had been flying that we were finding "tons of gold" every day and secretly smuggling it out on a submarine. When the rumors reached Bogotá, all hell broke loose and two police inspectors were rushed to the island to arrest us. Although I showed them the written permission from the director of the Institute of Culture, they claimed they had to take all three of us back to Bogotá for questioning. We were to leave the next morning, so we packed most of our personal possessions, with the expectation of never returning to the island. We had made many friends on the island during our three-month stay, and that night the Catholic priest held a rally at the church to stir up the people against the government in Bogotá. For years the citizens of Old Town had been talking about declaring themselves independent. They had little love for the "Spaniards," as they called all Colombian nationals. We were under house arrest, so we could not attend the rally, but around midnight the priest appeared and said: "My children, God will protect you tomorrow." The irony of it was that the priest was the only Colombian from the mainland besides the alcalde and a few police officers who lived on the island. Everything we had recovered to date had been put on the boat that was to carry us to San Andrés; we would go on to Bogotá by plane. When the two inspectors and the local policemen came to escort us to the dock, more than 300 of the islanders, led by the priest, suddenly appeared and demanded that the inspectors leave without us. Not only did they leave—in a fury—but the local policemen did, too. The alcalde, who was a good guy, in the eyes of the villagers, declared a fiesta and there was one hell of a bang-up. It lasted for two days and nights and featured a horse race around the island that resulted in broken limbs among several drunken jockeys.

Manolo, Nancy, and I fully expected the government to send reinforcements. We were sure that we would be tried for sedition or something even more serious. Manolo and I loaded everything on *Lady Alice,* ready to leave at a moment's notice. But when a month passed and still no ship with reinforcements on the horizon, we unloaded our gear and decided to start working in the water. The alcalde assured us that he didn't mind if we went to Serrana, but this was out of the question. A local boat returning from collecting turtles and booby bird eggs on Southwest Cay reported that six soldiers were living on the cay and that every few weeks a gunboat arrived to patrol the bank.

The alcalde gave us permission to work on any wrecks we found in the waters around Providencia, even though this could cause him a great deal of trouble when word reached Bogotá. As compensation for his kind consideration, we offered him a fourth of the treasure we recovered, which he gratefully accepted. Up till now, we had limited ourselves to a bit of spearfishing, because orders from Bogotá forbade us to dive to any wrecks until permission arrived from the Minister of the Navy.

Ever since we arrived, the priest had been telling us of the need for a new schoolhouse and how the government hadn't responded to his repeated requests for construction funds. Nancy, Manolo, and I decided that we owed the local people something for their act of defiance in preventing the police from taking us away. A large American racing schooner had wrecked on the barrier reef about six months before we arrived. She carried over 10 tons of lead pigs for ballast. In addition, on the same reef, about a mile from her, a small British warship, H.M.S. *Jackdaw,* carrying 20 tons of copper ingots, had been lost in 1835. Our thought was that if we salvaged the lead and copper, the islanders could sell it and build their school.

The sites of both wrecks were known to the local fishermen who took us to them, and we turned the project into a community affair. I even put Bandido to work. The diving wasn't difficult; it was just extremely dangerous. Both wrecks were just on top of the reef which was continually pounded by large, powerful waves.

We tackled the schooner first. Everything of value had already been stripped by the local people, and the sea had taken care of the rest. Except for her engine, generator, rudder, and the ballast, there were no traces left. The water was about four feet deep, and the closest we could get a boat to the wreck site was about 100 feet. Wearing high combat boots and thick clothes as protection against the sharp coral, Manolo, Bandido, and I would take hold of one of the 100-pound lead pigs and somehow crawl and walk with it through the pounding surf to the edge of the reef, where we would deposit it in one of the dugout canoes manned by the villagers. When each dugout was loaded with eight or ten pigs, they would raise their sails and head back.

The job took three days. Then we rested for a few more before tackling *Jackdaw,* which would be more difficult. Over the years, coral had grown over the copper ingots, cementing them to the barrier reef, so that most of them had to be pried loose with crowbars or chipped loose with hammer and chisel. We spent nearly two weeks at this task. When we finished, the whole island celebrated with another two-day fiesta which this time even included boat races with sail and oars. We estimated that the proceeds from sale of the copper and lead would be enough not only to build a new six-room schoolhouse but a library and recreation center, as well. The pigs and ingots were loaded aboard *Lady Alice,* and the alcalde offered to go. He had excellent contacts in Panama, he said, and would get the best price for the metal.

Days and then weeks went by, with no word from the alcalde or the crew of *Lady Alice.* The first news we had, via the monthly mail boat, was that when *Lady Alice* dropped anchor at San Andrés, she was seized by the local authorities and both crew and vessel were sent to Cartagena, charged with illegally transporting a cargo of lead and copper out of the country. We soon learned that the alcalde had disappeared with the money from the sale of the metal, and months later, heard that he had moved to Jamaica, leaving his wife and four children on Providencia to face the wrath of the islanders. So much for our act of goodwill. After leaving the island, we did manage to get several New York publishers to donate books for the island's schoolchildren, but the children had to make do with their cramped, rickety old building.

Now that Catalina Island was without government officials or police, things actually ran more smoothly, at least as far as we were concerned, but eventually a new alcalde arrived from Bogotá and with him a contingent of 20 soldiers and six policemen—which really set the islanders' teeth on edge. I offered the new alcalde the same deal as I had his predecessor, and he accepted, providing we worked secretly. Doing anything on Providencia secretly was out of the question, but this newcomer didn't know that yet. On the island, where the birth of puppies was an important event, we were the focus of curiosity and gossip.

The discovery of our first shipwreck took less than an hour, thanks to documents I had found in London. The English merchant vessel, *Seaflower,* carrying settlers and building materials to the newly discovered island in 1631, had struck a submerged reef and sunk several hundred yards off Catalina Island. According to the records, most of her cargo had been salvaged. Besides three iron anchors, ship's fittings, cannonballs, and thousands of red-clay building bricks, the only items of interest we found were two copper coins and a lead packing seal. We might have found more if we had made a thorough search, but from records I had seen in other European archives, I knew there were more valuable wrecks in these waters.

With the exception of Bandido, none of the inhabitants dived. This reflected sentiments I have heard expressed by island people all over the world; they thought we were crazy to "go down there with them monsters." One day we heard a local fisherman shouting, "the monsters have come back," and saw half the people on the island running to the dock to hear his tale. It seems there was a bank about 200 feet deep and surrounded by very deep water, located about six miles southeast of the island, which was the islanders' main fishing area. Every August or September, for as long as anyone could remember, "huge hundred-foot monsters" appeared on the bank, where they stayed for about a month. During this time, fish, the main staple of the island, were scarce because none of the fishermen would go out, not even to the reefs around the island. Nancy, Manolo, and I were eager to see the "monsters," and we even convinced a frightened Bandido to come along. The villagers tried to stop us, and as we headed out, many went to the church with the priest to pray for us.

The monsters turned out to be harmless whale sharks which swim lazily on the surface, feeding on plankton. They were more like 40 feet

long, not a hundred. It was an unparalleled experience to swim alongside them. When we realized that they didn't object to our presence,
we climbed on their backs and rode them. Bandido was too scared to
join us in the water, but when we got back to shore, he was still
something of a celebrity merely for having survived the experience.
Even this feat didn't convince the local fishermen that it was safe to fish
out there, however. It may be that they used the appearance of the
"monsters" every year as an excuse to swing in their hammocks and
nurse their rum bottles.

Momo made an unexpected appearance. Returning to Texas from Ethiopia, and suffering from malaria and dysentery, he learned that we were
on Providencia. So he hitchhiked to Nicaragua, then bummed a ride on
a shrimper, and finally turned up on our doorstep. Two days later, we
had another surprise: the director of the Institute of Culture had not
been able to get us a permit to work on Serrana, but he did get permission for us to work on wrecks around Providencia—providing that we
turned 50 percent of our finds over to the government for the National
Museum. Naturally, the alcalde wasn't very pleased with this, since he
would lose his 25-percent cut. To keep him on our side, I promised him
10 percent of our share.

Ever since we arrived, we had heard tales of a large ship wrecked off
the south side of the island, and I decided that this would be our next
target. The wreck was a large, steel-hull sailing ship that had sunk
during a hurricane in 1864 while carrying a cargo of general merchan-
dise from Norfolk, Virginia to Panama. Nancy and Momo had been
down only a few minutes when they suddenly surfaced, excited as hell,
blabbering about a "large treasure chest." It didn't take Manolo and
me long to reach the bottom where we found a safe measuring about
four feet on a side. Its weight indicated that it wasn't empty. We tied
lines to it, but it was too heavy to pull up by hand and get into our skiff.
The next day we hired a shrimper and with most of the islanders
following us in every available craft, returned to the wreck and raised
the safe. On the dock, over the din of dozens of suggestions on how to
open it, we worked several hours with a wide assortment of tools until
it finally opened. First, there was a rush of water, then out tumbled
more than $100,000 in Confederate paper currency and two ledger
books. A free-for-all ensued, with everyone trying to grab some of the

Manolo Darnaude attaching chains to a safe containing $100,000 in Civil War paper currency that the author found off Providencia Island

wet bills, until the alcalde, police, and soldiers took it in custody, "until it can be established if the legitimate owners are still alive," the alcalde said. Though this was a ridiculous assumption to make, it did keep the islanders from possibly harming each other over the useless currency. But the alcalde himself turned out to be either greedy or stupid or both. The next day he sorrowfully told us that he had placed all of the money and the ledgers in his wife's oven the night before, "to dry it out." He dried it a little too much: the money and ledgers were reduced to a pile of ashes. "Easy come, easy go," Nancy said when we heard the news.

A rather bizarre event took place the following day. Word went around the island that a lady in her eighties was dying on the other side of the island, and soon the muddy road was crowded with trucks and horses moving toward her home. The priest came by our house in his pickup and talked us into going, saying that a death was one of the most interesting social events on the island. By the time we got there, there must have been over 300 people crowded into her yard. Two lively calypso bands were vying with each other, simultaneously playing different tunes, and most everyone was guzzling rum straight, as though Prohibition were beginning the next day. In the slight shade of a coconut tree, two men were hastily knocking together a coffin. The priest said the tropical climate made immediate burial imperative.

About an hour after we arrived, the old woman died, her end perhaps hastened by the raucous festivities. The priest had a difficult time trying to lead the islanders in prayer. Then the dead woman was placed in the coffin and set out in the yard for a brief viewing before the trip to the cemetery. As one of the carpenters was about to nail the lid of the coffin shut, the woman's eyes opened. She sat up and said: "Where de hell all dese damn people come from?" In just a few seconds, the only ones left were Nancy, Manolo, the priest, and me. Everyone else had vanished, leaving behind a litter of musical instruments, rum bottles, horses, and trucks.

During the Spanish attack on the island in 1641, a Portuguese ship had been sunk. According to documents I had read in Lisbon, she was carrying two large chests of Colombian emeralds. We knew that the ship had hit a reef and gone down in 10 or 12 fathoms and that divers at the time had been unable to salvage her treasure or bronze cannon. None of the local fishermen knew of any wreckage in the area where she sank, so we started a visual search, with two of us at a time being towed on lines behind the skiff. After a week of searching, we finally picked up a trail of ballast at the spot where the ship had struck the reef. We followed it for nearly a mile until the reef ended and the water appeared to be the right depth, then we switched to SCUBA gear and underwater metal detectors. And there she was: in 65 feet of water, buried in the sand.

We made plans to use an "airlift," a type of excavation tool that works on the principle of the vacuum cleaner to dig down into the sand. But the next day, nothing we did could get the air compressor started. The compressor was needed to supply power to the airlift for sucking up the sand. The one we were using to refill our SCUBA tanks wouldn't work with the airlift. So we dug with our hands. It took us four days to reach the first bronze cannon, buried in seven feet of sand. My hands trembled when I saw the Portuguese markings on the cannon. I knew we had struck pay dirt, but without the airlift or some other kind of mechanical excavation tool, excavating the wreck was impossible. I cabled a friend in Miami to ship us a compressor as quickly as possible, but it never arrived; customs in San Andrés seized it without explanation. When we told the islanders that we planned to salvage the wreck later, they didn't believe us. Again, rumors so easily nourished on slender facts, began flying about, that we had found "tons of gold."

About this time, a yacht flying the colors of the United States put in to the harbor for fresh water and a little sightseeing. The captain, hearing that some of his countrymen were on the island, paid us a visit. During the conversation he mentioned that there was a bad leak in the bow of his vessel and asked me where he could get some cement for a temporary repair job. Glad to help him out, I borrowed a truck and scouted around until I found a bag, buying it from a man who was building a new water cistern. That evening, when the captain invited us out to his boat for cocktails, we took the bag of cement in the skiff with us, never imagining the trouble it would cause. We patched the leak, and the following morning, the yacht sailed away.

Some 10 days later, Manolo and I were diving around Morgan's Head where we had a pet manta ray, Mortimer. Our 10-foot-long friend was as playful as a puppy, and on this day we were taking pictures of him. Coming up from our first dive to change tanks, we noticed a Colombian Navy destroyer entering the harbor, but thought no more about it and continued diving. When we got home we found a naval officer sporting a chestful of ribbons and medals and carrying a sword, seated in the living room with my wife. Neither of them looked happy. When I came in, the officer snapped to attention and began reading a list of charges concerning my discovery of a skeleton and under it, the fabulous treasure of Henry Morgan. I asked him where he had obtained this information, and he replied that, after all, there were a few patriots on the island, and some of them had reported it. I said I was sure there were patriots on Providencia, but added that there were also some practical jokers. The officer said he hadn't come hundreds of miles to investigate a practical joke and demanded to know what was in the bag I had taken out to the American yacht. I told him it was cement—and that was all we needed. He whistled, and the room immediately filled with armed marines and sailors. They tramped through the house and out the back door to the garden which they began to dig up.

While this was going on, Momo, who had been exploring the caves up in the hills, appeared and in his usual undiplomatic fashion, began cussing out our visitors in both Spanish and English. Nancy dragged him away, probably saving him from getting his skull bashed in. Dig as they would, however, they found nothing in the garden except what was supposed to be there: vegetables. They came trooping back into the house, looking sheepish, which made their commanding officer even angrier. He ordered me to pack a bag and be ready to leave the next morning. He was taking me to Cartagena for questioning. A bit out of sorts myself, I told him he would need another destroyer full of men to carry me away.

At this point, the alcalde entered. He had evidently been standing outside, along with half the island's population, getting an earful. He sort of passed the peace pipe by inviting the naval officer and me to a party at his house that evening where, he assured us, things would straighten themselves out. And, over demon rum, they did. The officer gradually mellowed, especially after Momo apologized for his outburst, and bit by bit, the plan to take me to Cartagena was forgotten. The following morning, we waved as the destroyer left, but it wasn't total victory. We learned later that the destroyer had gone off in pursuit of the American yacht and that dubious bag of cement. The episode convinced me of one thing: our days on Providencia were numbered. Nancy and Manolo were all for leaving at once, fearing that the next time we had a problem, we might really end up in a dungeon some-where. I was about ready to agree with them when something very exciting happened.

A retired sea captain of about 80, whose face was a catalogue of sun-baked wrinkles, made me change my mind. At first, when he launched into the usual preamble about knowing the location of a gold hoard, I groaned inwardly, telling him I was too tired to listen. But he insisted that he had walked all the way across the island to talk to me, and I invited him in. At least his tale was more interesting than the "dreams" I had heard earlier. It concerned gold that lay on a shipwreck. I figured he was just a shrewder salesman than the others and, with some skepti-cism asked him to tell me about *his* dream.

He drew himself up with great dignity and assured me that this was no dream. He was talking about gold he had actually seen and touched. It had happened some 30 years earlier, right after a hurricane hit the island. He had been diving, without any gear (it reminded me of Aldo), to recover a fish trap and had come upon the remains of a shipwreck. Near it was a pile of what looked like golden suns. The water was about 50 feet deep, and with great difficulty he grabbed one and tied it to a line. But in attempting to bring it to the surface, the line came undone and it fell back to the bottom. Too tired to continue diving, he quit for the day. When he returned the next morning, he found that shifting sand had covered the gold suns and most of the wreck. About 10 years ago, he had hired several divers from Panama to come to the island, but they couldn't find the wreck.

I believed him. What convinced me were those "golden suns." It's a matter of historical record that gold was shipped from the New World to the Old in the form of disks, as well as the better-known bars, or ingots; but this is a fact known to few people outside historical circles. The captain agreed to a fifty-fifty split of any treasure found on the wreck, and we drew up a contract which was witnessed by the alcalde. Early the next morning we headed for the wreck. About four miles north of Catalina Island, he told me to stop the skiff, and squinting into the rising sun, motioned for me to move the skiff several hundred yards. I did, not believing he could find the exact spot so easily, but I had underestimated his seamanship.

Wearing tanks, Manolo and I went down. There was a reef that came almost to the surface and then dropped off to a sandy bottom at a depth of about 50 feet. Halfway down the side of the reef, we spotted an iron anchor almost completely buried in the coral, and nearby was a large, intact, Spanish olive jar. The Spaniards used these clay jars—which are similar to Roman, Greek, and Phoenician amphorae—to transport everything from liquids to gunpowder. At the base of the reef we found two more unbroken olive jars and several ceramic plates, neatly stacked, as one would find them in a kitchen cupboard. But on the bottom, where the old sea captain claimed to have seen "golden suns," there was nothing but sand and sea urchins.

The olive jars and plates dated from the second half of the sixteenth century. According to documents from the Seville Archives, the ship was probably a small merchantman lost in 1572 en route to Nombre de Dios, Panama. That meant it was unlikely that we would find any treasure aboard her, but this didn't bother us particularly; one of the things that makes treasure-hunting so fascinating is that you can never be sure of anything. Maybe the ship had made an unscheduled stop somewhere in the New World; perhaps it carried contraband gold; or maybe it was another wreck altogether.

Word that we were onto something big spread quickly. That evening I had a visitor, a man the islanders referred to sarcastically as "The Duke." They had warned me about him, telling me he was bad news. It seemed The Duke had once been the most powerful man on the island. During World War II he had helped a couple of Nazi agents who were sent to Providencia. They set up a lookout station on the highest peak and radioed the position of passing ships to German submarines in the area. The Duke was also suspected of supplying the submarines. When the agents were caught, his star fell, and now, more than 20 years later, he was still held in low esteem by his fellow islanders.

Here he was at my house, demanding that he be cut in as a partner in the treasure hunt. When I told him I already had a partner, he said I wouldn't be able to do anything without his permission. I remarked that the permission of the Colombian government was good enough for me and with that, went back in the house. His last words, shouted through the door, were to the effect that I would regret this, but I paid no attention.

The next morning I was the first overboard. As I descended, I saw about 20 sharks circling rapidly in the water. As fast as I could, I shot back to the surface, yelling at everyone to remain in the skiff as I climbed aboard. Sharks, of course, are a routine feature of the diving racket, but such a large number in one area is unusual. Even then, though, sharks don't usually act as if you were on the menu. It was the old captain, gazing down through his glass-bottom bucket, who discovered the reason for it: a wire fish trap filled with cow intestines!

On the way back to shore, I ran the outboard motor so fast that I almost overturned the skiff. I charged through town toward The Duke's house. Maybe I was jumping to the wrong conclusion, but from the way the door was slammed in my face, I knew I wasn't. I pounded on the door, but the Duke did not return. A crowd gathered. I began shouting through the door. My threats must have had some effect (at least, I thought so at the time), because that evening The Duke left the island.

For the next few weeks everything went well. I carried on a love affair with the beautiful island, working hard on the wreck by day and enjoying the balmy breezes with my wife and friends during the evenings. I was soaking up the island's relaxed, easygoing atmosphere which, I felt, would soon change. There were some difficulties, of course, such as the occasional squall that caused the sea to deposit enough sand on the site to undo several days' work. Despite this, though, we made good progress on the wreck.

After locating the main section of the ship with the metal detector, we found that most of it was covered by only a few feet of sand. Yet without an air compressor to run the airlift, we were again forced to excavate by hand. One person would dig into the sand, filling buckets, while the other two or three carried it about 100 feet off and dumped it. It was a slow, tedious process, but we had no alternative.

On our third day on the wreck we discovered seven pieces of eight and two 25-pound silver bars. By the time we were forced to throw in the towel, we had recovered a considerable display of interesting items, including 58 olive jars, all intact; more than 200 glazed ceramic plates which later sold for $300 to $500 each; cups, bowls, and chamber pots; wine and pharmaceutical bottles; iron pots and kettles; swords and other weapons, including four breech-loading swivel guns that fired a three-pound stone ball; a brass ship's bell and other fittings, as well as personal relics such as crucifixes, medallions, belt and shoe buckles, and even a pair of ivory dice. The old captain kept trying to get us off the wreck into the area of the "golden suns," but as long as we were making such good finds, we were reluctant to do so.

Then all at once, the love affair was over. The Duke returned to the island, and on the boat came two pieces of news that finally convinced me to call it quits. He had acted against me from a distance, having gone to Bogotá with a signed partnership agreement allegedly drawn up between the old captain and himself more than 30 years earlier. On the strength of this document (a forgery, according to the captain), The Duke started a lawsuit over the wreck, and we were forbidden to work on it until an investigation had been completed.

I was confronted with a choice. We could remain on the island and try to find other wrecks, waiting until the investigation was complete, or we could leave. Having seen the way justice was dispensed in the lawsuit involving Bandido, I realized that I didn't have much of a choice. As it turned out, the choice was made for us. In the mail one day was a letter from the government of Jamaica, offering me the job of excavating the sunken city of Port Royal, which had been a lifelong dream of mine.

Expecting problems when we reached San Andrés, I divided up what we had recovered into two parts, giving the alcalde his share and that for the Colombian government, and shipped the rest to the United States aboard an American shrimper. (I was later to regret that I didn't do the same with the diving equipment and our other things.)

As things now stood, I had a great deal of experience in this part of the world, when I considered all of the wrecks I had worked on around Serranilla, Serrana, and Providencia. At the time of writing this book, after 10 years of effort, I have finally obtained leases for the wrecks in these three areas. Now it's just a matter of finding the time to go after them.

5: The Sunken City
of Port Royal

To a marine archaeologist, the name Port Royal generates as much excitement as Pompeii does to his land counterpart. Both cities met with sudden destruction, one sinking into the sea while the other vanished under molten lava, and it has long been recognized that excavating them would produce important clues to the past. Pompeii yielded its historic treasures some time ago, but that of Port Royal was still waiting when I was contacted to take on the challenging task of excavating it.

Port Royal was a legend from its beginning to its end, a period that spanned less than four decades. In the closing years of the seventeenth century, tales of the wealth and wickedness to be found there circulated throughout the civilized world. It was said that in Port Royal there was "more plenty of running cash proportionately to the number of inhabitants than in London." The town got its start in 1655 when Jamaica was captured from Spain by the English who recognized that its position in the center of the Caribbean made it an ideal base from which to attack Spanish treasure fleets returning to Spain. Soon after the town was founded, buccaneers, pirates, and privateers arrived in large numbers. These men were the heaviest contributors to Port Royal's reputation for boozing, wenching, and brawling. Some of them, accepting privateering commissions, served the English crown. Among these was Henry Morgan whose expeditions to Panama City and other ports of the Spanish Main earned him a knighthood. Others served only themselves, among them the infamous and volatile Roche Brasilano whose fondness for shooting up the town made him feared by friend and foe alike.

Port Royal continued to prosper even after the departure of the buccaneers in 1675, when the English crown, then at peace with Spain, rescinded all letters of marque and made a determined effort to suppress piracy in the Caribbean. Port Royal's strategic location assured its success as a seaport. The greatest source of wealth was the contraband trade with the Spanish colonies, but the town had other irons in the fire, as well. There was the traffic in slaves; there was the new industry of treasure-hunting, or the "wracking trade," as it was called; and there was the legitimate trade with England and the English colonies in North America. So many people flocked to where the money was that at the time of the disaster, the town had more than 8,000 inhabitants and 2,000 buildings, and some of the buildings were three or four stories high. These were crowded together in what appeared to be a solid mass, its edge reaching out into the harbor where houses stood on pilings driven into the sand. As fine as any in London, many of the houses were stocked with gold, silver, pewter, jewels, porcelain, silks, laces, and brocades from all over the world. Small wonder that everyone referred to Port Royal as the "Store House" or "Treasury of the West Indies" —everyone, that is, except a minority of moralizing, God-fearing souls who predicted that the town would be punished for its wickedness. The majority expected the boom to last forever. But it didn't.

Shortly before noon on Tuesday, June 7, 1692, disaster struck. In a matter of minutes, there were three strong earthquakes. The third and most severe was followed by a huge tidal wave that broke the anchor cables of ships riding in the harbor, wrecked ships near the wharves, and caused about 90 percent of the town to sink or slide into the harbor. By the time the sun went down on Port Royal that day, more than 1,800 buildings had disappeared. All that remained above water was a mere 10 acres of land in the shape of a small cay. The property damage was incalculable, but not the toll of lives: more than 2,000 perished, and an additional thousand survivors died from epidemics that soon followed.

A few years after the 1692 disaster, part of the town was rebuilt, but it suffered from one natural disaster after another, and few wanted to live there. Except for some importance as a naval base during the eighteenth and nineteenth centuries, Port Royal never regained its former glory; only the legend survived. A new legend grew up around it, that of a sunken city with streets of gold, silver, and precious stones, waiting under the sea for some brave adventurer to find. Through the years, currents and hurricanes deposited such a large amount of sediment in the area that more than half of the sunken city was covered over, forming the base for a new land mass and connecting it once again to the Palisadoes peninsula.

Today the Caribbean Babylon is a small, sleepy town of less than 500 people and an apparently equal number of skinny, hungry dogs. Most of the residents are engaged in fishing. They are fiercely proud of the town's former glory, and many of them claim to be descendants of Henry Morgan or other swashbucklers who once lived there. In a lifetime of traveling around the world, I have found the hardy Port Royalists (as they prefer to be called) to be the most honest and friendly people I have ever encountered.

The prospect of excavating the sunken city would excite anyone, but for years I had an interest in Port Royal that amounted to an obsession. It dates back to when I was 10 and happened to read a book written by a treasure-hunter who claimed to have dived to the sunken city. At that age I could hardly swim. The thought of someday becoming a professional diver and marine archaeologist had never entered my head; but that book of fiction masquerading as fact changed all that. The author spun a good yarn about what he had seen under the sea: the standing cathedral, taverns in which skeletons sat at tables with tankards in their bony hands, chests of treasure everywhere, ready for the taking. I don't think I swallowed it all even at the age of 10, but the parts about the sunken cathedral and treasure, I never doubted for a minute. Only when I eventually visited Port Royal did I discover that the book catalogued under nonfiction in the library should have been under "Fiction."

After learning how to dive in the murky lakes and rivers around Pittsburgh, I made several unsuccessful attempts before I was 13 to reach Port Royal by running away from home. The farthest I ever got was Miami. I finally got to Port Royal in the spring of 1954 while serving in the Marine Corps. A strong north wind was blowing, driving great, crashing waves against the seawall. Undaunted and wearing snorkeling equipment, I plunged into the water and headed out to the buoy known as the Church Beacon, under which the local fishermen claimed the cathedral stood. The jellyfish were as numerous as snowflakes in a blizzard, and the visibility underwater was a mere one or two feet; but nothing was going to stop me from seeing the sunken cathedral. I knew that I could *feel* the walls of the cathedral even if I couldn't see them. I gulped air into my lungs, jackknifed, and descended. I felt something, all right: the seafloor. Groping around in the darkness, I suddenly felt as if a thousand needles had been driven into my right hand. I had caught hold of a large, black, spiny sea urchin! The excruciating pain forced me out of the water to get medical assistance.

When I was finally able to dive again, conditions were more to my liking. The sea was flat calm and the visibility was over 10 feet. Unable to find any SCUBA equipment on Jamaica, I almost killed myself by free diving for eight straight hours before giving up from sheer exhaustion. I saw no sign of the cathedral or any other building—only some coral-encrusted projections on the seafloor which, due to my lack of experience, I didn't recognize as being the walls of buildings. The only artifact I found was a whiskey bottle dating from the late nineteenth century. The next few days were virtual repetitions of that one, and I became increasingly depressed. I was beginning to doubt that Port Royal had ever sunk into the sea. Convinced that I was wasting my time, I left to join some friends who were salvaging a shipwreck off the coast of Florida.

My interest was revived the following year after reading that amateur divers had found some interesting artifacts at Port Royal, dating from the time of the 1692 earthquake. Still in the Marines, I had already used up most of my leave for the year, but managed to get back to Port Royal for a few days. This time I brought several SCUBA tanks with me and hired a fisherman to take me to the place where the divers said they had located a standing building. I almost capsized the skiff in my haste to get down. Visibility was good this time, and I spotted the ruins at once. During the first hour of diving I found several clay smoking pipes, two intact onion bottles (so named because of their shape), a cannonball, and numerous pottery shards in the mud. I could hardly believe it; I had been over the same area the year before and had found nothing. In a daze, I climbed aboard the skiff, almost overturning it again. But the fisherman didn't share my bewilderment. He thought the building had probably been uncovered by a recent storm or current which carried the sediment away and suggested that I search the area for other buildings that might have been uncovered. I took him up on it, and before exhausting my air supply, discovered the walls of several other buildings.

The next day, while the tanks were being refilled at the local oxygen-supply house in Kingston, I paid a visit to the Institute of Jamaica where I met the director, an American named Bernard Lewis who was very interested in Port Royal. He showed me files filled with documentation on the sunken city. By the end of the day I was aware of the importance of doing historical research on underwater sites before undertaking any exploratory work on them. Little did I realize that eventually I would spend four years doing primary research in libraries, archives, and museums in Europe and North and South America. (One of the first documents I came across was an account by a British Royal Navy diver who had discovered Fort James in 1859 under the Church Beacon buoy. Any last bit of faith I had in the author I had read as a boy vanished.) Before leaving, I thanked Lewis, assuring him that someday I would be back to excavate the sunken city.

The next day I was back at the Church Beacon, and this time didn't dismiss the projections on the seafloor as coral reefs. For hours I chipped with a crowbar through almost a foot of coral. I couldn't have been more jubilant about the discovery if I had been the first to make it instead of coming along a century later. There was a fort there, as the diver had claimed. Digging in the sediment near one of the fort's walls, I found a large iron cannon, cannonballs, and other artifacts. My air supply exhausted, I surfaced with the feeling that I had done a good day's work. My childhood dream of finding treasure was soon replaced with a new one, that of excavating Port Royal and learning about its famous past. I wasn't ready then, however, and I knew it. I was a good diver, but I had no knowledge of the way to excavate an underwater site properly, not that very many others at the time did, either. During the intervening 10 years, before I began serious work on the sunken city, I devoted myself to learning all I could about archaeology and maritime history.

When I received the letter from the Jamaican government in November 1965, asking me to direct the excavation of the sunken city, there was a certain amount of urgency about the project. Plans to turn modern

Port Royal into a tourist center had been proposed. This entailed dredging a deepwater port there, which would result in the destruction of over half of the sunken city. The month before, Port Royal had suffered a series of minor earth tremors, which was another reason for prompt action. Diving enthusiasts who rushed to Port Royal immediately afterward discovered that the seafloor had been affected by the tremors, exposing dozens of walls. Many lightweight artifacts had been forced to the surface of the seafloor and were lying there exposed. This precipitated a stampede, something on the order of the California gold rush.

When I arrived in Port Royal, it wasn't with the expectation of finding treasure. Salvors were on the scene with nets and grappling hooks immediately after the 1692 earthquake, recovering valuable artifacts from submerged buildings. No part of the sunken city lay more than 50 feet below the water's surface, a depth the divers based in Port Royal could easily penetrate, either with diving bells or with their own breath. Anything valuable that had been overlooked by the salvors would have been recovered during the salvage efforts that continued for years after the disaster. Despite the numerous articles by divers who claim to have recovered gold from the sunken city and who bolster their claims with tales of entering taverns to find skeletons seated at tables or of entering the town's cathedral (which happens to be buried under land), there is only one recovery of treasure that is a matter of historical record—three leopard's teeth covered with gold, found in the belly of a shark in 1788. The other claims are romantic fiction.

I wasn't interested in fiction; I was interested in recovering artifacts and relics of old Port Royal, with a view to reconstructing life in the sunken city. That this *historical* treasure was there was proved by the Edwin Link expedition of 1959, which recovered a number of interesting artifacts, including a small cannon and a brass pocket watch. From the start, I was determined to carry out the excavation according to established archaeological principles. I knew I couldn't hope for the spectacular results achieved at Pompeii where archaeologists had uncovered a fantastic time capsule of history. Because the site had been quickly covered with volcanic ash and had remained virtually untouched for almost 2,000 years, houses were found with their furnishings intact and impressions of the inhabitants at their daily occupations were preserved in the solidified ash. Old Port Royal is less than 300 years old, but during those years the area has been ravaged by upheavals and hurricanes, to say nothing of man-made disturbances.

I discovered how far I was from Pompeii during my first week of exploring the site in December 1965. A large freighter dropped anchor near my position, and its anchor dragged on the bottom, gouging a trench four feet wide and five feet deep over some 200 feet of the site. Scattered on the seafloor were hundreds of artifacts dating from the 1692 earthquake, while in the trench lay Coca-Cola bottles, tin cans, automobile hubcaps, and other modern debris. Obviously, how far beneath the seafloor an object was found would not be a certain indication of its age. Nevertheless, I intended to excavate layer by layer, plotting the locations of the major finds as precisely as I could.

After spending the first week exploring the site, I decided the next move would be to remove all of the modern debris: automobile chassis, stoves, sinks, and incredible amounts of other junk that had been thrown into the sea by the inhabitants of modern Port Royal. For nearly a month, working alone except on weekends, when I had a few volunteers, I brought tons of modern trash to the surface, put it in a small skiff, and took it to an area some distance from the site of the sunken city. It was hard and not very exciting work, but it had to be done. I tried using divers from the local chapter of the British Sub-Aqua Club to assist me, but I soon found out that they were more interested in artifacts than in raising trash—which wasn't surprising, really. Two members of the club—Stan Judge and his teenage daughter, Louise— were a cut above the others. They eventually resigned from the club and worked with me as volunteers on the project. Along with my wife, Nancy, who soon became a history professor at the University of the West Indies, Stan and Louise contributed every free minute they had.

Several cocky American divers whose yacht had been anchored over the site for almost a year came under suspicion, but though they were watched closely by the local police, no one could figure out how they were getting the artifacts from the sunken city, which they were selling to tourists. Then one day, while on a routine dive, I encountered one of them in the murky water. I was ascending with an armful of trash when I spotted a diver swimming with a bulging gunnysack. I pretended I hadn't seen him and gave him a head start, following him back to his yacht. Then he entered a hatch in the boat's hull and disappeared. I had to admire the James Bond ingenuity of the maneuver, but, ingenious or not, what they were doing was criminal. I reported my discovery to the authorities, and the American divers were deported. Their exposure discouraged others from making illegal dives, and I had no further need to play detective. I had a large sign erected on the outskirts of the town, notifying divers that they would be prosecuted for taking anything from the seafloor around Port Royal.

In the center of Port Royal was a tumbledown bar—the Buccaneers' Roost—which was the town's focal point. Most of the men hung out there, and I soon made it my headquarters while in Port Royal. It was the only place to get a decent hot meal, but the selection wasn't very large. One ate either delicious, fresh fried fish or filling conch chowder, the latter so richly spiced with hot peppers that few of my visiting friends could stomach it. Actually the place was far from what one could call a tourist facility; rum flowed like water, and brawls were a daily occurence. There were even occasional knife fights, mostly precipitated by Kingston fishermen who were not welcome at Port Royal. But, I was accepted by the local people, who were interested in what I was doing, and I rarely had any problems with the fishermen. In fact, on a number of occasions, when bad types came over from Kingston and began giving me a hard time, they were driven off by the residents of Port Royal.

From the beginning, the main problem was lack of money. Although the Jamaican government was eager to get the project started as soon as possible, the necessary funds just weren't available. Consequently, it was a one-man operation—which it remained for the first five months.

When "Operation Junk Removal" was completed at the end of December, I was ready for the next phase of the operation. This entailed mapping the site now that the trash had been removed. The waters were so murky that aerial photography or any other aids dependent on visibility were out of the question. If funds had been available, I could have used a magnetometer and two types of sonar—side scanning and subbottom profiling. Instead, to locate metallic deposits, I relied on a hand-held metal detector, and to locate walls and other large nonmetallic objects buried in the sediment, I used an eight-foot metal probe. I had the Jamaican Survey Department put up permanent markers ashore, which enabled me to plot locations with a fair amount of accuracy. Another major problem was the sheer magnitude of the task:

it required at least five or six people to be accomplished efficiently. After four months of diving between 10 and 12 hours a day, I had mapped only a small portion of the site, an area roughly 200 by 300 yards in the section of the sunken city, where the jails, fish and meat markets, shops of craftsmen, and private homes had stood. Although the water was never clear, the weather was rarely a problem during most of the three years I worked there, because the site is inside the harbor where it is protected from both wind and seas.

Around the middle of April I was told that money for the project would soon be available, so I set about assembling a team and enlisted two good diving assistants. Kenute Kelly, an amateur swimming champion and a commercial salvor by profession, became my chief lieutenant by virtue of having had more experience underwater than Wayne Roosevelt.

Now I had my divers and my equipment. Instead of SCUBA gear, we would use a recent invention consisting of a small air compressor set inside a floating tube, with hoses carrying air to the divers below. I decided on this device, called an Aquanaut, because it freed us from the need to wear the cumbersome air tanks on our backs and from the need to surface to replenish the oxygen in the tanks. With a skiff attendant to put fuel in the Aquanaut every hour, we could remain submerged all day.

Selecting the proper excavating equipment presented difficulties because of my determination to avoid any tool that might endanger fragile objects such as glassware which, in view of Port Royal's renowned thirst, I expected to find plenty of. In digging by hand, the safety of the artifacts would have been assured, but while I anticipated that the Port Royal project would take years (it was the largest marine excavation project in terms of scale and duration ever attempted anywhere in the world), I had hopes of finishing it sometime before I was 92. I decided to use an airlift with a tube four inches in diameter, which was smaller than those normally used in underwater digs. A screen on the bottom of the tube would prevent objects from being sucked up before the diver could retrieve them, and an even finer screen on the barge, the receptacle for the sediment and debris coming up the tube, would snag very small artifacts such as pins or beads so they could be retrieved by the four boys manning the barge.

Plotting the position and stratigraphical depth where the artifacts

The airlift in operation at Port Royal

were found wasn't easy when working in such dirty water, but we finally found a method that worked quite well. At the beginning of each day's excavation, four buoys were placed in a square around the work area. As each major artifact was brought up, the skiff attendant would record the position of the top of the airlift tube in relation to the four buoys, and at the end of the day, the exact position where each artifact was recovered could be plotted on a grid chart. To obtain the stratigraphical depth, the skiff attendant merely had to record the length of airlift tube protruding above the seafloor. By knowing the depth at which we were working, the status of the tide, and the depth of the airlift tube beneath the sea, we could establish the stratigraphical depth of each major artifact. The only problem occured when the sides of a hole being excavating collapsed and artifacts fell deeper into the hole, with the sediment making it impossible to determine the original position and depth of the artifact or artifacts.

On May 1, 1966, at seven in the morning, the dig began at a spot about 120 feet from shore. After removing only a foot of sediment, we turned up one artifact after another and by the end of the first hour had filled three baskets with clay smoking pipes, ceramic shards, some unbroken onion bottles, and various coral-encrusted iron objects. We were off to a good start.

Our first major discovery was a fallen wall. If the wall had fallen during the earthquake, I thought there was a good chance of finding valuable artifacts underneath, since the early salvors might not have been inclined to go as far as lifting walls. I was right. As I excavated along one side of the wall, objects began dropping into the hole I was making: a pewter spoon and then a pewter meat platter, with four pewter plates stacked neatly on top of it. Suddenly I noticed that the wall was tilting over the hole. I shut off the airlift, debating whether to disassemble the wall before proceeding. Quick as a flash, Kelly, eager to make a find of his own, crawled under the wall and emerged with a pewter tankard and a pewter plate.

That settled it. I was happy about the finds, but I didn't want Kelly displaying any more recklessness around a wall that might fall on top of him at any moment. Signaling to the team to keep hands off the wall until it was level again, I went around to the opposite side and began pumping away sediment there. At once uncovered four pewter spoons.

Now it was my turn to be reckless, and I began pumping deeper than I should have. Before I knew what hit me, the wall slid over on top of me, pinning down my head and torso. Luckily, it didn't break my air hose, but it did smash the airlift tube. That told the boys on the barge that something was wrong, and they sent Kelly to find me. It took him awhile (visibility was less than a foot), but as soon as he did, he disconnected the air hose from the broken tube and used it as an air jet to blow away the sediment that was pinning me down. It was a risky maneuver; there was every chance that the wall would slide farther, trapping him, too. But it worked. After that, the rule was: *take a wall apart before it can take you apart.*

In the vicinity of the first wall we found six others of similar construction, along with seven roof beams. I was convinced that we were working on the site of a single house. But whose? We had a clue in the initials on two pewter plates and two pewter spoons found under the first wall. Consulting a map of old Port Royal at the Institute of Jamaica, I learned that at the time of the earthquake in 1692, a Richard Collins owned property near where we found the pewterware bearing his initials; so it was a reasonable assumption that the house belonged to him. Aside from the fact that he owned property, nothing is known about Collins, but I believe I have found out something interesting about him —that he either kept a tavern or rented part of his land to someone who did. In the area around the house we found quantities of onion bottles, ceramic beer mugs, broken wineglasses, and more than 500 clay smoking pipes. The drinking paraphernalia could have belonged to a tippler with a lot of friends, but the clay pipes were another matter. No one man would have owned so many. Since many of the pipes had been smoked, they couldn't have been stock from a shop that sold pipes. The most plausible explanation was a tavern. In those days a man owned several clay pipes and customarily left one at each of his favorite taverns.

Fairly soon after this exercise of my powers of deduction on the tavern site, I had a real mystery on my hands. For a couple of weeks we excavated an area roughly 50 feet square, in which we came upon few clay pipes or household relics. Instead, we found thousands of artifacts from a ship—iron nails and caulking tools, brass ship's fittings, copper wire and patches for covering holes in the hull, and lead draught markers. The evidence pointed to a shipwreck, but where was it? As a

The author and Kenute Kelly with artifacts found at Port Royal

rule, no matter how much sediment might cover a wreck, the pile of ship's ballast protrudes above the seafloor. (Ballast is a heavy substance used to improve the stability and control the draft of a ship.) We didn't find any ballast, and who ever heard of a ship without ballast? I was baffled. The English "broad arrow" marked on the brass and copper artifacts, proof that they were property of the crown, told me that they couldn't have come from a ship chandlery; no shop would have been allowed to sell crown property. The draught markers—Roman numerals VII and IX (or XI)—indicated that the wreck we were looking for was a large one, because a small sloop never drew more than four or five feet.

A week later we found the keel and ribs of a ship of 250 to 300 tons. The size of the cannons found nearby, along with the absence of barrel staves and other artifacts normally carried by merchant vessels, indicated that she was a warship. The brick walls we found above and below part of the keel showed that she had sunk during the earthquake. What ship was she? A period of detective work began, involving a search through contemporary documents and extensive correspondence with the British Admiralty. The only English warship reported lost during the earthquake was HMS *Swan.* She measured 74 feet in length, and with a normal load, her depth in the water was 10 feet and her weight 305 tons, statistics that matched our wreck perfectly. The most exciting information to come to light about *Swan* was that she was being *careened* at the time of the earthquake. "Careening" involves turning a ship on its side, for example, to clean the ballast from it. But we didn't find any explanation of why this was being done. Without ballast (at least a hundred tons of it for a ship this size), *Swan* would have been light in the water, light enough to be flung by the tidal wave from her original position into the middle of the town. There was little doubt in my mind that our wreck was HMS *Swan.*

Invariably any major discovery such as *Swan* gave us a big lift. The average working day consisted of gruelling labor, and on some days the bucket came up with nothing but clay pipes and ceramic shards. But there were hazards, too. We had to expect the unexpected, because the water was usually so black that we could see our reflections in our face masks. Our hands were frequently lacerated by sea urchins and slivers of glass caught in the airlift screen. More serious than the cuts though, were objects that fell from the collapsing sides of the hole. Despite a tour of inspection every morning, groping around the hole for anything large, a few times we overlooked large coral heads. Two of them seemed to have eyes; the target of one was Kelly's knees, and the target of the other was my back.

Adding to the hazards were some uninvited visitors. More often than not, they were upon us before we saw them. One day Kelly felt himself nudged from behind as he was surfacing out of the gloom, and an instant later, a manta ray 12 feet wide embraced him with its "wings." Manta rays are by nature playful, but now and then their romps in the water have carried them onto a ship's deck where they have crushed people to death with their weight, a fact Kelly was well aware of. He remained perfectly still until the manta ray, probably deciding that Kelly wasn't much fun as a playmate, unfolded its wings and swam away. Another time, I felt myself being nudged from behind as I was working on the bottom. Intent on my task, I reached out a hand to push the intruder away and touched something with the texture of sandpaper. I whirled to find myself looking doom in the eye: a large hammerhead shark was only inches away! Possibly my sudden movement frightened it, or maybe my rubber suit and glass face mask didn't make me a very appetizing morsel. In any case, it departed.

Not every shark was so obliging. One particular hammerhead, over eight feet long (by measurement), arrived one morning and refused to leave, letting us know it was around by nudging us at intervals. Twice its fins caught my air hose and ripped it off. The necessity of posting a guard slowed work down considerably, but the only alternative was to kill the shark. Fearing that its blood would attract other sharks, I preferred to get on with the job rather than invite out-and-out warfare with a shark gang. But not Kelly, a born gambler! Deciding that the emphatic nudge he received was a little too unfriendly, he went to get a spear gun. While I worked the airlift, unaware of what was going on, Kelly lured the shark to the surface where the water was clearer. He knew he would have to kill it instantly (merely wounding it would have insured retaliation, and no man is a match for an angry shark), so he fired his first shot into the brain. Then with the help of the surface team, he heaved the dead shark into the skiff before the blood could spread.

Despite the dangers and delays that once in a while forced work to a standstill, we made numerous discoveries. A pestle and wooden chest containing 21 small glass medicine bottles and two ceramic medicine vases told us we were on the site of an apothecary's shop. Awls, pieces of leather, heels, soles, and completed shoes were signs of a cobbler's shop. Hammers, saws, adzes, chisels, files, scrapers, nails, tacks, and a wooden table and chair indicated a carpenter's shop. Ship's rigging and fittings (not marked with the "broad arrow" this time) were the signs of a ship chandlery. We came upon an area about 40 feet by 15 feet on which bones were piled two and three feet deep. One section contained the bones of fish and the other the bones of cows, horses, pigs, goats, and wild boars. We had found the fish and meat markets.

The shops and markets were what I expected to find in the part of the site we were excavating, and I wasn't surprised, though, of course, I was overjoyed at the wealth of artifacts recovered. One find that did surprise me was the uncovering of two turtle crawls side by side. I knew that turtles, which provided the meat staple for Port Royal's inhabitants, had been kept in fenced areas awaiting slaughter, but I assumed that the wooden fences would have been swept away by a tidal wave powerful enough to lift *Swan*. Instead, most of the fence posts were still standing, and there we found thousands of turtle bones. Why the turtles didn't swim to safety when the area sank under the water is a mystery. Were their legs bound together (a common practice at the time)? Were they buried under an avalanche of mud before they could escape? Whatever the reason, I was delighted with them, as I was with other relics that had miraculously survived for almost three centuries: a handful of human hair, a complete tobacco leaf in a remarkable state of preservation, and a petrified chunk of butter.

A high point of the dig was the discovery of two standing buildings. We excavated around the exterior of the first, as well as a portion of the interior, before we had to quit for the day. The next morning we were disappointed to see that the walls had collapsed during the night. Soon afterward, we came upon the second standing building. I decided to excavate differently, removing no more than a foot of sediment outside the walls before doing the same inside, thus equalizing the external and internal pressures. I hoped to brace the walls after the excavation so that the building would remain standing. It was a full day's work just to excavate the top five feet of the building which was 34 feet long and 17 wide and had walls two feet thick.

The next morning we were happy to see that the building was still standing. It was the only happy event of the day. The first unhappy one was the breakdown of the Aquanaut. Descending with SCUBA gear, we had been down only a few minutes when Kelly cut his hand badly on a piece of glass. I sent him to the doctor and continued the excavation with Wayne's help. But when the building was almost excavated, Wayne complained of a headache, so I sent him to the surface.

Before stopping work myself (as a rule, we never dived alone, for reasons of safety), I decided to complete my sketch of the building, since I knew there was every chance of its collapsing during the night. I went to examine the wall near the entrance, and the next thing I knew I was pinned under the wall. My mask was gone, and my eyes were smarting from the salt and dirt in the water. Fortunately, the weight of the wall, plus my own, pressed my face against the purge button of my mouthpiece regulator, and I got all the air I needed while unconscious. As soon as I realized where I was, I tried to push the wall off my back, but it was impossible to move. A solid mass of wall had fallen on me. I knew I couldn't count on being rescued, so the only thing to do was dig straight ahead with my hands. After what seemed like years, my fingers touched the end of the wall, and I crawled through the handmade tunnel until my arms and head were free. I could see a glimmer of sunlight filtering down through the murky water as I crawled out a little farther. Then suddenly, my regulator got caught between two bricks in the wall.

I wasted precious minutes of my dwindling air supply attempting to free the regulator, but couldn't. With most of my body still pinned to the bottom, I couldn't maneuver well enough to ditch the tank. Every second it became more difficult to breathe. There was only one chance. I jerked my body forward with every ounce of strength I could muster. The regulator snapped, and I found my torso clear of the wall. Another jerk and I shot upward to the surface.

For several days after that narrow escape, walls were my enemy. There was a reconciliation when I excavated a fallen wall and came upon the single most valuable artifact recovered during the entire dig. It was a round object so thickly encrusted with coral that I didn't have any idea what it was. An x-ray revealed the outline of a man's pocket watch, removal of the coral showed the substance from which it was made—silver—and cleaning, its remarkable state of preservation. The watch face shone like a mirror. On it was the name of the maker, Gibbs, and the place of origin, London, both as legible as they were the day the watch left the workshop.

Almost immediately after the recovery of the watch, the supply of artifacts ran out on us. Most days we surfaced emptyhanded. We expected a quick end to the run of bad luck, but it continued for more than a month. It was bewildering. All along we had been recovering artifacts steadily. The pewter we had already amassed was the most extensive collection of pewterware of the period to be found anywhere in the world. Now we found no pewter and few other artifacts. We were working in an area that contained no fallen walls. Even onion bottles, clay pipes, and pottery shards—things we usually found strewn over the seafloor—were becoming rarities. Accustomed as we were to feasts, we became discouraged by the famine every day. Seeing how miserable I was, Nancy suggested that I move the dig to another area, but I was determined to stick to my plan to enlarge the original hole. As the morale of the team steadily declined, however, I changed my mind and handed Nancy a chart of the site, asking her to pick a spot. She chose an area about a hundred feet north of the area we had been working.

I moved the dig, but for hours it seemed as though the jinx had followed us. The Aquanaut was being serviced that day, so to conserve air in the SCUBA tanks, I excavated alone, instructing Kelly and Wayne to descend at intervals on their own breath to carry up artifacts. I didn't find any artifacts, though, only pieces of coral. Then I had to surface for another tank. Deciding that I had to make a phone call, I sent Kelly down to pump and then swam ashore. I had been on the phone no more than a minute when one of the boys from the barge came running toward me, shouting that Kelly had found something great.

The find was great, all right—four silver Spanish pieces of eight, so well preserved that the markings were still clearly visible. I could hardly believe my eyes. Ordinarily coins found underwater are so badly sulfated that even after cleaning, their impressions are barely discernible. Making out the date on one coin in a hundred is cause for rejoicing among numismatologists. I asked Kelly whether there were any more coins below. He said he thought so. And he was right; we found hundreds more, all beautifully preserved. This was explained when I found the remains of the wooden chest that had protected the coins over the centuries.

The unexpected discovery of this treasure temporarily raised our spirits, but in the long run, it proved to be a nuisance. Up till then our project had gotten little publicity on the island, but as soon as it leaked out that we had found the coins, their value was magnified a hundred times and eventually resulted in our losing several weeks' work while the police chased away the curious local inhabitants.

We entered the new year 1967 faced with two big mysteries: it was the first time we had found anything of value on the site that wasn't located under a fallen wall; and the keyhole plate on the chest bore the coat of arms of the king of Spain. We wondered how it had gotten to Port Royal. The first mystery we were never able to solve, but research in the Archivo de las Indias in Seville soon told us how the chest of coins belonging to the Spanish crown had gotten there. At first we thought it was plunder obtained by some enterprising Port Royal seadog, but documents revealed that in 1690, just two years before the earthquake, three Spanish galleons had wrecked near the island, and a great part of the treasure on them was salvaged by Port Royal divers and fishermen.

Things returned to normal, with the usual, daily interesting finds and occasional unavoidable accidents, some of them serious. The wear and tear on those of us who were diving began to show, and early in February, doctors forced us all to take a two-week break. None of us got much of a rest, however. We were behind in the preservation aspect of our work, and the respite from the long hours of diving was used to do preservation work and catalogue the thousands of artifacts we had found.

Early in March we discovered another shipwreck, broken in two sections, lying fairly close to the surface of the seafloor. From the artifacts recovered from this wreck and documents in the local archives, we learned that this was a French warship that had sunk during a hurricane at Port Royal in 1722. The main cargo was thousands of 150-pound iron mortar balls. After raising a few dozen balls, we decided to move the remaining ones to an area we had already excavated, so we could excavate deeper in the sediment. And there under the wreck we discovered numerous fallen walls and a large number of artifacts.

Moving the mortar balls, which took several weeks, wasn't the end of the hard work, however. Between the two sections of the shipwreck was a veritable forest of tree branches and trunks which also had to be removed by hand. This area proved to be a warehouse containing tons of dyewood, probably awaiting shipment to England.

April started off well when we discovered a cookhouse containing hundreds of kitchen implements. Two items of special interest were a large, intact barrelful of lime, with the shipper's mark still visible, and a large wooden mortar containing cornmeal. We also accidentally found our first artifact of gold. By this time we had over 50 large tanks of coral-encrusted iron artifacts, the majority of which were unidentifiable unless x-rayed or broken open. The former was impossible because of the lack of money, and the latter was out of the question, as we didn't have the proper means for preserving the iron. One day, to test my underwater metal detector, I grabbed at random a piece of coral-encrusted iron and set it in front of the detector head. To my surprise, it gave a nonferrous reading. Out of curiosity, I broke the encrustment off and discovered a gold ring among some badly oxided nails. I wondered how many other interesting artifacts lay hidden among the thousands of artifacts in those storage tanks.

Throughout the excavation we found most of the artifacts dating from the 1692 earthquake buried in the sediment at a depth of four to nine feet, although we usually excavated as deep as 12 feet. On several occasions, below the stratigraphical level of the artifacts dating from the time of the earthquake, we discovered a few Arawak Indian artifacts such as pottery shards and a stone metate. However, we now found an area in which there were seven intact Arawak pots, hundreds of pottery shards, fishing sinkers, axe heads, one projectile point, and a limestone mold of unknown use. The volume of these Indian artifacts certainly indicated that Port Royal had once been a settlement and not just a fishing outpost for the Arawak.

I suffered my most serious accident that month. Wayne was beached with sinus trouble, and Kelly and I were working alone. Lying on the bottom of the hole, we were excavating a large coral head that we had overlooked in our black environment, when it fell out of the wall of sediment in front of and above me and rolled right on top of my back. The coral head was about 12 feet in diameter and must have weighed at least a ton, but fortunately most of its weight rested on piles of loose house bricks I had piled on both sides of me. Kelly, finding that he was unable to move it after nearly an hour of labor, gave diving equipment to two of the boys on the barge, neither of whom had used the equipment before, and told them to help him roll the coral head off me. After considerable effort they were finally successful, but I had slipped a disc from trying to help them by arching my back, which resulted in my being out of action for several weeks.

May and June were the only two months of excavation that were free of accidents or loss of diving hours due to colds, cuts, or other mishaps. The excavation became more difficult, however. About 80 percent of the sediment consisted of fragments of house bricks and small pieces of dead coral—all too large to be sent topside through the airlift tube —and therefore they had to be excavated by hand and sent up in buckets. Still, from beneath the fallen brick walls, we recovered thousands of priceless artifacts such as plates, bowls, tankards, spoons, porringers and other items of pewter and silver; many intact cups, mugs, bowls, and plates in ceramic; candlesticks, pots, skimmers, ladles, buckles, buttons, and an apothecary's mortar and pestle in brass and copper; and many other artifacts of iron, lead, glass, wood, bone, and leather. Up until that time, we had recovered about six tons of bones, most of which were the turtle bones from the area of the turtle crawls, as well as fish, fowl, and domestic animal bones from the site of the fish and meat markets. During these two months we found several hundred human bones, most of which came from under fallen walls and were probably those of people who had been trapped under the walls in the disaster.

During the first two weeks of July we excavated the area of another tavern and cookhouse. Then, unfortunately (or fortunately, depending on how one looks at it), we discovered another big treasure. This time, similar to the first find, we found several thousand Spanish silver coins in a remarkable state of preservation, as well as a large amount of silverware, gold rings, and cuff links, and fragments of a large clock. The most exciting find of all was a beautiful 14-inch-high Chinese porcelain statue of a woman holding a child in her lap. Research has shown that it was the goddess of fertility and childbirth, dating from the Kuan-Yin dynasty and that it was made in Tu-Hun. All evidence pointed to this being the site of a pewterer's or silversmith's shop.

Once again our work was interrupted. Word of our find spread through the island like wildfire. The police were not only needed to keep people from interrupting our work but to protect us as well. The local criminal element became involved, threatening our lives if we didn't share our find with them. To add to the problem, the opposition party of the local government claimed that the find was much larger than had been reported in the press. They accused the party in power of stealing the treasure and using part of it in various illegal ways. By the time the issue came up for debate in Parliament, the party in power was forced to virtually call a halt to the entire project. Finally, however, the matter was resolved, and we got back to work again.

September was a routine month except for Hurricane Beulah passing nearby and causing a few days' loss of work, but October was the most frustrating month. By this time another diver had been added to my work force, making three besides myself. One morning, as we were preparing for the day's work, all three announced that they were going on strike unless they got a raise. (This may be the first known strike by divers!) Besides demanding an increase in salary, they thought they should get a large bonus because of our recent coin find. (It had been announced in the press that the coins were worth several hundred thousand dollars.) Two of them came back to work when they got a raise, but since they weren't given a bonus, Kelly, who was like my right arm, quit. His loss was the lowest point of the excavation.

Our most remarkable find the next month was a large, brass oil lamp of Mediterranean origin, which we think came from the site of the Jewish synagogue. Early in December my two divers announced that they could not keep up with the pace at which we were diving, and would thereafter dive only half a day each day. To overcome this obstacle, and since I still had the threat of the proposed dredging operation for a deepwater port, I was able to get more money from the government and hire two additional divers, with each team working half-day shifts.

Early in January 1968 I threatened to go on strike myself if something weren't done to hire one or more preservation experts to tackle the massive job of preserving the thousands of artifacts we had brought up. Even though stored in waterfilled tanks, many of them were showing signs of disintegrating. The Jamaican government went to the United Nations for assistance, and the UN eventually found two experts to cope with the problem.

Our excavation continued with good results until the end of May

1968 when, for various reasons, I finally called a halt to the project. It was announced officially that the proposed dredging operation would not take place after all, thus the site was no longer threatened. By devoting most of my efforts to excavating, I had neglected to write as many archaeological reports as I knew should have been written; and realizing that much of the valuable archaeological and historical data would be lost if it wasn't done while so much was still fresh in my mind and in the hundreds of pages of daily notes I had kept, I decided to devote full time to this aspect of the excavation.

After two and a half years of work we had barely made a dent in the site, having excavated less than 5 percent of it. Judging from the huge amount of archaeological material we had recovered from the site, most experts in the field agreed that to date this is the most important underwater archaeological project undertaken in the Western Hemisphere. Someday I hope to return and pick up where I left off.

6: Columbus' Shipwrecks

Although I have long been convinced that the Phoenicians and other peoples reached the New World long before Christopher Columbus did, anything dealing with Columbus and his voyages continues to fascinate me. Before sailing on the *Niña II* in 1962, I was involved in another "Columbus caper." During the summer of 1960 the late Dr. John Goggin, an archaeologist at the University of Florida, paid me a surprise visit in Seville where I was doing research in the Archivo de las Indias. I had worked with him on several land excavations in Yucatán and on the island of Margarita, a pearl-fishing center off the coast of Yucatán. Goggin's specialty was Spanish ceramics, and he was the leading expert on the subject.

One day Goggin heard a rumor that a large jar containing human bones had been dug up from the crypt of an old Carthusian monastery outside Seville. The monastery had been abandoned for over a century, and workmen from a nearby pottery works were extracting clay from beneath it when they stumbled on the jar. I knew from my own research that Columbus had been buried in this monastery. Although many claim that his bones were shipped to Santo Domingo for burial in the cathedral there, there is no evidence to prove this. When we arrived at the old monastery, we found a crowd of excited people. What we had not heard was that on the jar was a Latin inscription stating that these were the bones of Columbus.

While I was photographing the jar and bones, the mayor of Seville and some other government officials arrived. They had a policeman confiscate my film, and refused to give Goggin a bone sample for carbon dating and spectroanalysis. We were ordered to forget about the matter for the time being, until they investigated and decided what to do. One reason, the mayor informed us, was that there was a large monument to Columbus in the Cathedral of Seville, which supposedly also contained Columbus' bones. Goggin hung around for a few more weeks, but we couldn't learn anything more about this exciting find. Months later, I learned that the bones had been turned over to the head of the medical school of the University of Seville. Somehow the bones were accidently mixed in with others being studied by medical students and burned along with the rest at the end of the school year. As preposterous as this sounds, it seems to have really happened, and nothing has appeared about the discovery in the Spanish press since then.

Years earlier, I had met Dr. Harold Edgerton, a physicist and electronics wizard, at the Massachusetts Institute of Technology. He is internationally known as the inventor of the electronic strobe for photography, as well as many devices used in oceanography, including two types of subbottom, penetrating sonar units called "Boomer" and "Pinger." In a lecture I gave in Boston about my work at Port Royal, I covered the period in which I made a preliminary exploration with the metal probe and metal detector. After the lecture, Dr. Edgerton— or "Doc," as he is known to friends—said I had done it the hard way. I should have used either his "Boomer" or "Pinger." I explained that I knew of his equipment, but that lack of money had kept me from using it. Ever since then, I had been begging for funds with which to rent one of his units and make a complete survey of the underwater city. With the primitive method I used at the time, I must have missed many objects hidden beneath the seafloor. Nor had I been able to plot those I did find as accurately as I should have. Doc magnanimously offered to come at his own expense and make a complete sonar survey of the site, but it was nearly a year before I could get permission for him to do it from the Jamaican government.

Doc Edgerton arrived in January 1968 with two assistants—Dr. Tsuneyoshi Uyemura, of the University of Tokyo—and Dr. Louis Wolfson, a medical specialist from Boston, who had worked with Edgerton on several marine archaeological sites in the Mediterranean. The first two days were lost because of problems with customs, involving bringing his equipment into the island, this despite the fact that he was doing the survey for the government. Fortunately, one of the senior officials in the Jamaican Survey Department was an active member of the Jamaican Historical Society and was very interested in my work at Port Royal. He was able to provide a team of surveyors to assist us and even provided us with a small survey boat named *Chart*. Ivan, my watchman, and another man worked from a skiff, setting and picking up the buoys we needed for the survey. For a week we worked from sunrise to sunset every day, completing the survey sooner than expected.

Running between buoys offshore and markers set up by the surveyors ashore, we made more than 300 runs at right angles to the shore, each spaced 10 to 15 feet apart and each between 500 and 800 feet in length. The surveyors had the hardest job of all. In addition to plotting the position of each shore marker used on each run, they had to plot the position of each offshore buoy used, so we would know the precise course we had run and the area surveyed. Aboard ship, I ran CHART while Doc and his assistants operated the "Boomer" and recorded the exact time that each run took, which was essential to establishing the position of each object we located.

The runs gave us a graph showing the water depth, bottom contours, and geological information, to a depth of about 150 feet below the seafloor and indicated the presence of solid objects that were either protruding above or hidden beneath the seafloor. They didn't identify the type of object, though. That would come later. By the time we completed the survey, we had located more than 4,000 solid objects of considerable size. The easier part of the survey was over, with the most difficult yet to come. All of the data obtained on the sonar graphs now had to be transferred and plotted on four large charts of the site, which was a ticklish undertaking, because we had made the runs at varying speeds to counteract winds and currents; in addition, the length of each run varied considerably.

On the afternoon that we finished the sonar survey, Doc said he still had several days left and asked if I wanted any other sonar surveys made on Jamaica. Immediately Saint Ann's Bay, on the north coast of the island, came to mind. After telling Doc what I hoped to find there, he was eager to help.

In April 1502 Columbus sailed from Spain with four small caravels on his fourth and last voyage of discovery. It turned out to be his most dangerous and least profitable voyage. He spent almost a year in the Caribbean, cruising along the Central American coast but discovering little of importance. Meanwhile, the teredo worms caused such damage to the hulls of his ships that two had to be scuttled on the coast of Panama. With his two remaining ships—*Capitana* and *Santiago*—in deplorable condition, he finally had to admit failure and start for home, heading first for Santo Domingo where he hoped to repair the caravels before making the long ocean crossing. By the time he was between Cuba and Jamaica, he was suffering not only from an acute shortage of water and food, but both vessels were leaking so badly and were so near sinking that his son Ferdinand, who chronicled the voyage, wrote: "Day and night we never ceased working three pumps on each ship, and if any broke down, we had to supply its place by bailing with kettles while it was being patched up."

The vessels were so full of water that they made slow progress, and when the wind swung around to the east and blew against them, it was too much. On June 25, 1503 they were forced into Saint Ann's Bay which Columbus had visited on his second voyage and had named "Santa Gloria." There both vessels ran aground, "about a bow shot distance from shore." There was fresh water nearby and an Indian village from which Columbus hoped to obtain food with which to feed his 116 men. With only the fore and stern castles protruding above the water, there were insufficient accommodations aboard for everyone, so many of the men had to live ashore.

Soon after his arrival, Columbus bought a dugout from the Indians and sent it to Santo Domingo to notify the authorities there of his plight. But because the governor of Santo Domingo was his enemy, Columbus and his men spent a year and four days on the island before being rescued. Things went well at first. The Indians were glad to trade food for Hawks' bells, glass beads, and other items, but after they had accumulated a substantial quantity of these items, they began bringing less and less food to the marooned Spaniards, and conditions deteriorated. When months passed and there was still no aid, several of the expedition's leaders enlisted a majority of the men in mounting a mutiny. They plotted to assassinate Columbus, blaming him for all of their problems. But Columbus, though bedridden with arthritis, was able to quell the mutiny.

When the rescue ship finally arrived on June 29, 1504 and picked up the Spaniards, leaving behind the two now worthless caravels, Columbus was a discouraged, heartbroken man and died not long after his arrival in Spain.

From the book written by Ferdinand, as well as other contemporary accounts, the location of the two wrecks is well known, unlike that of other Spanish ships lost in the West Indies. In 1940 an expedition sponsored by Harvard University and led by Admiral Samuel Eliot Morison, one of the world's leading authorities on Columbus, used this information in attempting to establish the location of the wrecks. Morison's book, *Admiral of the Ocean Seas,* which won a Pulitzer Prize, contains a chart of Saint Ann's Bay, marked where he thought the wrecks lay. He was almost right about the location, for we found both wrecks within a hundred feet of where Morison estimated they were.

One person who helped Morison when he visited Saint Ann's Bay was a Jamaican plantation owner, Charles Cotter, who for the past 40 years has been conducting land excavations at the site of New Seville, the Spaniards' first settlement on the island. New Seville was situated on the shore opposite where Columbus' ships were abandoned. For years Cotter has dreamed of someone locating the site of the wrecks, but until I arrived, he had been unable to get anyone interested in diving to the site, including the Smithsonian Institution. He was overjoyed when we met and I told him that I was interested in searching for the wrecks.

I was especially interested in these two wrecks because, unless someone finds a Viking or Phoenician shipwreck someday, these two wrecks are the oldest that will ever be found in this hemisphere. Although Columbus lost other ships during his four voyages, all were lost under conditions which make it highly unlikely that any trace of them will ever be found. A good example was *Santa Maria* which was wrecked on Columbus' first voyage off Cap-Haïtien, Haiti. The wreck was stripped of its timbers and other items and was used to build a fort ashore for the men from the wreck who were left behind when Columbus sailed for home. On the other hand, because the two wrecks in Saint

Ann's Bay were so heavy due to the vast amount of water in them, most of the lower sections of their hulls were pushed deep into the silt and mud, thus preserving them from the ravages of the teredo worm. If I was right about this, the wrecks could provide invaluable information about the construction of ships of that period, as well as other data.

Although my primary work was at Port Royal, I considered these wrecks of even greater archaeological and historical importance and repeatedly asked permission to mount a small expedition to find them. The government showed no interest, especially when I told them there was no likelihood of finding treasure or valuable artifacts. I finally convinced Edward Seaga, my boss, to let me spend one day searching and went to the bay one Sunday in March 1966 with my wife and Stan and Louise Judge. About a month earlier, I had a friend take some aerial photographs of the bay. I knew that even if Morison and Cotter were wrong in their location of the wrecks, there was only one small area in the entire bay that fit Ferdinand's description and where the water was shallow enough for the ships to have run aground. A series of charts of the bay, some dating as far back as the middle of the seventeenth century, showed that the coastline and shape of the bay, except where the massive landslide had occurred during the 1692 earthquake and which I knew was at the opposite end of the bay from where the wrecks lay, hadn't changed over the centuries.

As we were preparing to dive that Sunday, several residents stood by, claiming that this part of the bay was a mating ground for large sharks and that it would be suicide to dive there. Just the night before, a fisherman had caught a 14-foot tiger shark and was there on the beach, skinning it when we arrived.

With 10-foot metal probes we swam along in a line underwater, forcing the rods into the bottom sediment, trying to locate solid objects that might indicate a wreck. Using this method, by which we located several large, dead coral heads, we spent five hours before finally striking pay dirt. Nancy motioned to me that she needed help. Her probe, which was about eight feet down in the sediment, was stuck in something solid. It took three of us to pull it out and six hours of excavating by hand and with buckets to reach the solid object, which turned out to be a wooden beam. When we relayed this information to Cotter, who was pacing up and down the beach in anticipation, he said it was probably a piling from an old wharf that had sunk in a hurricane in the area over 20 years before. I thought we should forget about it and continue searching, but Nancy said I might be making a mistake, that it could be part of a wreck. As usual, she was right. Feeling around in the pitch-black hole in the sediment, I discovered treenails (wooden pegs) in the beam, the method of fastening ships together in the old days, and not one that would have been used on a modern wharf or ship. The hole was large enough for only one person to squeeze into, and because of the danger of a cave-in, we began enlarging it. Nancy, who was the smallest, got the honor of probing the bottom of the hole. When she came up with several pieces of obsidian, a type of volcanic glass found in Mexico and Central America, I was sure we were on the verge of the most important marine archaeological discovery ever made in the Western Hemisphere.

Even though dark was fast approaching, I decided to see what I myself could find in the hole. Besides some more obsidian, I recovered several pieces of Spanish pottery which dated from the time of Columbus' shipwreck. Then, as I was about to call it a day, the dive came to an abrupt dramatic end. Stan Judge, who was above me, grabbing the objects I handed up from the hole, was bitten on the neck by a two-foot-long sea snake, reportedly often deadly. In 20 years of diving, I had never seen one, nor did I know of any other diver who had seen one in the Caribbean. As luck would have it, we had just encountered the first one during what could be the most important dive of my life. Stan was in considerable pain, so we rushed him to a hospital where he was given an injection of serum. By the next day, he had recovered and was laughing about the experience.

During the next month, while awaiting confirmation from various experts concerning the identity and date of the shards and the origin of the obsidian, I petitioned Seaga for permission and money to do more work in Saint Ann's Bay. When the confirmation came, I took it and confronted Seaga, but all he would promise was that sometime in the near future—"soon come" again—he would send me back up there. I was convinced that I had found one of Columbus' wrecks, or at least a section of it, and it was damned frustrating not to be able to do anything about it.

Doc Edgerton was excited—as I had been two years earlier when we first dived in Saint Ann's Bay—at the prospect of discovering the *Capitana* and *Santiago,* so the morning after finishing our work at Port

Royal, we asked to have a meeting with Seaga. He was quite satisfied with our sonar survey of the sunken city but not very happy when we asked for permission to search for Columbus' wrecks. Only when] promised that we would spend no more than a few days searching and that we wouldn't undertake any excavation work, did he reluctantly grant us permission.

I lined up a boat by telephone, and we drove to the coast the same day. There we found Cotter who thought I had given up my search for the wrecks. The next morning, we were off to a poor start, though. It was pouring rain, and the boat I had engaged was nowhere in sight. After several hours, during which I nervously chain-smoked, the rain stopped, the sun came out, and the boat finally appeared.

Doc and his Japanese assistant had the "Boomer" operating in a few minutes, and within an hour we had two positive sonar contacts. From the sonar graphs, we knew they were shipwrecks. More important, they were in the right area (where the documents said they should be and where we had found the wooden beam, obsidian, and shards) and about the size we knew the wrecks should be. To be on the safe side, after marking both sites with buoys, we made a complete sonar survey of the other areas in the bay where the wrecks could possibly lie. When there were no contacts, I was certain we had located Columbus' wrecks.

We returned to Kingston the next day as happy as though we had found a million dollars in gold. Doc and his two assistants caught a plane for the United States, and I notified Seaga of our discoveries. Although he had shown no interest in the wrecks so far, he now became very excited and wanted to hold a press conference and announce the find. I talked him out of it, convincing him that more work must be done before we were sure of the discovery. He instructed me to mount a major expedition to excavate the site. When I told Mrs. Hart, the secretary of the National Trust Commission, about our discovery and Seaga's instructions, she said it was just like him to do that without making provision for financing the project. She promised to find the money somewhere.

Before returning to the site of the shipwrecks, there was some planning to be done; many factors had to be taken into consideration. First, since the wrecks were of such great historical importance, the best scientific methods of excavation would have to be used, and at the moment I had neither the best equipment and personnel nor the money to obtain them. Furthermore, every sliver of wood from the wrecks would be of immense importance. Without an adequate preservation laboratory, I could go down in history as the man who destroyed the Columbus shipwrecks, because, once the wood was exposed to the air, if it wasn't properly treated, it would disintegrate and be lost forever. I finally convinced Seaga that it would take a lot of money to excavate the wrecks properly and build a good preservation lab, that we would have to seek funds from outside sources such as UNESCO or from a foundation. I pointed out that before any foundation would give us the money, we would have to establish beyond any doubt that these *were* the Columbus wrecks, and to do this, I would have to recover a substantial amount of material from the sites, for identification and scientific dating.

For a project of such importance, I decided to enlist the help of experts in my field; they agreed that we should do as little as possible to disturb the sites. Rather than excavate a large hole to recover the sample material for testing—which would not only disturb the archaeological context of the wrecks but might expose the wooden timbers to the teredo worm, from which they had been protected in their muddy grave—another method should be used. Dr. George Bass, of the University of Pennsylvania, suggested that we use a coring device and found one which had been invented by Dr. John Saunders, of Columbia University. Saunders offered to loan it to us and to send one of his assistants down to help us use it.

I expected daily to leave for Saint Ann's Bay but did not get there at all in February. I was told that no money could be found with which to finance the project. After several weeks, I offered to pay all the expenses myself, but Seaga refused. Dr. Saunders' assistant, Bob Judd, had his bags packed and was ready to come at a moment's notice, and I had to phone him every few days to tell him to wait a bit longer. News of the find leaked to the press, and worldwide attention focused on the Columbus ships; but even this did not produce the funds for the job.

We were scheduled to leave for Saint Ann's Bay on the first of March, but a few days before that, I was told that we would need a special permit from the Beach Control Commission. Knowing all too well the snail-like pace at which the Jamaican bureaucracy functioned, I spent a whole day anyway, sitting in the office of the Permanent Secretary of the Beach Control, until he was so tired of seeing me that he finally issued the permit. He told me to come back the next day to pick it up. But when I did—as I should have expected—it hadn't been signed yet. In fact, it took three weeks just to get the Chairman of the Beach Control to sign it. Remember, I was actually working for the government; had I been requesting the permit as a private citizen, I might have had to wait months or even years merely for a signature.

I had invited Dr. Bass to come to Jamaica in early February and work with me on the site, but he had to decline the invitation. He never flies, and he thought it would take too long to get there by ship. As it turned out, he could have sailed around the world and still had plenty of time to arrive before we finally got permission to start. He said he would send one of his assistants, Larry Joline, who, like Robert Judd, had to wait for word to come. Then, after nearly two months of waiting, when I phoned Joline and told him that we would be starting the next day, he had flu!

On March 21 our permit from the Beach Control Commission was signed, and I made plans to leave immediately for Saint Ann's Bay. I had asked for a minimum of $500 to finance the project, which would last one to two weeks, but instead was given only $168. This called for a drastic change in plans. I couldn't put up five or six people in a hotel, feed them, pay for the rental of a boat, and meet the other expenses with a paltry $168. Was that all the memory of Columbus—who had discovered the island—was worth to the Jamaican government?

Coral and Alphonso, my diving assistants, were on vacation. When I told Coral that we would be leaving the next day and asked him to find something to sleep in on the beach, at first, he refused to go, saying: "In all my years of poverty, I've slept between white sheets and with a girl. I refuse to sleep on a beach and leave my girl behind in Kingston." It took a lot of convincing to get him to go, especially when I wouldn't let him bring his girl along. When he showed up, wearing a patch over his eye like a pirate, because of a bee sting, Alphonso gave me an even stranger reason for not wanting to go. "I don't like Jamaicans. I don't want to live around them, because they are bad people." In all his 17 years, like so many other Port Royalists, the only place on the island he had even been to was Kingston.

We planned to set up camp on the beach near the wreck site. From the local chapter of the Boy Scouts, I borrowed three tents and some other camping equipment. When Alphonso heard that Coral was refusing to sleep in a sleeping bag, he too refused. So from a junk pile on the grounds of the police training school I got six rusty beds and filthy matresses which Ivan covered with canvas before Coral and Alphonso saw the condition they were in.

We were scheduled to leave at seven the following morning, but the Public Works truck that was to carry us and our equipment—which included an aluminum skiff since I couldn't afford to rent a boat—caused an unexpected delay. While we were loading the truck, the driver and his two assistants, all of whom appeared to be drunk, disappeared, and it took me two hours to get them out of the Buccaneers' Roost, and only then by convincing the owner not to sell them any more rum. The driver careened over those narrow, dangerous mountain roads like a lunatic, managing to force a dozen or so vehicles off the road before we somehow reached Saint Ann's Bay. My draftsman, Walter, jumped off about halfway there and hitchhiked the rest of the way.

We spent the rest of the day setting up camp and putting markers on the beach. Alphonso had been right about Jamaicans being bad people—or at least one of them. Hundreds of curious persons from the nearby town came up the beach to see what we were doing, and by the end of the day two of my cameras and several tools had disappeared. Charles Cotter had found someone to stay with us and serve as watchman, and the man took the job seriously. Every time someone approached the camp, he would fire a shotgun over their heads! Not surprisingly, nothing else was stolen.

I was delighted when Bob Judd arrived and amazed when I found out what a voracious appetite he had. He was six-feet-eight, weighed 260 and during his first meal consumed seven huge sandwiches and four soft drinks. We named him the "Jolly Green Giant." When we went into town everyone gazed at him as if he were the eighth wonder of the world.

We had planned to start making the cores first, but Judd's luggage, which included the coring device, had been lost and didn't turn up until late that night. So, instead, we took turns using the water jet to blow away a few feet of overburden around the area of the two wrecks. The next morning, all the overburden was back where it had been before, because of strong winds (and therefore, currents) during the night. My plan was to get core samples from the sites of both wrecks, but we were able to work on only one site before the money ran out and we headed for home. We started off using ropes—which were easily visible in those waters where the average underwater visibility varied from 10 to 30 feet, depending on how much we had stirred up the muddy bottom—and laid out a grid pattern on the bottom. We also circled the area with buoys that rose to the surface. With this system, we would know exactly where we had gotten each core.

The coring device was simple and ingenious. It consisted of a steel tube four inches in diameter, made up of four detachable sections, with an overall length of 16 feet. After this had been forced into the seafloor by hand, another small section of thicker tubing was placed on top, which had a steel rod projecting upward for three feet. The tube was pounded into the sediment with a 50-pound, two-handled hammer which rode up and down on the steel rod. It sounded easier than it was. Because divers are almost weightless underwater, trying to hover in the water while manipulating that hammer was quite a feat. Once most of the tube had been driven into the sediment, it was a bit easier. The diver could stand on the bottom and wrap his legs around the tube; this way, he had more leverage for working with the hammer. After driving all but about a foot of the tube into the bottom, the heavier section of tubing and the hammer were removed and a rubber plug was screwed into the top of the tube to maintain suction (otherwise everything would drop out of the tube as it was being pulled up). Then came the hardest part. It usually took an hour to pound the corer into the sediment, but sometimes twice that long to pull it out. For the first few days, Judd and I worked on the bottom, twisting and pulling on the tube, while Coral, Alphonso, and Walter worked from the skiff, pulling on lines. The work became easier when Stan Judge brought one of my portable lifting bags from Port Royal. By attaching it to the top of the tube and filling it with air, we could exert additional pulling force, which helped considerably.

Once the tube was extracted, another plug would be placed on its bottom, and we would swim it ashore atop an inner tube. On the beach both plugs would then be pulled out and the contents of the tube carefully shaken out onto a piece of canvas. Then we would gingerly separate the sediment, searching for objects from the wreck. Those we found were placed in water inside plastic containers, with tags denoting

The author's team inspecting the mud that was brought up in the coring tube while they were working on the Columbus shipwrecks in Saint Ann's Bay, Jamaica

the location and stratigraphical depth we found them at. The first day, we took seven cores. Five cores produced a number of pieces of wood, several of which were two to three inches thick. They had been cut from larger pieces of wood by the sharp edge of the tube bottom. The two other cores we had started had struck solid objects at a depth of four feet and couldn't penetrate any farther. Using the water jet, we found ballast rock to be the solid objects that had stopped the corer.

That night we dined on fried fish speared during the day, as well as beans and rice—delicious and nourishing—and repeated every day. After sunset the mosquitos and sandfleas were so thick that we had to sleep with our rubber diving suits on, to keep from being devoured. During the day, the local people had worked on Alphonso and Coral, scaring them with tales of man-eating sharks in the bay. Twice during the night, Alphonso woke us up, screaming from shark nightmares. Early the next morning, unfortunately, we sighted a large tiger shark hovering nearby. Both Alphonso and Coral shot out of the water, refusing to dive again. From then on, Judd and I had to dive alone, except for the few times when Nancy and Stan Judge were there to lend a hand.

The next day we got eight good cores. In addition to more pieces of wood (which, I later learned, were oak and pine), we found fragments of animal bones (pig and chicken), pieces of charcoal, a striking flint (either for a weapon or to start a fire with), and a small coral-encrusted nail. During the day, several more inquisitive sharks appeared, and one suddenly began butting me with its snout while I was trying to measure the distance between the last core hole and the one we were then making. I smashed him on the head with a crowbar, and he took off.

Our problems weren't confined to the water, however. Before we had arrived, a rumor had started that we were after a large quantity of gold on the wrecks. The mayor of the town and four police officers appeared that afternoon and tried to arrest us—until I produced the permit from the Beach Control Commission and the letters from Seaga. When they realized their mistake and saw that they were losing face with the townspeople who had come with them, they decided instead to arrest Coral and Alphonso, who were brazenly smoking ganja cigarettes right in front of the mayor and policemen. I had to talk fast to keep them out of jail. It was really strange that both Coral and Alphonso considered the Jamaicans who lived on the northern coast to be foreigners, and would have nothing to do with them. On several evenings when they went into town for a few beers, they returned with cuts and bruises from fights with the locals.

On the third day we struck solid objects at a depth of about nine feet, and three times forced our way through them. We came up with samples of ballast rock that were different from those we had found near the surface. In addition to more wood, bone, and charcoal, we found several coral-encrusted tacks, a few ceramic shards, a fragment of green glass, and a black bean of the kind called *frijole* in Spain. Although we lost time whenever we had to cut our way through ballast rock (because it entailed resharpening the cutting edge at the bottom of the tube), we managed to get nine good cores this day.

During the next four days we got 34 additional cores, each one of which yielded wood and other material. We now had enough samples with which to properly identify and date the wreck. I didn't want to disturb the wreck anymore, so we stopped using the coring device. Nearly all of the material we had recovered came from a depth of eight to ten feet beneath the seafloor; only a few pieces of wood were from farther down, and these may have been pushed deeper into the sediment by the coring tube before it cut through them. Judd came up with a better system for defining the limits of the wreck, than my system of using a metal rod as a probe. We attached one of the hoses from an Aquanaut unit to a 20-foot piece of one-inch galvanized water pipe, and it worked beautifully. The air rushing down the pipe enabled the pipe to go down rapidly and without much force, and it was easy to extract. When solid objects were encountered, we turned off the air. Tapping the object, both by feel and from the sound, we could tell whether it was wood or ballast rock.

Before heading back to Kingston, we spent another day diving at the site. All the evidence indicated that the wreck lay at a stratigraphical depth of eight to ten feet below the seafloor, but I was curious about the ballast rock we had found at a depth of only four feet in a small part of the site. My curiosity was satisfied by blowing away a large area of mud covering the rock. I was able to date the artifacts we found among them, including clay pipe stems and bottle fragments, to the mid-seventeenth century. The absence of wood and ship's fittings indicated that a ship had probably been anchored here and, before taking on a heavy cargo of sugar, rum, or molasses, had jettisoned some of the ship's ballast overboard, a common practice at the time.

An amusing incident occurred during our last evening there. Judd announced that he refused to eat fish, rice, and beans again, and offered to take everyone out for a good meal. Walter and the two divers had dates with some local girls, so Judd and I went alone. Barefooted and attired in dirty shorts and jerseys, we chose one of the fanciest restaurants on the island, one in nearby Ocho Rios. When the headwaiter refused to seat us because we didn't have a jacket and tie on, we asked to see the manager who apologized after we explained our situation and produced two ties and dinner jackets. We brought all talk to a stop as we walked into the packed dining room. The dinner jackets hung lower than the shorts; it looked as though we had forgotten to put our pants on. Several tourists laughed so hard that we fled for the exit, with stomachs growling, especially when we saw the fantastic food being served. We then went to the Playboy Club where things were a bit more informal and where they were serving a smorgasbord which we attacked voraciously. Judd went through 11 heaping plates of food before even tackling the dessert.

We left for Kingston the next morning. At one point Judd leaped from the cab of the truck after yelling to the driver to stop. His shorts were on fire. He had pushed the seat down so that it touched the batteries underneath, and the seat had caught fire. After applying first aid, we continued on our way.

The waiting game that now began took longer than expected. The material we had recovered had to be sent to experts in England, Spain, and the United States, a process that took almost three months. Most of the ballast rock had come from Central America, though a little of it was from Spain. This didn't surprise me. I knew Columbus had careened his vessels several times during his voyage along the coast of Central America. According to many documents written by persons of other nationalities who had sailed aboard Spanish ships, the Spaniards were very messy and cared little about sanitation. Rather than throw trash (and sometimes even human waste) overboard, they frequently tossed it into the hold as ballast. Consequently, when Spanish ships were careened, the old ballast was replaced with new.

According to experts at the Corning Glass Museum, the fragment of colored glass had been made in Venice and was probably from an hourglass; it definitely dated from the time of Columbus. I knew that the pottery we had found was Spanish, which was confirmed by experts, but it was of a type commonly in use for several centuries and therefore wasn't easy to date. A new method called thermoluminescence, for dating ceramic and other material fired in a kiln, had recently been developed, but it wasn't as useful as it was purported to be. I sent two shards to the Museum of Applied Science Center for Archaeology at the University of Pennsylvania, which dated the pieces at circa 1637, plus or minus 150 years. Shards sent to Oxford University in England were dated at 1475, plus or minus 100 years. Both the striking flint and the black bean were thought to have come from Spain.

The fragments of wood were identified as having come from Spain, but the date I received for the first piece of wood that had been dated by the carbon-14 process presented a problem. It was said to be 1,200 years old, give or take a hundred years. I figured that it might have been a piece of firewood which they found on land, which would furnish a reason for its age. So I sent several more for carbon-14 dating and received the same date. Was there a Viking ship lying beneath the Columbus wreck? I knew carbon-14 dating produced more accurate results for organic material dating in the thousands rather than hundreds of years, but even so, the date shouldn't be off that much. The mystery was solved when I consulted some dendrologists (tree experts). It isn't unusual for an oak tree to reach the age of a thousand years or more, so it was conceivable that an oak tree 700 years old had been cut down and used in building one of the ships lost in Saint Ann's Bay.

As a final test of the authenticity of our discovery, I submitted the findings to Samuel Eliot Morison and three other experts on Columbus in Spain and Colombia. All of them were convinced that we had found one of Columbus' wrecks.

7: The Viking Voyages

While appearing on a Spanish television program in 1963, shortly after my successful crossing in the replica of Columbus' ship, *Niña II,* I made the mistake of saying that "Columbus was not the first to discover America." The next morning headlines in Madrid's largest newspaper thundered: ROBERT MARX IS A DISGRACE TO HISTORY. The writer of the front-page article went so far as to suggest that the government withdraw the knighthood they had granted me after the voyage of the *Niña II.* I was pretty much a persona non grata in Spain until the following year when my voyage in a Viking ship turned out badly. This cheered the Spaniards, who interpreted my failure as proof that Columbus had indeed discovered America and that the Vikings and others couldn't have done so. The truth was, it was a miracle that the Viking ship made it as far as it did.

The history of early navigation in the Atlantic is a matter of heated controversy among scholars, chiefly because of the lack of sufficient original documentation; but history must often be interpreted from bits of oral tradition and archaeological evidence and not from written sources alone. In 1963 a noted Norwegian archaeologist, Dr. Helge Ingstad, uncovered archaeological proof the Norsemen had founded colonies on the North American continent more than 500 years before Columbus arrived. Soon afterward, the famous Vinland chart substantiated this. Even the most skeptical scholars had to agree that the Vikings had beat Columbus across the Atlantic. In fact, the Norsemen were only one of many peoples who reached America in early times.

Archaeological evidence has been found throughout the Western Hemisphere, proving the presence of Old World visitors even before the heyday of the Norsemen. The Spanish conquistadores were greatly aided in their conquest by the belief prevalent among the Indians that they were the "bearded White Gods" who had visited their lands and had promised to return. Were these white gods Irish missionaries who left Christian symbols in pre-Columbian buildings after the fall of Rome? Were they Carthaginians whose architectural characteristics are incorporated in many pre-Columbian buildings? Or were they perhaps Phoenicians whose distinctive robes, high-bridged noses, and long beards are similar to those portrayed in many frescos and on ceramic and stone artifacts?

Scholars have long ignored this evidence, primarily because they believed such voyages were impossible, given the small ships and primitive means of navigation used then. We know that the Phoenicians, whose genius in trade and seafaring in the ancient world was unmatched, sailed well beyond the Pillars of Hercules, or Straits of Gibraltar, going to the British Isles, the far-off Azores, and even circumnavigating the African continent. It is probable that the first sailors to reach the New World were accidently blown across the Atlantic when they were caught in the prevailing northeast trade winds and westerly flowing current while sailing off the west coast of Africa or venturing out to such outlying islands as the Canaries, Madiera, or Azores. From all the archaeological evidence to date, however, it also seems that there was a two-way traffic between the Old World and the New.

While working as a technical consultant on a Hollywood movie about the Vikings in August 1963, I conceived the idea of demonstrating that such voyages could have been made by the Phoenicians as long ago as 3,000 years. Because iconographical representations on coins, lead seals, and pottery and stone carvings were not detailed enough to provide sufficient information to build a replica of a Phoenician ship, I had to settle for one of the tenth-century-replica Viking ships being used in the movie, which the producers of the movie donated to me for the publicity value they would derive. A Viking ship was the most authentic representative of a pre-Columbian vessel. Actual tenth-century A.D. ships were discovered on land during the nineteenth century

The tenth-century replica, *Long Ship,* under sail in 1964

Replica of the tenth-century Viking ship which the author sailed in 1969

and have been preserved in a museum in Oslo, Norway. The most complete one, known as the "Gokstad Ship," was the model for constructing the three used in the movie. Rather than duplicate an ocean crossing by the northern route, as had been done by the Norsemen who reached America by stages, island-hopping and rarely out of sight of land for more than a few days at a time, I chose the longer southern route which I believed was used by the Phoenicians and mariners of other Mediterranean cultures. My intention was not just to prove that such a ship could make the ocean crossing, but that it could be done with no charts or navigational aids (particularly since we aren't sure that ancient seaman used them). I would use the moon, sun, and stars to steer by.

All three vessels had been constructed in Denmark under the supervision of a leading maritime historian. Although for a movie, they were built authentically and accurately, except for the most crucial part—the keel. I didn't discover this defect until it was too late and the ship was sinking beneath me. After the filming was completed, I ran sea trials on all three ships and selected the best one, which I named "The Long Ship," after the title of the movie. My plan was to begin the official voyage in Lisbon (which had been founded by the Phoenicians), then sail down to the Canaries, cut across to the Caribbean, and eventually land at Yucatán. The voyage from Yugoslavia to Lisbon would be a shakedown cruise.

Returning to Yugoslavia five months later, to prepare for the voyage, I found the ship under six feet of water, with only her masts and two elaborately carved figureheads at the bow and stern sticking above water. Somewhere along the line, there had been a lack of communication. The Yugoslav representatives of the Hollywood movie company had ordered the three ships stripped and destroyed. It was midwinter and cold as hell, with four feet of snow on the ground, but I had no intention of abandoning the voyage. Luckily I had brought along a good rubber wet suit and some diving equipment.

My first problem was raising her. There were no cabins or holds to fill with air or in which to put floatation gear. I decided to sling cables under the hull and attach buoyancy tanks to the gunwales, using the powerful winches on several large fishing boats to provide the main lifting power. But after three frustrating days, I had to give up this plan, because I couldn't find the necessary materials, and the boats put to sea whenever the weather was good for fishing.

The next plan worked. With the help of men from the local shipyard, I collected all the car jacks available on Punat Island and at each low tide lifted her a few inches at a time off the bottom. Finally, after four days, we got her gunwales above the water and could start pumping her out, but first we had to seal the 32 oar holes and the gapping holes that had been knocked in the sides to sink her. We made other repairs and fitted her with a new 45-foot mast. Covered with ice and snow, she was ghostlike, but at least she was afloat again. Her lines were graceful— 72 feet long, with an 18-foot beam and a draft of only three feet.

The five-man crew I had selected from more than a thousand applications was a mixed group: an Englishman, Bill Holmes, who was a chemist by profession and an enthusiastic amateur sailor; two Viking descendants from Norway, Knut Adeler and Per Christiansen; and two Yugoslavs, Jevtic Slobodan, an artist and sculptor whom we called "Jumbo" because of his size, and Plavsic Slavoljub, called "Bell," for short, who had worked as a stunt man in the movie for which the ship was used. The five men arrived one day during a whirling blizzard and immediately set to work sweeping the snowy shroud from the ship's deck and examining every inch of her structure. Neither Jumbo nor Bell had had any sailing experience. They had been told by workmen at the shipyard that the vessel was actually a toy made for the movie, that it wasn't fit to sail across a lake, much less the Atlantic. The 220-pound Jumbo started jumping all over the gunwales to test their strength, while the others inspected other parts of the vessel skeptically.

That night, while we sat around consuming nearly a gallon of *slivo-witz* (a local brandy made from prunes), to drive the chill from our bones, I explained the background relevant to making the voyage. The two Norwegians were perturbed to hear that it wasn't, strictly speaking, a *Viking* voyage, but one that could have been made by other seamen 2,000 years before the Norsemen reached America. I warned them that it would not be a pleasure cruise, especially at this time of year, and that to save time in reaching Lisbon, we would use an auxiliary motor when we met with contrary winds.

All of them said they were game, however. The next day, the snow melted, and we made final preparations—checking out the new motor, filling the fuel tanks, and loading the ship with enough supplies to reach

Lisbon, including 50 gallons of *slivowitz* donated by the good islanders. We were ready to cast off when our first stroke of bad luck occurred. The port authorities and customs officials abruptly announced that we would have to pay a 20-percent export duty on the ship, which had originally cost $30,000 to build. I was panic-stricken, but the movie company eventually came to our rescue and paid duty.

For those who are superstitious—and most sailors are—our bad luck was preordained. In the film, "the Long Ship" was a funeral ship stolen by a band of Vikings, which ended its career shipwrecked on the North African coast. Both Per and Knut were adamant about not using the black funeral sail; they were sure that unless we changed to a sail of a different color, we would meet a similar fate. My main worry wasn't dictated by superstition, however, but rather by the fragile condition of the patched-up ship and the realization that we would be sailing through the Adriatic and Mediterranean during the worst months of the year. "Well, hell," I said to Bill, "it will be a good test for the men and ship. If we reach Lisbon, then crossing the Big Lake should be a breeze." I had no way of knowing then that out of 30 days of sailing, 26 would be spent battling gale-force winds and mountainous seas.

That first evening, as we were running south under sail along the Yugoslav coast at more than eight knots, a sudden squall with winds over 60 knots hit us. The threat we had feared most—heavy seas breaking over the low gunwales and swamping us—turned out to be a minor one; the Vikings had designed a good ship, and we rode the big-tail seas like a gull bobbing on the wavelets of a bay, hitting the astonishing speed of 15 knots. But although the design was good, the construction wasn't. Whenever we were hit by head or cross seas, the entire hull shook violently and the sides heaved in and out like a bellows. Instead of the heavy brass spikes and walrus-hide thongs the Vikings had used, this replica was fastened together with small iron nails. After several hours of running before the gale, with the crew frantically trying to keep up with the small geysers spouting from the places in the hull where nails had popped out, we dined on a sardine, onion, and ketchup salad prepared by Jumbo, the ship's "cook."

When fair weather returned at daybreak, I decided to cross the Adriatic to the Italian coast. Then, late that afternoon, we were hit by another gale which forced us into the Italian port of Vieste. This was pretty much the pattern throughout the voyage: sail in the morning in reasonable weather, then run into bad weather that would force us into port for the night. Working our way down the rock-strewn, windy coast of Italy was more dangerous than crossing open water. One day when fog had reduced visibility to less than a hundred yards, Bill, who was interested in the navigational aspects of the voyage, said: "Chief, do you really know where we are?"

"Bill," I answered, "I have built-in radar. There's nothing to worry about."

Just then, Per, who had overheard, shouted: "Your radar isn't working so well. I can see the bottom."

And at the same moment, we heard babbling voices which I thought were coming from a passing fishing boat. But only seconds later, we discovered that they were from people on shore. We had almost run aground!

After three miserable weeks, we somehow reached the western tip of Sicily and put in at the ancient Phoenician port of Mazara del Vallo where we stayed for a week, due to the terrible weather. I kept busy diving to several Greek and Roman shipwrecks which the local fishermen showed me. When we left port, it was with the best weather we had yet experienced. The sea was flat calm, and the sky so clear that we could steer by the stars. But the Viking curse hadn't left us. I was serenely taking a fix on the shimmering North Star when we were suddenly swallowed by a dark cloud driven by 70-knot winds. Tunis was 130 miles to the south, while Mazara del Vallo was only a few miles behind us, but we decided to go ahead. For the next 30 hours all we could do was pray and force our aching muscles to keep bailing. The diminishing force of the gale announced our entry into the Gulf of Tunis, and, exhausted but thankful, we crept into Tunis and immediately fell asleep.

We spent about a week there, making additional repairs. At the request of the local director of antiquities, I spent most of the week diving off the ruins of ancient Carthage, and located several old wrecks and sunken harbor works. Meanwhile, Per went to a fortune-teller who predicted that we would be in a disaster at sea within a week. We laughed it off, but the crystal ball was right.

At sunup on Good Friday, we sailed for Algiers where we planned to spend Easter Sunday. The weather was good (rarely did we start under poor conditions), but there were unusually high swells running from the northwest, which I assumed were the aftermath of a recent storm, since the local meteorological department had predicted good weather. Several hours after passing the port of Bizerte, however, we were struck by a ferocious gale, this one more savage than any so far. Once again, our poor, valiant ship was lifted high on the crest of one wave, dashed into the trough, and pounded by the next wave. We began hearing strange noises which we later discovered were caused by the keel coming apart. Unknown to us (since the keel was covered by a thick coating of tar when I had inspected it on various occasions), it had been constructed of 13 laminated sections rather than from a solid piece of wood. I now regretted bitterly that I had not looked the gift horse in the mouth!

It grew so dark, I thought the end of the world was coming. One by one, the planks began to separate from the ribs, the nails flying out like bullets. As each sea hit us water came gushing in through six-inch gaps and the entire hull began to twist and squirm. The mast worked loose from its step, and the gunwales heaved in and out as much as a foot and a half. Realizing that there was no hope of reaching port, since the water was rising so high that the ship was on the verge of sinking, I made for shelter in a small cove off a rocky headland.

After dropping anchor we frantically began patching the holes below water level with anything from slabs of ham to our own clothes. Then, when we thought we had sealed off the leaks as best we could, we began the fruitless task of bailing her out by hand. After six fatiguing hours we gave up. The water level hadn't gone down an inch. We fervently hoped that because of her wooden construction, the ship was buoyant enough to stay afloat even when half full of water. For two days the gale continued, and she miraculously stayed afloat; but we were in a miserable state. We had jettisoned most of our provisions and all the casks of water. Fortunately, we had kept the jugs of the brandy, which made living in waist-deep water just bearable.

After two days, the storm subsided enough to permit us to weigh anchor and make a slow, tedious voyage back to Bizerte, thanks to a fishing smack that came to our rescue and gave us a tow. Safe in port, our sad and final task was to dispose of the hulk that had once been a ship. I had planned to sell the auxiliary motor and other equipment, but the Tunisian authorities said I would need to get special permits

Crew of the *Long Ship* jumping aboard Tunisian fishing boat after setting fire to their ship

(which, of course, would involve a great deal of money and time). They forbade me to give the ship away or even abandon it where we had run it ashore on the beach. The shabby treatment the police inflicted on my exhausted crew—who were repeatedly searched and forbidden to leave the ship unless they left their personal possessions, coupled with the arrogance of the customs officers who threatened to keep us all in Tunisia until the ship was disposed of to their satisfaction—forced me to take drastic action.

With the exception of Jumbo, who chose to go ashore and not risk imprisonment, the disconsolate crew approved of my plan, which was helped along by official incompetence and the de rigueur Tunisian siesta. The ship was under constant guard except right after lunch when the police would sprawl under a tree for a siesta. The captain of a fishing boat agreed to tow us to sea at noon and after we sank the ship, carry us back to shore, in return for anything he and his crew could take off the ship before she went down. The decrepit wreck, straining and creaking simply with the effort of reaching open water again, had failed us, but she still deserved a proper Viking funeral. We dropped anchor about two miles out, aware that we couldn't possibly reach international waters (beyond the 12-mile limit) before the police caught up with us. Giving vent to all the frustration and disappointment we felt, we took axes and started smashing everything in sight: motor, planks, and deck, and set her afire as the fishermen scrambled aboard to grab anything of value. Once the flames reached the sail, she became a towering inferno. We hastily scrambled aboard the fishing boat as a police cutter headed toward us. By the time the law arrived, only thick, tarry smoke and a small portion of the stern remained of the "Long Ship." Since we didn't have time to take much more off the vessel than our personal belongings, she sank with a large number of Roman and Greek amphorae which I had recovered off Mazara del Vallo. One of the crew remarked: "Some poor underwater archaeologist will probably discover her in years to come, and boy, will he be surprised to find both Roman and Greek artifacts on a Viking ship—and one with a motor at that!"

During the trip back to port, escorted by two police boats jammed with furious, gesticulating officials, we were sure our curse-ridden voyage would end in a Tunisian prison. But a benevolent genie in the person of the resourceful Jumbo was waiting with two taxis. First, the police arrested the hapless fishermen who had helped us. While they were thus occupied, we piled into the taxis and sped off toward Tunis and the freighter that was to take us to Marseilles, leaving the officials on the pier more irate than ever.

Our voyage had failed, but not our determination. Before we split up in Marseilles, each of the crew offered to sail with me again if I ever attempted such a voyage. I vowed that I would indeed sail another Viking ship—the next time, one better constructed—and successfully cross the "Big Lake." Five years were to pass before my chance came again.

In 1968 Metro-Goldwyn-Mayer had two replicas of the Gokstad Ship built in Denmark by the same firm that had built the other three. This was for a movie entitled *Alfred the Great,* which was being filmed in Ireland. For their publicity value, MGM sold me one of the ships for a dollar. In August I went to Ireland to make sure this ship was built better than the one I had lost off Tunisia, as well as to test her seaworthiness. Although the keel was solid oak, she was fastened just like the "Long Ship" had been. International law forbids the killing of walrus, so she couldn't be lashed together with walrus thongs. Consulting various Viking ship experts, I decided to use wooden treenails and bronze spikes to refasten her before sailing for America.

My original plan was to duplicate a Phoenician voyage by sailing from Lisbon to Yucatán, but two things made me change my mind. A fellow underwater archaeologist, Peter Throckmorton, who lived in Athens, had been working for nearly a year, trying to determine how we could build a Phoenician ship of the type that existed around 1000 B.C. Just about this time, he produced what looked like a good set of plans, so I deferred taking the southern route until I could build such a ship. In addition, several naval historians assured me that more historical information could be obtained by sailing in the wake of the Vikings. Two such historians who specialized in the construction of Viking ships wanted to sail with us to study the seaworthiness of the vessel and the navigational methods of the Norsemen. Two oceanographic scientists from the Office of Naval Research asked to come along to collect marine specimens in the north Atlantic and to study the effect of such a hostile environment on the crew. So the die was cast: I would take the northern route.

My plan was to pick the ship up in Ireland and take her to Bergen, Norway where the voyage would officially start. There we would take on Viking-period provisions, from victuals to clothing. The only modern items would be lifesaving and photographic equipment. From Bergen, using only the sun, moon, and stars as our guide, we would sail for America, with stops at the Faeroes Islands, Iceland, Greenland, Labrador, Newfoundland, and the United States. During several months of research on the Norsemen and their voyages, I learned several important facts. In their era, the earth was going through a "warm climatic optimum." Greenland, which is practically a solid sheet of ice today, was verdant and fertile, with many varieties of vegetation. Not only were the air and water temperatures much warmer, but there were virtually no icebergs, not even the thick pack ice that surrounds the island today. Furthermore, the wind patterns were much different and more advantageous to those rugged mariners. With weather conditions as they are today in the areas where they sailed, I doubt that even the Norsemen could have reached America.

By the time I had found this out, however, there was already so much publicity about the voyage along the northern route that I had no choice but to go through with it. Meteorological experts in Europe and the United States told me that the only feasible time to attempt the voyage was between early February and the middle of May. That was the only time when we would have easterly winds to carry us across. Also, after May, the glaciers begin to break up, making the seas in those areas unnavigable because of icebergs and pack ice. So I rushed preparations, planning to sail from Bergen no later than mid-February.

At the end of January, just a few days before I was to fly to Ireland to pick up the ship, which I had named *Alfie,* and take her to Bergen, the first of many problems arose. According to its lawyers in London, MGM couldn't provide me with ownership papers to the ship unless it was first registered. Registering a ship is normally an easy procedure, but registering a replica of a Viking ship is quite another matter; it had never been done. The lawyers in London couldn't seem to make any headway with the British Admiralty. Days of impatient waiting slid into slow weeks and then frustrating months. I was going out of my mind with desperation, aware that every day of waiting reduced my chances of getting across the Atlantic before the winds changed. Finally, in mid-April, I had had it. I notified MGM that I was heading for Ireland and would sail without the ship's being registered and without ownership papers. Reluctantly, they gave me a bill of sale after first clearing themselves of any legal connections with the ship.

By this time, I had received nearly 2,000 applications from volunteers all over the world. Of my previous crew, I was able to locate only Bill Holmes who gladly accepted. In the last four weeks before we sailed, over 50 men cancelled for various reasons, some with such excuses as being reluctant to give up smoking on the trip or an allergy to fish. The irony of it was that the four (the two from the Smithsonian and the two from the navy) who had helped convince me to take the northern route also chickened out. Just four hours before we left New York, three others deserted. I replaced one with a German photographer named Dietrich Truebe who claimed to be an expert seaman. Another last-minute volunteer was a 95-pound Greenwich Village hippie, 10 pounds of whose weight was in his hair. He said he first wanted to consult his astrologer, Madam Bird Feather, and called shortly afterward, saying she felt vibrations of disaster; so he withdrew.

When I finally flew from New York, I had a crew of only three with me: the German photographer; George Belcher, a strange, rather intense chap who had just returned from a tour of duty in Vietnam; and my tried and true friend, Neal Watson, who was worth three men. I had met Neal about six months before, when he broke the world's record for the deepest dive on compressed air. In addition to being an experienced diver, he was a karate expert and pilot. At the time he was running a detective agency in the Bahamas. In London we were joined by Bill Holmes who looked perfect for the role; he had just finished playing St. Paul in a British movie, and had an enormous beard and hair down to his shoulders.

I got the shock of my life when we arrived at Lake Athlone in Ireland, where I had left the ship the previous summer. I had made arrangements for a shipwright to change the fastenings and make other modifications and repairs, but except for applying a bit of caulking here and there, he had done nothing. Instead of my paying his outrageous bill of almost $2,000, Neal found the shipwright in the local pub and broke a bottle of whiskey over his head—which precipitated a hasty departure on our part. I had already heard that the ice was breaking up around Greenland much earlier than expected, that we would have to rush to Bergen or the voyage would be impossible that year. The nearest seaport was Limerick, about 70 miles down the Shannon River. There I hoped to find a shipyard in which to make the necessary repairs. Because of rain that had been falling for weeks, we had an exciting and dangerous ride down the river. We passed through one set of rapids at a speed of over 20 knots—without sail up or the use of two outboard engines I had had mounted on the stern in case we needed help getting down the river. Dietrich Truebe decided, on the basis of this preliminary phase of the voyage, that it was too dangerous, and deserted when we reached Limerick.

Needing more crew just to get to Bergen, I advertised in all the major Irish newspapers for volunteers, but could find none who were suitable. Then a German freighter put into port, and her first officer, Otto Washchkau, fell in love with *Alfie*. So I signed him on as my first mate.

Limerick was once a great seaport, even used by the Vikings; but today there is very little shipping. There wasn't a single shipwright in port, and I had to head for Bergen with the ship as she was. Just trying to leave, however, took another two weeks. First we were told by the harbor master that because the ship wasn't "exactly what one could call a seaworthy craft," we would have to wait while he consulted the Admiralty in London. After a long delay, they gave us permission, providing the ship and crew were adequately insured. I took a plane to Lloyd's of London. No soap. Nobody in their right mind would insure us. Through a close friend, I managed to get a forged set of insurance papers, and with them, hurried back to Limerick. Then I learned that the lord mayor had laid on a celebration in honor of our departure. The celebration consumed three precious days and left us with Gaelic hangovers which lasted for several days.

The festivities were launched with a grand medieval banquet in an old castle, during which my crew managed to seduce most of the young serving wenches and even our lovely hostess who was in her sixties. When this feast ended around sunrise the next morning, we were whisked off to the cathedral for a high mass performed by the archbishop who threw another party after the mass. Somewhere along the line, Neal and Bill kidnapped three Pan Am stewardesses who had a day's layover in Ireland. Naturally, they missed their plane: the two carousers tied them to a tree when their departure time came and then forgot about them for about 10 hours. After threatening to file charges against Neal and Bill, the stewardesses were talked into forgetting it and joining the festivities—which they did. On the morning we were to sail, the archbishop blessed the ship, with most of the town present, and we christened her with a bottle of tequila and one of Irish whiskey. As we were about to leave, a truck appeared, with the lord mayor shouting at the top of his lungs. As a present from the port of Limerick, "to get ye safely to America," as he put it, they gave us a hundred gallons of mead (a very potent liquor made from fermented honey which the Vikings drank), 20 cases of Irish whiskey, and 25 cases of Irish stew in tins.

With expressions of thanks for Limerick's hospitality, we rode the outgoing tide to the sea—and immediately our problems began. Leaks sprang all over the place, which we had one hell of a time patching. Between our throbbing hangovers and the work at hand, no one slept that first night.

For the next three days, despite contrary winds, rough seas, and a Russian trawler that almost ran *Alfie* down, we made good time. Then it happened. Off the northern tip of Scotland we ran into a gale. With only the storm sail up, we were forced to run before it for three days until it finally abated and we found ourselves close to Iceland. Two days later we were off northern Scotland again and were once again struck by a gale. This one lasted for eight days and nearly carried us all the way to America. We were west of Iceland when it dissipated, and would have kept on going if I known what the future held. It was like a stuck record: no sooner had we sighted Scotland again than another gale caught us, and back to Iceland we went, and this time we were almost wrecked off its east coast.

By the time we reached what I thought was Scotland again, we had been through hell. Fortunately *Alfie* held together better than the other Viking ship had. We were too busy fighting the elements to worry about plugging leaks. By now, we had lost 26 days being blown back and forth between Scotland and Iceland, and the highest temperature we had encountered was 34 degrees Fahrenheit; most of the time, it was closer to 10 or 15 degrees. Only large doses of the mead (which we blessed the people of Limerick for) kept us from freezing to death in the open vessel. Once, when I tried to open a can of Irish stew with a can opener, the skin on my hand came off and stuck to the can opener.

Things weren't much better when we reached Scotland for the fourth time. Visibility was down to less than a mile when we finally sighted land. Both bitter wind and dark seas were blowing us onto a rocky coast which seemed as barren as the moon. We tried dropping anchor, but the water was too deep even when we were only a few hundred yards from shore. In desperation we cranked the two outboards we had used to get down the river, never really expecting them to start. They saved the ship—and probably our lives, as well.

Finding a bit of sea room, we went down the coast for several miles until we sighted a small, partially protected cove and dropped anchor. It was just in the nick of time; we had run out of gasoline for the outboards. The crew was a sorry sight. Everything was soaked, and the ship was a shambles. Neal had fallen off the mast top and sprained his ankle, I sprained my arm pulling on the halyard trying to raise the sail, and Bill slipped on some ice and broke his leg. Just a few hundred yards away was the shore, but we didn't have a skiff. We were too exhausted to row *Alfie,* and the freezing water ruled out any thought of swimming ashore.

It was a crazy, exasperating experience. After a brief perusal as we entered, the villagers, who lived in the 20-odd cottages, paid us not the slightest attention. It was as though Viking ships came to that tiny, isolated cove every day. We did everything we could think of to attract their attention. Nothing. For three days we lay in that cove, not even knowing exactly where we were.

With only a Boy Scout compass and a Michelin road map of the British Isles, I couldn't figure our location. I did know that if we headed north and then east, we would eventually round Scotland and could cut across to Norway. We departed from that strange village and after a three-day sail against contrary winds were still heading north off the western coast of Scotland when we sighted what turned out to be the port of Tobermory.

After getting everyone patched up by the local doctor, I decided to take a shortcut to Norway—through the Caledonia Canal which cuts across northern Scotland. Compared to what we had been through recently, it was a calm but memorable trip. It took a day to reach Fort George, a small village on the western end of Loch Ness, where we anchored for the night. Early the next morning we started across the

23-mile lake, using the outboard motors (we had to lower our mast to pass under many of the bridges over the canal). There was a thick fog lying about 10 feet above the surface of the lake. To see where we were going, one of us would periodically crawl onto one of the dragon figureheads for a sighting. When we reached Inverness on the other side of Loch Ness, there was quite a bit of excitement in the town. An unusual number of sightings of the Loch Ness monster had been reported that day, but what they had seen were our Viking figureheads.

After a brief stay in port to have the mast stepped and minor repairs made, we started across for Bergen in reasonable weather. Twenty hours later, as we neared the Norwegian coast, gale-force winds struck from the north. With only a small storm sail up, we had to run before it, and by the time it abated three days later, we had been blown so far south that we were off England. We entered Scarborough, which had been a Roman and later a Viking seaport. While there, I learned of the voyage Thor Heyerdahl planned to make in his raft, *Ra*.

Heyerdahl believes Mediterranean cultures reached Yucatán and that the Egyptians reached the New World in papyrus rafts. Although I agree that inhabitants of the Mediterranean accomplished this, I can't agree that the Egyptians ever did so on papyrus rafts. These rafts were for use on rivers and were never intended for ocean voyages. Furthermore, the Egyptians weren't a seagoing people. Although they built some wooden ships, they hired Phoenicians to handle their far-ranging maritime commerce. If the Egyptians did reach the New World, they did so in much sturdier, wooden Phoenician vessels and not in flimsy paper boats.

This development, coupled with advice from the weather experts that it was too late in the season to attempt the northern route, caused me to decide to head for Lisbon and take the southern crossing, hopefully catching up with *Ra* and beating it across.

Twelve hours after leaving Scarborough, we were hit by another gale. *Alfie* developed several leaks so serious that we had to put into another port, running the ship aground to keep her from sinking. When the tide went out and she was high and dry, we found that several planks near the keel had worked loose. We repaired them, using brass spikes.

Things looked good for the next two days as we made fair progress down the coast. Then another of what seemed like an inexhaustible series of gales caught us, and the situation became critical. Running with a storm sail, we were fighting huge cross seas; sometimes two would strike at the same time from different directions. *Alfie* was twisting so violently that the gunwales began heaving in and out, as they had on her predecessor. She was acting like a drunken snake, making very strange noises. The iron nails holding the planking to the ribs flew out faster than we could replace them. At one point we heard a sharp snap. Two ribs below the waterline had broken in half. While we were trying to cope with this, loud and unfamiliar noises assaulted our freezing ears, and we discovered that whole planks above the waterline on both sides of the ship had worked loose from the ribs as much as six inches. We were, quite literally, falling apart. We quickly passed lines under the keel and all the way around the hull of the ship— holding her together like a soggy Christmas package. To prevent further strain on the hull, I had the storm sail taken down, and we threw out a makeshift sea anchor. Then we rode out the storm, which subsided about 12 hours later.

When we crawled into the port of Lowestoft, I had reached the conclusion that it was plain suicide to go back out on the high seas with the ship in that condition. We had *Alfie* hauled out of the water, and I hired a bunch of shipwrights to completely refasten the ship with brass spikes. I also had several of the planks and the two ribs replaced, as well as a new mainsail to replace the one that had been torn to shreds in the last storm. As an added safety precaution, I even bought an emergency radio and rubber life raft.

When we left Lowestoft, our luck had to change, or so I thought. At first it looked as though the fates were smiling on us. A lovely, stiff 20-knot breeze enabled us to average 12 knots sailing to Dover. George Belcher deserted there when I sent him ashore to purchase some food; but I didn't have time to try to find a replacement. From the newspapers, I knew that *Ra* had already started across the Atlantic. Leaving Dover for the crossing to France, we again had a tail wind and for the first 12 hours made remarkable time. Then, when we were within sight of Cherbourg, another gale struck. Unfortunately, but in keeping with our rotten luck, the wind came from the south and we were blown back across the English Channel. We had to put into a small fishing port on the Isle of Wight. Two days later, in midchannel, we had a repeat scenario, this time ending up in Weymouth. On our third attempt, after waiting a week for reasonable weather, we made it across and put into

St.-Peter Port on the Isle of Guernsey, one of the Channel Islands owned by Great Britain which lies near the coast of France.

We landed to find most of the townspeople at the wharf. Neal addressed the crowd: "We Vikings have come to rape, pillage, and plunder." As it turned out, he meant it. Early the next morning we were given the option of leaving port immediately or facing 30 days in jail for disturbing the peace and numerous other misdemeanors. We had gotten in three brawls in various pubs the night before, and four men who had the misfortune to tangle with Neal ended up in the hospital. A police launch towed us out of port and left us nursing monumental hangovers and facing 30- to 35-knot winds and high seas. Lisbon was more than 1,000 miles away, and on the way there, we would have 350 miles of open sea, crossing the Bay of Biscay. I put it to a vote, and everyone agreed that we should go for bust—reach Lisbon or sink trying. I threw my Boy Scout compass and Michelin road map of Europe overboard; we would sail or sink as the Vikings had, without modern aids.

Three and a half days later, we were off Lisbon in record time. We had averaged almost 12 knots, a feat few racing yachts can lay claim to today. It was downhill all the way, or rather, more like riding a surfboard, due to tail winds of 25 to 35 knots. At times as we were flying down a huge sea, it seemed that only the keel was touching the water. It was thrilling, but none of us slept more than a few minutes at a time. We were aware of being in constant danger. One miscalculation on the steerboard and we could easily capsize. I have always loved sailing, but for sheer thrills, nothing equaled this.

We received a great reception from the Portuguese when we entered the port of Lisbon. In fact, it was a little too great. As we were dropping anchor, a tugboat full of the press accidently rammed us, cracking the stern post and putting a large hole in the hull at the waterline.

There was so much to do, and all of it quickly, before starting the transatlantic crossing. I felt pressed; *Ra* had already passed the Canaries and the hurricane season was fast approaching. One of my major tasks was to raise more crew. I figured that eight was the minimum for an ocean crossing. When we arrived, there were only four of us. Then Neal had to rush home to his wife who was seriously ill, and Otto Washchkau announced one morning as he was being tortured by a wicked hangover that he didn't think the ship could make it. He departed as suddenly as he had come, without even picking up his personal effects. Now, with only Bill Holmes left, I had serious problems.

I appealed for volunteers in the newspapers and even on Portuguese television, to no avail. Then I decided to hire professional seamen, but none were interested, no matter how much I offered to pay them. Bill finally talked his younger brother, Dick, into join us. As ludicrous as it sounds, the three of us sailed the morning after Dick arrived from London. Five hours later and 30 miles south of Lisbon, I knew it was futile. It was virtually impossible for the three of us even to raise and lower the mainsail. The Vikings had used crews of 20 or more. So, with broken hearts we returned to Lisbon.

I spent the next 24 hours and over $400 on the phone, trying to raise a crew, calling to places as far away as California. After another wasted week in port, we finally recruited two crew members—Trevor Whitehouse, a 120-pound Englishman who had never been on a sailing ship, and Manuel Santos, a Portuguese draft-dodger with about the same qualifications. Within minutes of leaving Lisbon, both were wretchedly seasick, and they remained so for days.

With a good northerly breeze during the first three days, we made excellent time toward the Canaries. Then, about a hundred miles from Lanzarote Island, a sudden gale came out of the southwest. It struck so suddenly that, before we could get the mainsail down, the mast had cracked along its entire length. The large fish-shaped block that holds the mast in place also cracked. There was nothing to repair; both parts had to be replaced before the sail could be used again. While trying to put up a jury rig so we could run before the storm wind, I fell on the wet deck and slipped a disc in my back, which put me out of action but good. We wallowed around on the stormy seas for three days until a Spanish fishing boat appeared and towed us back to Cadiz.

Once more the Spaniards were jubilant because I had failed to discredit Columbus by crossing the Atlantic in a Viking ship. Soon after this came news that *Ra* had also sunk before reaching Barbados. Lying in traction in the Cádiz hospital, I came to the decision to end the voyage right then and there. The ship needed extensive repairs (which I didn't have the money for), and my doctor said I wouldn't be able to walk—let alone sail a Viking ship—for several weeks. Since it was already the end of July, it would be sheer stupidity to cross the Atlantic during the hurricane season. Old *Alfie* had been through hell; it was time for her to go into retirement.

Although I failed to cross the Atlantic Ocean—first on the northern route, following in the wake of the Norsemen, and then twice on the southern route used by the Phoenicians and other early Mediterranean mariners—I considered both voyages partly successful. I had learned first hand much about the Viking ships and many important aspects of the Norse voyages. By the end of the second Viking voyage, I had logged nearly 7,000 miles sailing Viking ships and had tested these ships under practically every sea and weather condition, experiencing some of the worst storms imaginable. I am convinced that a properly built Viking ship could even sail around the world with no problem.

Our most important discovery was the impressive speed of this class of vessel. The Norsemen did not measure distances when relating their voyages in the sagas. Rather, they said something like: "After so many days' sail from [one place], we reached [another place]." This has been an area of controversy for years. Some historians believe the Viking ships could average about four knots, or roughly 100 miles a day, while others believe that six knots was a more realistic figure. Using this rough estimate, plus descriptions of the places they reached on the North American continent, some historians claim that the farthest south the Norsemen went was Newfoundland, while others think they got as far as Chesapeake Bay. With the speed we averaged between Guernsey and Lisbon, they might have even reached Florida or Mexico.

Another widespread misconception we disproved was that these ships weren't seaworthy under poor conditions at sea. Most experts have stated that because they were open-built, like a large canoe, the waves would break over the gunwales and they would fill with water and sink in rough weather. After going through some of the roughest seas in the world and countless gales, I can honestly say that isn't so. Except for spray, we did not take a single sea over the side. Still another interesting discovery was how close to the wind these ships could sail. Most armchair historians have believed that the Viking ships could sail only with a following wind, but we found that, with light winds and the aid of whisker poles, we could sail our ship as close as 70 degrees to the wind, although she naturally had a bit of drift because of her shallow draft. With stronger winds, which meant rougher seas to plow into, this figure decreased proportionately to the wind's velocity.

On balance, these insights into Norse seafaring made up for the dissapointments, the aches, the freezing, and the soaking.

8: *The Sunken Continent of Atlantis*

The possible existence of the sunken continent of Atlantis, whose golden spires, Plato wrote, once lighted the whole world, have tantalized men for more than 2,000 years. One of the great mysteries of the past is the apparent suddenness with which highly developed prehistoric cultures disappeared, leaving no clues as to the fates that befell them. Today, many scholars and scientists theorize that these civilizations were abruptly terminated by geophysical events involving earthquakes, volcanoes, floods, tidal waves, and the submergence and emergence of land. Others are equally sure it is all a myth.

I first got involved in the Atlantis controversy in 1962, while working in the Archivo de las Indias in Seville. A noted historian from the University of Vienna approached me, claiming that he had proof that Atlantis existed in the shallow waters off Cádiz. Skeptical at first, I refused his offer to conduct an underwater survey of the area. Several weeks later, he returned with letters from some high-ranking government officials in Madrid, asking that I help him; so, as an act of goodwill, I consented. A secretive man, the historian never really told me what proof he had, not that it mattered; I didn't find any sign of a sunken continent, the earthly paradise of antiquity.

The Spanish government provided me with a boat, the necessary equipment, and six good divers. Since the depth of water ranged from 75 to 250 feet, I decided that we should first conduct a sonar survey of the area and attempt to locate positive targets which the divers and

I would inspect visually. Using side-scanning sonar—which would indicate the presence of any objects protruding above the seafloor, and subbottom profiling sonar, which would indicate the presence of solid objects buried in sediment below the sea floor—we spent 12 days covering an area of six square miles. The sonar located 13 "possibles," an unlucky number, as it turned out. It took us three days to dive and identify the first 12 targets, which were: seven rock outcroppings, three fishing vessels, a tanker sunk during World War II, and a Dutch warship of the eighteenth century.

On the morning of the fourth diving day, I had a funny feeling in the pit of my stomach, a premonition that we would have trouble. Our thirteenth target was the deepest of all. It lay in 245 feet, and the sea was exceptionally rough that day. As I was preparing to make the dive with two of the navy divers, the captain of the ship suddenly ordered me to stay on board. He said that because of the depth, he couldn't take responsibility for the life of a civilian, preferring instead to send down his two best divers. Of course I was upset about this, but I complied with his order.

Both divers were to make what we call a "bounce dive"—go down quickly, spend only a few minutes at the assigned depth, then surface to 30 feet and undergo decompression there, and again at the 20- and 10-foot levels. Two other navy divers were stationed at the 30-foot level to meet them on their ascent and aid them if necessary. About 10 minutes into the dive, one of the safety divers surfaced and said there was no sign of the two deep divers. They were then only two minutes overdue, so he went back down, only to surface five minutes later with the same alarm. Over the protests of the captain, I quickly grabbed my SCUBA tank and started down. At 200 feet I saw the remains of a large steel-hulled vessel and headed for it. About 20 feet lower, I was swimming along the deck of the ship when I came upon one of the divers. He was entangled in some steel cables. After determining that he was still alive, I took a big gulp of air and stuck the regulator from my SCUBA tank in his mouth while removing the cables that were wrapped around his tank and head. On the way to the surface, he perked up a bit, and we shared the same air source until reaching 50 feet and getting fresh tanks from the safety divers.

After spending 20 minutes decompressing, we surfaced and learned that the other diver had not come up. Surely he was dead by now. His air would have run out long before. I was against risking our lives to go back down after him. Making two dives to that depth in such a short period of time is extremely hazardous. Furthermore, the diver I had rescued said that the last time he saw his companion, he was apparently suffering from "raptures of the deep," or nitrogen narcosis, and was swimming away from the shipwreck. None of the other navy divers had been down to this depth before, and the chap I had rescued was still too shaken from his close call, so I had to go down alone. Before jumping in, I arranged for safety divers to meet me at 100 feet, and we worked out a detailed decompression schedule, starting with a stop at 60 feet for 20 minutes and taking a total of almost three hours of decompression before surfacing. One thing I certainly didn't want was a dreaded case of the "bends."

Going down, I carried a line to attach to the diver's body in the event that I found him. All went well at first. After two minutes on the bottom, I found him and tied the line to it. I jerked the line three times to signal the men in the boat to pull him up and then started up, pulling myself hand over hand on the same line. At 180 feet, the line suddenly became taut. I knew it had snagged on the wreck and made the mistake of heading back to unsnag it. This went off without a hitch and all was well until I reached the 60-foot stop where I began to feel faint. My body began to tingle all over. This was the first stages of the bends, and I knew I was in trouble. At the 50-foot stop, I blacked out, and the divers rushed me to the surface.

Still unconscious, I was taken from the deck of the boat by helicopter to the U.S. naval base at Rota on the far side of the Gulf of Cádiz. There I came to, only to find that I was totally paralyzed. Thanks to the quick action of the U.S. Navy doctors, my life and mobility were saved. They packed me in ice and flew me to the U.S. Air Force base in Wiesbaden, West Germany, which was the nearest place with a recompression chamber. After 96 miserable, claustrophobic hours in that hot chamber, I emerged in a weakened condition from the ordeal, cured and very thankful.

This fiasco should have sated my curiosity about Atlantis, but six months later I was involved in another search for the sunken continent. When we stopped at Las Palmas, Grand Canary Island, on the *Niña II* voyage to America, the director of the museum on the island told me that a fisherman had reported finding a "sunken city" off the southern side of the island. The director thought it might have some connection with the Atlantis theory. Expecting another wild goose chase, I dived to the site and was amazed to find the remains of more than 50 stone buildings in the middle of a large bay at a depth of 60 feet. Although it wasn't Atlantis, it was a remarkable find, and I hope to return someday and carry out further exploration. From the materials I recovered and the historical research done later, the buildings appear to be the remains of a fishing village that was submerged by an earthquake in 1607.

In 1968 I really caught the Atlantis bug. In August, while searching for shipwrecks on the Little Bahama Bank north of Grand Bahama Island, I made two important discoveries. On a shallow sandbar about three miles north of Memory Rock, in 15 feet of water, I found over 50 fluted marble columns. At first I assumed that they were part of the cargo of a shipwreck, but when I didn't find any signs of a wreck, ballast, or other type of cargo, I was mystified. How did they get there? I finally surmised that a ship had run aground there and that, to lighten the ship and get it off the bottom, the columns had been jettisoned. Then two weeks later, about 10 miles to the south, near Sandy Cay, I located several hundred round marble balls, each two to four feet in diameter. Again, no shipwreck or other material. This time, the water depth of 50 feet precluded the possibility that a ship had run aground and jettisoned the heavy balls. The water was too deep. Now I was really baffled! How *did* these balls get there, and even more interesting, what were they used for? Prior to the seventeenth century, stone balls were used as projectiles in cannon, but they were never more than a foot in diameter.

I chipped off samples of marble from the columns and balls, which I sent to several geologists. Knowing that a date couldn't be obtained from marble, I still hoped that the place of origin could be established. All I could learn was that the marble wasn't of North American origin, that it was most likely from somewhere in the western Mediterranean. Had it been brought over by Phoenicians or some other culture that had reached the New World long before Columbus? I decided to turn over my findings to someone more qualified to study the matter. First I consulted scientists at the Smithsonian Institution, but they weren't interested. Then I met Dr. Manson Valentine—curator of the Science

Diver inspecting one of the many marble columns on the "Atlantis" site near Bimini in the Bahamas

Museum of Miami, who had devoted his life to seeking explanations of mysterious phenomena—and soon after that, Dimitri Rebikoff, a well-known inventor of underwater photographic products and an underwater archaeologist. To my astonishment, I discovered that both were involved with a number of interesting underwater sites in the Bahamas. They had recently formed the Marine Archaeological Research Society (MARS) and invited me to become part of their group.

While flying over the Grand Bahama Bank in 1967, Rebikoff had sighted a rectangular object about a quarter of a mile long at a depth of about three fathoms, which, from his more than 20 years of experience, he identified as definitely being manmade. Several weeks later, he returned with Dr. Valentine to investigate further and photograph this strange site, but shifting sands, something common in the area, had covered the site. On subsequent flights in that general area, Rebikoff and Valentine discovered many other suspicious bottom patterns around the chain of islands extending from Bimini south for about 60 miles; but lack of time and money prevented further investigation by diving.

During July 1968 Robert Brush, a pilot flying between Miami and Nassau, reported sighting a square structure in shallow water off the northern tip of Andros Island in the Bahamas, not far from where Rebikoff had made his original sighting. He passed this information on to Rebikoff and Valentine, but before they could mount an underwater investigation of the site, the press learned of it and various articles appeared, stating that a sunken temple of Atlantis had been discovered. A few months earlier, a book by the son of the clairvoyant, Edgar Cayce, had been published. In it, Cayce predicted (in 1933) that a temple of the sunken continent of Atlantis would rise out of the sea in the area of Bimini in 1968. Naturally, many of his followers associated this discovery with Cayce's prediction, and the press was only too happy to agree with them.

Valentine and Rebikoff made a preliminary exploration of the site and discovered that the structure *was* manmade; that it measured 60 by 100 feet, with walls three feet thick; and that the limestone blocks, of which the walls were constructed, were laid with an accuracy not to be expected of recent inhabitants of the area. Nor was there any reason to believe that it was the work of the Lucayo Indians who lived in the area when Columbus first visited it; they weren't stone-builders. Nevertheless, many "experts" jumped on the bandwagon, stating that the structure was probably a pen used by modern inhabitants of the Bahamas for storing turtles, sponges, or conch shells.

Although Valentine does believe in the existence of Atlantis and has publicly said that this structure may be associated with Atlantis, further investigation convinced him that the site belongs to the Mayan civilization or to some other American Indian culture. By a strange coincidence, the site duplicates the floor plan of the Mayan "Temple of the Turtles" at Uxmal, in Yucatán, even to the extent that both sites have their east end and southwest corners partitioned off. Other scientists agree with Valentine that, due to the relative water level over the site, the site is certainly pre-Columbian.

On subsequent expeditions to this general area, Valentine and Rebikoff located several other submerged, manmade structures. One day, when Rebikoff was showing me these sites from the air, we discovered another large, rectangular, manmade structure near the others.

One of the sites Valentine discovered is close to a small sandy key where he found hundreds of cut stone discs about eight inches in diameter, lying in a heap on the beach, no doubt thrown there by storms. From these discs he followed two parallel ranks of identical discs into the undergrowth. The discs were partly buried in the sand in straight lines that made several abrupt, right-angle turns and appeared to delineate definite boundries, perhaps that of a ceremonial court. The top half of the discs, which were protruding from the sand, were so weatherworn that there is little doubt that they have been there for centuries.

On September 2, 1968, while searching for other submerged sites off Bimini, Valentine and his associates were taken to an area near the northern shore of Bimini by a local fisherman who said he had seen many "square stones" on the seafloor at a depth of three fathoms. There Valentine was astonished to find two extensive, parallel walls of rectangular and polygonal, flat stones of varying thickness and size. They had obviously been cut by men and were accurately aligned to form a convincing structural pattern. These stones had evidently lain submerged for a long time; their top edges had been rounded off by weathering, giving them the appearance of giant loaves of bread. The main orientation of the site was parallel to the coast for about half a mile, and the tops of the massive blocks, which protruded some three to four feet above the sandy seafloor, were in a pattern that averaged 17 feet in thickness.

Before visiting the sites Rebikoff and Valentine were investigating, I researched lost civilizations and found that, whereas many had met with cataclysmic fates, others took centuries to disappear beneath the sea. For example, only 3,000 years ago, there was a land bridge between the British Isles and the European continent; today the English Channel flows over vast forests covered by the sea. In the Mediterranean alone, there are more than 180 known sites of sunken ancient cities, the majority of which were covered by a rise in the sea level of the world. Rebikoff, who had spent years investigating these phenomena, found that the oceanic level of most of the world's oceans has risen 16 feet in the past 2,000 years. This has resulted from the general warming of the earth since the last ice age, due to the melting of the polar ice.

There is also considerable geological evidence that large land masses in the Western Hemisphere have been inundated by the sea. Many early-sixteenth-century maps of the New World show various islands in the Atlantic and Caribbean which no longer exist. While some of them may never have existed, there is evidence that some did. Many early Spanish navigators mentioned sailing passed a large island about 200 miles west of the Cayman Islands, which are shown on the early maps. Later mariners did not see this island, and it was eventually named Isla Misteriosa, or Mystery Island. Modern maps show a Misteriosa Bank in this same area, with depths as shallow as four fathoms. No doubt, this is the site of the island that disappeared beneath the sea. In recent years divers have discovered intact sunken Mayan temples on the coast of Yucatán, and I am certain other submerged archaeological sites—possibly even complete cities of ancient civilizations—will be found elsewhere in the Western Hemisphere.

Some traces of ancient civilizations may eventually be discovered right off the coast of the United States. In 1959 the U.S. Coast and Geodetic Survey reported that during hydrographic surveys off the Florida Keys, they found sinkholes as large as a half-mile in diameter at depths of 900 feet about 14 miles off the Florida Keys, which are presumed to have been freshwater lakes in an area that subsided beneath the sea.

According to the *Dictionary of Anthropology,* Atlantis is "a hypothetical land in the Atlantic Ocean where civilization is alleged to have begun." Many scholars believe that it is a mythical land, that it never existed, while others believe the opposite. The existence of Troy, the legends of the sacrifice of maidens in the Sacred Cenote of Chicen-Itza, and the tales of King Arthur and his knights of the round table were also believed to be mythical legends until recent archaeological evidence showed otherwise.

The oldest known, written mention of the existence of Atlantis is found in two dialogues of Plato, which date to around 335 B.C. In a discussion between Solon and certain Egyptian priests, Plato introduces Atlantis, whose disappearance they put at about 12,000 years ago. Plato wrote:

. . . and there is an island situated in front of the Straits [of Gibraltar] which are by you called the Pillars of Hercules; the island was larger than Libya [Africa] and Asia put together, and was the way to other islands, and from these you might pass to the whole of the opposite continent which surround the true ocean, for this sea which is within the Straits of Hercules [the Mediterranean] is only a harbor, having a narrow entrance, but the other is a real sea, and the surrounding land may be most truly called a boundless continent. Now in this Island of Atlantis there was a great and wonderful empire. . . . But afterwards there occurred violent earthquakes and floods; and in a single day and night of misfortune all the warlike men in a body sank into the earth, and the island of Atlantis in like manner disappeared in the depths of the sea.

Since Plato's time, hundreds of books and articles have been written about Atlantis, some denying its existence. But the important fact is that many scholars have compared his writings with historical and archaeological data and have substantiated his narrative.

The earliest known maps that are still in existence place Atlantis in the Atlantic Ocean, but later ones, published before Columbus' discovery of the New World, place a massive land mass in the Atlantic, calling it "Antillia." Some scholars believe that the present islands of the Caribbean, which the early Spanish explorers first called "the Antillies," are remnants of Atlantis which are higher land masses of the sunken continent.

We need not rely on the misty surmises of these controversial myths

The author with a second-century B.C. Roman amphora discovered off Cádiz,
Spain in 1961

or legends; we can look at more recent geological evidence. Most geologists believe that an Atlantean continent did at one time exist between the European and American continents. The question still being debated is the precise period in geological history that this continent existed.

The bed of the Atlantic is the most unstable part of the earth's surface. It would have taken only a relatively small warping of the earth's crust—only 1/8,000 of the earth's diameter—for a considerable portion of the ocean floor to rise above the water and another large land mass to sink beneath the sea. Scientific evidence that this did indeed happen has come to light only recently. In the past decade, we have witnessed the emergence of two islands—one off the Azores and the other off Iceland—due to volcanic action.

In August 1964 two French naval officers, Captain Georges Houot and Lieutenant Gerard de Froberville, reported an amazing discovery. While diving in the research submarine *Archimedes* at a depth of five miles off the northern coast of Puerto Rico, they found a gigantic stairway hewn from solid rock on a sloping seafloor, obviously man-made. Two years later, the research vessel *Anton Bruun* was engaged in oceanographic investigations off the coast of Peru under the direction of Dr. Robert J. Menzies of Duke University. Their deepsea underwater cameras unexpectedly focused on what is believed to be the site of an ancient civilization. On a muddy plain at a depth of 6,000 feet, they found elaborately carved columns with some sort of inscriptions on them. Nearby, the sonic depth recorder detected strange "lumps" on the otherwise level bottom. These were thought to be ruins of ancient buildings. "Although the idea of a sunken city in the Pacific seems incredible," Dr. Menzies said, "the evidence so far suggests one of the most exciting discoveries of the century."

Soon after I met Dimitri Rebikoff we made several flights in his plane to the Bahamas, where we investigated the sites that had been found. Flying with him was an experience in itself! On one flight, which originated in West Palm Beach and ended three hours later on a rather sour note, I survived two near midair collisions, a serious fire, and an emergency landing. (I chose to return to the States on a scheduled airline.) On another flight with Rebikoff, between Fort Lauderdale and Nassau, over the Gulf Stream, one of the plane's two engines quit.

Losing altitude, we had to jettison the expensive diving and photographic gear in order to stay airborne.

With the backing of a number of universities and the promise of funds from the National Geographic Society, we decided to make a proper survey of each site and submit detailed reports to various experts. With Rebikoff and Andy Pruna (an expert diver who had just left the U.S. Navy Sealab III Project and joined Rebikoff's underwater equipment firm), I flew to Bimini. On arriving, we were surprised to hear that only three weeks earlier, two divers were reported to have discovered two stone statues, as well as fragments of a carved column, and spirited them away in a yacht to the United States. Such stories are always floating around, but this time we located over a dozen people who swore they had seen the artifacts.

While Andy, who is an excellent draftsman and cartographer, made drawings and measurements of the site, Rebikoff and I did an extensive survey. Everything he and Valentine had said, I found to be true. Our first goal was to ascertain that none of the blocks was attached to the seafloor, and in doing so, we made two further discoveries which substantiated their early findings. By fanning away the sand on the sides of the blocks, we discovered that the buried part of the blocks was square-cut and that it did not appear to be attached to the seafloor in any way, but instead was lying on top of other massive, square-cut blocks.

Our first day of diving came to an abrupt halt with the appearance of a 12-foot mako shark. The remora fish on the shark, which itself measured over three feet, tried to attach itself to Andy's back while he was sitting on the bottom, drawing. Boarding our small boat, we found the reason for the shark's sudden appearance. Anchored only a hundred yards away was a yacht owned by the late congressman, Adam Clayton Powell, who had a home on Bimini. The people fishing from his boat were using chum to attract fish and had inadvertently attracted the mako shark.

A well-known expert on prehistoric architecture, who asked to remain anonymous, studied the photographs and Andy's mosaic drawings. He said that the construction used on this site is known as "Cyclopean," which was the type used by the earliest civilizations of man. Cyclopean architecture was used not only in Europe and Asia, but by early American civilizations.

The Bimini area has always had a bit of mystery about it. It is the site of the legendary Fountain of Youth sought by Ponce de León. Forty years ago, there were reports of stones with carvings being found on land, but the location is unknown. Neither the Spaniards nor any other Europeans built anything on or near Bimini; so this at least rules out the possibility that it was constructed by modern man.

As soon as we returned to Florida, we applied to the Bahamian government for excavation permits for the Bimini and Andros Island sites. Unknown to us at the time, another group, dominated by Edgar Cayce psychics, had applied for the same permits. The press played up the discoveries, claiming that the sunken continent of Atlantis had been discovered. Quite a lot of people got in the act, which inevitably complicated our work. Eager as we were to return to the sites, months dragged by with no word from Nassau about our request for permits. Valentine and I agreed that it would be prudent to wait for government permission before doing anything, but Rebikoff, who was impatient, made frequent trips to the sites. During one, he reported seeing a number of marble columns that some amateur divers had found in only four feet of water near Entrance Point on North Bimini Island and which we later verified.

In early November 1970 I was surprised to read in the newspapers that the North American Rockwell Corporation, which has substantial land holdings on Bimini, had been granted exclusive exploration rights on all underwater ruins in the Bimini area. Included in this agreement with the Bahamian government was a plan to construct an underwater restaurant and bar near the sunken walls. When he heard about this, Rebikoff rushed to Nassau, demanding an explanation; but none was forthcoming, nor would the authorities there tell him whether they would grant us the permit to explore the sunken buildings off Andros Island. Two months later, the Rockwell Corporation got an exclusive permit for the Andros Island area.

Around this time two interesting discoveries were made. A Pan Am pilot phoned me one day to say that he had found still another large wall off Bimini—this one in 60 feet of water—which had a large archway extending through the middle of it. Three days later a charter-boat captain named Pat Delaney, working out of Bimini, reported that he had discovered a large, steep, pyramidal structure with a rectangular base in 60 feet of water. He claimed that a psychic with an excellent reputation for finding oil for petroleum companies had rented his boat and from a psychic impression had located the sunken pyramid. Although both the pilot and Delaney refused to reveal the location unless we paid them an outrageous sum of money, Rebikoff and I made several trips to Bimini but failed to find either the new wall or the pyramid. When I gave up, sure that both were hoaxes, Rebikoff kept searching. During one trip he found an underwater, fresh-water spring, or well, pouring out of the seafloor. It was enclosed by a stone wall close to the two parallel walls we had already surveyed.

As an archaeologist, my main objective was to identify and date these sites through careful and systematic excavation, with the help of other experts. I didn't put much stock in the Atlantis theory, but I did think they might be tied in with some pre-Columbian culture, and this, in itself, made them interesting. From dealings I had with representatives of the Rockwell Corporation, I gathered that they weren't eager to prove or disprove the authenticity of the Atlantis theory. Soon after they obtained the lease for the Bimini area, they hired a geologist who had experience in the area. After a brief trip to Bimini, during which he didn't even go in the water, he announced that the walls were not manmade and that the columns were probably from a shipwreck. Unhappy with his report, the Rockwell people engaged scientists from the Marine Laboratory of the University of Miami. One of these, Dr. John Gifford, a geologist, made a thorough survey of one of the walls and reported that "the blocks were something of a geological enigma; none of the evidence conclusively rules out the possibility of human intervention in their formation."

As a result of Gifford's encouraging report, Rockwell decided to mount a major expedition to uncover one of the walls. With astronaut Edgar Mitchell as the leader of the expedition, about 25 people were invited to participate, including Rebikoff and a number of psychics from the Edgar Cayce Foundation. Until just three days before the expedition was to begin, I thought I was to be in charge of the actual excavation of the wall; then my invitation was withdrawn on the pretext that there wasn't enough room on the boat. However, I discovered that, in fact, the Rockwell people were afraid I would publish an unfavorable account of the excavation that would make their stockholders unhappy.

Fortunately I was able to interest a diving friend of mine, Art Hartmann, in taking me over in his boat while the Rockwell expedition was in progress. Their salvage vessel, *Venture,* was anchored over one of the walls where just a month earlier, Rebikoff had reported sighting 16-foot-high pillars holding up some of the massive 15-ton blocks. We anchored alongside their vessel despite shrill warnings that we would be arrested for diving in an area for which they had exclusive rights to excavate. But we had already gotten permission from the Bahamian government to dive to the site, though not to excavate.

In any case, nature had already done the excavating. The bottom was clear of sand. *The wall wasn't a wall at all.* The stone blocks, which were three to four feet thick, rested on the hard seafloor. If anything, the site resembled a road or causeway similar to many I've seen in Yucatán and elsewhere. When challenged about the 16-foot-high columns he had reported sighting, Rebikoff claimed he had really seen them on another wall which, unfortunately, had been covered again by sand. The most important information gleaned from this expedition was that none of the blocks was attached to the seafloor, thereby proving that they are not natural formations.

Before leaving Bimini, I talked to some of the fishermen and asked them if they knew of any other underwater walls or ruins near the island. One showed me a bronze coin he claimed to have found on the beach near where most of the walls and columns were found. The coin, which is not necessarily connected to the ruins, was Phoenician and dates from the fifth century B.C.

Although Rebikoff and others still believe the walls are manmade, I am now convinced that they are the work of mother nature, since I have seen similar underwater formations in other areas of the Bahamas, for example, off the coast of Yucatán and near the Dry Tortugas Islands west of Key West. As for the marble columns and Phoenician coin: the columns were probably dropped off a ship that ran aground trying to enter the port, and the coin was probably a "plant" arranged by someone trying to convince me that the site was the real McCoy.

The buildings off northern Andros Island are another matter. They are certainly worth further investigation. Unfortunately, to date, nothing has been done except for a brief hit-and-run trip I made there shortly after the Rockwell expedition. I had a friend fly to the site in a small amphibious plane, and we spent several hours exploring with snorkeling gear. Alongside the largest building I dug down more than seven feet, but did not reach the bottom of the wall. Walls made of square-cut stone of this height and covered as they are with a mortar-like substance would never have been built as turtle pens by the modern-day inhabitants of the Bahamas, nor were they in an area where the Spaniards or other Europeans had settlements. Even more tantalizing was a ceramic face of a man, which I found in the sand there, in addition to a carved piece of marble and more than a dozen ceramic shards—none of which appear to be New World in origin, according to the experts I have consulted.

On a small cay near this submerged structure off Andros, Valentine had reported finding hundreds of wheel-like stones with holes in their centers, ranging from two to five feet in diameter. I visited the cay and verified their existence. On a reef nearby, I found several more of these perfectly cut stones buried deep in the coral, which indicated that they have been there a long time. In appearance, the stones are identical to the stone currency used for centuries by the natives of Yap Island in the Pacific.

One of these days, the sites around Andros Island will be thoroughly investigated and important archeological evidence will be uncovered, perhaps proving that the area was once settled by some ancient people from the other side of the Atlantic who reached these waters long before Columbus.

9: Montezuma's Treasure

In March 1971 I was involved in what might eventually turn out to be the greatest treasure discovery of all times. During the past five centuries there have been numerous searches for the fabulous and immense treasures of Montezuma, the emperor of the Aztecs, but all have ended in failure. From the results of the expedition I participated in, however, I am convinced that this treasure has been found and that it will eventually be recovered. The mystery surrounding the disappearance of the treasure is in itself fascinating.

In 1519, when Cortez and his soldiers landed near the port of Veracruz to begin their conquest of Mexico, their goal was the accumulation of great wealth. But few if any had any idea of the incredible treasure they were to see when they eventually reached Tenochtitlán, Montezuma's capital, a city of canals on an island in Lake Texcoco, which has since been drained and is the site of present-day Mexico City.

According to ancient Aztec prophecies, Montezuma believed that the white god, Quetzalcoatl, would return to the land and that Cortez was indeed the white god that had been prophesied. On hearing of Cortez's landing, Montezuma sent the Spaniards many valuable gifts, including gold, silver, precious stones, and jewelry. Excited by the gifts, Cortez drove his men relentlessly to overcome the hardships of marching over the mountains to the capital, while fighting hostile Indian tribes along the way. As news reached the emperor of the atrocities committed by the Spaniards, he began to have second thoughts about their divinity. After sending Cortez several large bribes of treasure and asking him not to enter his city, but seeing that Cortez was determined to enter Tenochtitlán, Montezuma reluctantly permitted the Spaniards to enter unmolested.

The Spaniards were astonished at the beauty and high degree of development of the city. They were amazed at the large amounts of treasure decorating the Aztec temples and shrines. But they soon learned that this was only a small part of the treasure stored in the city. Realizing their insatiable greed for wealth, Montezuma had had most of his treasure hidden before the the Spaniards arrived. One dark night soon after reaching the city, Cortez and several of his men broke into a treasure storehouse. One of them later wrote: "I took it for certain that there could not be another such store of wealth in the whole world." Tons of golden idols, ingots and jewelry, much of it tribute exacted from tribes which paid allegiance to the Aztecs, were stacked in piles. There were also thousands of finely wrought pieces made from gold, silver, and precious stones. After resealing the building and returning to their quarters, Cortez and his officers decided that, even at the risk of their lives, they would attempt to get the fantastic treasure they had seen, as well as more which they knew was hidden elsewhere in the city.

Several days later they seized Montezuma and held him prisoner, demanding a huge ransom for his release. The treasurehouse the Spaniards had previously broken into was turned over to them, but Cortez wasn't satisfied and demanded still more, which the Aztecs were reluctant to deliver. Not long afterward, while Cortez was out of the city, some of his soldiers, disobeying his orders to respect the Aztecs, attacked and massacred priests and worshippers at a sacred temple. Incensed over the desecration of their temple, the proud Aztecs rebelled en masse, and Cortez rushed back to the city to find his men fighting against overwhelming odds.

During an attack on the building where Montezuma was being held hostage, the emperor was accidently stoned by one of his own people and died soon after, which made the plight of the Spaniards even more perilous. Forced to flee, they were able to take only a small part of the treasure they had already amassed, and a large part of that was lost as they fought their way out of the city.

After weeks of fierce fighting, Cortez and what remained of his army reached the coast near where they had first landed. Months later, after licking their wounds, training friendly tribes in combat, and being joined by reinforcements from Cuba, Cortez and his men returned to Tenochtitlán and recovered the lost treasure. After a three-month siege, the city fell on August 13, 1521. The city was leveled by the Spaniards in their search for treasure, but not a single piece of it was found.

Under cruel tortures, Cuauhtemoc, the new emperor of the Aztecs, and all of his aides refused to reveal the location of the treasure and were put to death, carrying the secret with them. Hundreds of other Aztecs were also killed. Although the Spaniards did learn that the treasure had been thrown into a lake, they were never able to discover which one. Over the years they used divers and in some cases even drained whole lakes in a vain effort to find the treasure.

In 1954, when skin diving was still in its infancy, Pablo Bush Romero and some of his diving buddies began using their skills for historical and archaeological pursuits. Pablo, who had been fascinated by the legend of Montezuma's treasure since childhood, convinced his friends to help him hunt for it, and over a period of years they made hundreds of dives in various lakes within a large radius of Mexico City. In 1959, when CEDAM was founded by Pablo, he had a larger number of divers to aid him in the search which by now had become something of an obsession with him. Although they did not find the Montezuma treasure, they did recover hundreds of important archaeological artifacts from the lakes.

After systematically exploring and eliminating many of the lakes in which the treasure might be hidden, Pablo resorted to logic. Knowing that Cuauhtemoc had originally come from the town of Izcateoban before being named to succeed Montezuma as emperor, Pablo theorized that he probably would have tried to have the treasure hidden near his native town. Since the treasure was known to have been thrown in a lake, Pablo at first assumed that this was done because the Spaniards were closing in too rapidly. Near the road that once connected Tenochtitlán and Izcateoban were numerous lakes, but all of them had been thoroughly explored without finding any trace of treasure.

Flying over the area between the two ancient cities, Pablo noticed two small lakes in the crater of the Toluca volcano that had not been marked on the maps of the area he had used in his earlier explorations.

At first he disregarded the possibility of the treasure being in the two lakes. At an elevation of 13,828 feet, they are the highest lakes in the world, and Pablo thought it would have been impossible for the Aztecs to carry the treasure to the top of such a height. Soon afterward, however, as a result of research, he changed his mind. He learned that the volcano had been called Xinantecatl by the Aztecs and that it was sacred to them. The larger lake was called the Lake of the Sun and the other, the Lake of the Moon. The Aztecs believed they were the home of their rain god, Tlaloc. Did the Aztecs make offerings to the rain god in these two lakes, as the Mayans did at the Sacred Cenote of Chicen-Itza in Yucatán? Besides preventing their treasure from falling into the hands of the Spaniards, did the Aztecs throw all of it into these lakes as an offering to their rain god?

Upon checking, Pablo learned that some divers had already made dives in both lakes and on almost every occasion, there had been near fatal accidents. After surfacing from their dives, the divers would lose consciousness from anoxia, or lack of oxygen. Little was known about SCUBA diving at high altitudes in those days, and it is a miracle that no lives were lost. Questioning Raul Echeverria, one of the first to dive in the lakes, Pablo was glad to hear that he had found several large pieces of copal, a ceremonial incense used by the Aztecs and Mayans as offerings to their rain god. Pablo knew he was on the right track; the presence of copal showed that the Aztecs had made offerings in the lakes. The discovery of copal convinced Edward Thompson, the American who in 1904 had recovered several million dollars in treasure from the Sacred Cenote of Chicen-Itza, that the legend about the treasure in the Cenote was true.

Before serious search of the two lakes could be made, though, Pablo knew something would have to be done about the hazards of high-altitude diving. For seven months, extensive tests were performed under the supervision of doctors from the Mexican Navy and Dr. Miguel Guzman, one of the early divers in the lakes. A polygraph was taken up to the lakes, and Dr. Guzman, Raul Echeverria, and other CEDAM divers were wired to the polygraph during their dives. From the pulmonary ventilation and cardiographical data obtained from these experimental dives, the doctors were able to determine the cause of the accidents and find a way to prevent them. The surface air at the lakes, because of the high altitude, contains 25 percent less oxygen than at sea level; but underwater, the diver breathes normally, since the compressed air in his tanks contains sufficient oxygen. As a result, the diver surfacing in these lakes goes from an equivalent of sea level to an altitude of almost 14,000 feet in only a few seconds. To overcome this problem, Dr. Guzman and the others recommended that a diver ascend and breathe very slowly upon surfacing. When a diver is severely chilled by the cold water and can't control his breathing rate, however, anoxia cannot be avoided and he must quickly be supplied with pure oxygen on the surface.

Another potential source of trouble at such an altitude is the dreaded bends. Although the maximum depth of the lakes is only 60 feet, the difference in air pressure between the compressed air in the diver's tank and the surface pressure makes a 60-foot dive the equivalent of a 100-foot dive at sea level; decompression stops must be compensated for accordingly.

While the medical tests were going on, Echeverria made an interesting discovery. At a depth of only a few feet, near one edge of the Lake of the Sun, he found the mechanisms of several dozen old pocket watches. On subsequent dives, he and other CEDAM divers discovered more mechanisms, as well as a gold ring and several tin boxes with *Monte de Piedad de Madrid* inscribed on them. Pablo soon discovered their origin. Near the end of the Spanish Civil War, the yacht *Vita,* carrying Spanish Republican officials and a large amount of loot they had taken from safety deposit boxes in Madrid, reached Mexico. Using some of their treasure to obtain Mexican citizenship, they settled near Mexico City. The exact amount of money and treasure they brought was never revealed, but Franco claimed it was in the millions of dollars. As a result of Mexico not returning either the fugitives or the loot, to this day the two countries do not maintain diplomatic relations. Apparently in an attempt to cover up the theft, the safety deposit boxes and watch mechanisms (stripped of their gold cases) were thrown in the lake.

During many dives made by CEDAM members, hundreds of other copal fragments and many wooden and ceramic artifacts were found, including two ceramic heads of Tlaloc. In certain sections of both lakes, the mud is over 15 feet deep, so the divers were able to dig down only a few feet by hand and recover the lighter artifacts of copal, ceramic, and wood. Heavy objects such as gold had settled on the hard bottom

Handing up artifacts found in the Toluca volcano in Mexico—on the left, a piece of copal and on the right, a ceramic mask of a rain god under the mud. To determine whether the treasure was really there and, if so, in which of the two lakes, as well as to pinpoint its location, Pablo decided that the next step was to make a thorough electronic metal-detection survey of the lakes, and he asked me to undertake the job for him. Since I heartily dislike diving in cold water, I would use a metal detector which could be towed and operated from a boat, and thus eliminate the need for diving.

Upon arriving in Mexico City, I learned that the detector, which I had shipped via air freight, had been lost in transit. Realizing that it might take days for it to be found and because I had another expedition scheduled to start in Yucatán in a few days' time, I reasoned that I had no recourse but to use the hand-held underwater metal detector I had brought with me. It would do the same job as the other one, but it would mean diving in the frigid lakes. Consulting with Raul Echeverria, I learned that the best months for diving were July and August when the water was warmer—like 40 or 45 degrees! Since I already had other commitments for those months, I was determined to do the job right away. Raul reluctantly agreed to dive with me and talked two other CEDAM divers into coming along as safety divers.

Pablo was leading another archaeological expedition at the time, so he had made arrangements with Alfonso Romero, the vice-president of Club de Exploraciones, Deportivos, Aquaticas de Mexico, or CEDAM, to provide the necessary logistical support for my survey of the two lakes. Within a few hours of my arrival Alfonso had me over the site in a small plane. The jagged peaks of the extinct volcano, which were covered with snow, towered above the precipitous and barren cliffs that encircled the crater and lakes. There was no sign of vegetation; the entire area looked forbidding. Down in the valley, five miles from the volcano, archaeologists were excavating a newly discovered Aztec site called Tenango del Valle.

The following morning we set off for the lakes in jeeps. A narrow dirt road strewn with fallen boulders led to the crater. The air temperature was a brisk 34 degrees, gusts of wind blew at high velocities from all directions, the shore around the lakes was covered with ice crystals, and the water temperature was 28 degrees, with sections of both lakes covered with surface ice. To make matters worse, I was having great difficulty breathing at that altitude and was tempted to call the dive off. But pride kept me from doing so. My friends suggested that we wait a few hours until we were better acclimatized to the dense air and the sun rose above the surrounding mountain peaks, which would increase the surface temperature and melt the ice on shore. Within an hour, however, everyone was having difficulty breathing and were suffering from severe headaches (which was alleviated somewhat by taking gulps of pure oxygen).

By noon the air temperature had risen somewhat, and we decided to make our first dive in the Lake of the Sun, which had yielded most of the artifacts that had been recovered from both lakes. Right from the start, everything went awry. I discovered that I had left my rubber diving boots and gloves behind and that my rubber suit was torn in several places. Two of the diving regulators failed, even though they had been checked that morning, and the valve on one of the air tanks had a bad leak. While I was adjusting the controls on the metal detector, Raul entered the water and minutes later emerged with a deep cut on his hand. He had been probing in the mud for artifacts but instead had cut his hand on a broken beer bottle. With Raul out of action, our two safety divers, Genaro Hurtado and Oscar Bush, decided to accompany me. Alfonso Romero would follow our bubbles in a small boat in the event any of us surfaced in trouble.

In the water I soon began suffering from the intensely cold water which entered my rubber suit through the torn places. Within five minutes my hands were so numb I could barely grasp the detector. Nearby, Genaro and Oscar, digging in the mud, located several chunks of copal, one of which had been made in the shape of the two volcano peaks. After about 10 minutes I was so cold and breathing was so difficult that I decided to surface. I pushed myself off the muddy bottom; but to my astonishment, I didn't have the strength to kick my way to the surface. In a state of near panic, I began crawling on all fours toward shore which I reached after what seemed like an eternity. Seconds after emerging from the water, I blacked out, and Raul rushed to my aid with the emergency oxygen bottle. I came out of it in a few minutes, but had to continue breathing oxygen for over an hour.

We decided to quit for the day and head home, but our problems weren't over. After descending the mountain, our headaches and breathing difficulties disappeared, but when we had to climb over a 10,000-foot mountain range before reaching Mexico City, Raul blacked out at the wheel of the jeep. If his wife hadn't reacted quickly and grabbed the wheel, we would have been in a serious accident.

The next day I returned to the lakes with the same group, plus an additional 10 divers. This time I was better prepared. Wearing not one but two good rubber suits and equipped with good rubber gloves and boots, I made three hour-long dives that day and three on the following two days. With the divers working in teams of two, alternating between holding the metal detector and rubbing the numb parts of their bodies, we completed the metal detection survey in three days' time and without further serious problems. A doctor was standing by each day, and we used a new system to prevent the divers from being affected by the lack of oxygen when they surfaced. Each time a diver neared the surface, a small bottle of pure oxygen was lowered to him, and he switched from breathing from his SCUBA tanks with compressed air, to the oxygen bottle. On the surface he continued breathing the pure oxygen until the doctor felt he could cope with the rarefied air.

That first day we concentrated on the Lake of the Moon, which was the smaller one. Twice we got good readings on the metal detectors, indicating the presence of metal under the mud, and each time we were able to dig down and locate the sources, because they were buried only a few feet deep. One that we discovered turned out to be a fishing tackle box, and the other was a geologist's pick.

We began our survey of the Lake of the Sun after stringing colored lines across the bottom of the lake in a grid pattern. Our only discoveries during a long cold day on the bottom were several beer cans which were fairly close to the surface of the mud bottom. We were a bit worried, because we had surveyed all of the areas bordering the lake, which, we estimated, was the maximum distance heavy objects could be thrown into the lake from shore. In an attempt to cheer everyone up (and make sure they returned the next day), I said that maybe the Aztecs had boats on the lakes and had dumped the treasure in the middle of the lake.

It was getting dark the next day and most of the divers were already preparing to go home when Raul and I went into the lake to complete the survey. Only an area about the size of a tennis court remained to be surveyed. After only a few minutes, Raul motioned to me, and I swam over. At first I thought the detector had gone on the blink. After testing it, I realized that Raul had found a large mass of metal right in the middle—and deepest part—of the lake. When we surfaced and bearings were taken, two other divers went down with 10-foot-long metal rods but were unable to reach the bottom of the mud deposit. Against the wishes of the doctor, Raul and I—very excited by our discovery—decided to dive again. Using longer metal probes, we soon established that the mud was some 20 feet deep in this area. Without proper excavation equipment, there was little likelihood of finding any of the treasure. We decided to dig a hole by hand, on the off chance that we would find something. At a depth of only two foot in the mud, we started hitting a bonanza: two jade axe heads, four obsidian spear points, and two 10-inch-high figurines of Tlaloc, the rain god. Working frantically, and forgetting about the cold that had numbed our bodies and senses, we soon discovered two more jade axe heads, 11 ceramic figurines of Tlaloc and seven small gold bells. About this time, Raul ran out of air and had to surface. I stayed on the bottom alone, breathing as slowly as possible. Just as I was exhausting my air supply, I saw the glint of gold in the dark water. Quickly I grabbed it and rushed for the surface, grasping a beautiful 10-inch jade figurine of a bird-like object; but the doctor sent me back down with chattering teeth to a depth of 20 feet to begin the 30-minute decompression sequence.

That night we met with Pablo and excitedly planned to go after the treasure the next day, using an airlift to remove the mud. But getting a boat up to the lake that would be large enough to hold the necessary air compressor and other equipment turned out to be next to impossible. Instead, we took up a dozen 55-gallon drums and lumber and built a barge, which took three days. Meanwhile, we had kept our discovery secret—or so we thought. CEDAM had obtained a permit to explore the lake from the Mexican government, but when word of our planned excavation leaked out, the same authorities suddenly announced that the permit did not cover any actual excavation. They told Pablo we would have to apply for an excavation permit and that until it was issued, we could do no more diving in either lake. I waited around for a week, champing at the bit to get back to the treasure on that lake bottom. Finally, when it appeared that the permit wasn't forthcoming in the foreseeable future, I returned to Florida, with the intention of coming back as soon as Pablo and his team had the permit.

Five years have passed, and the permit still has not been issued, nor has Pablo been given an explanation why it hasn't. From several sources

I learned that political intrigue is involved. Some members of CEDAM are apparently in disfavor with a high-ranking government official who has used his power to prevent the permit from being issued. Sooner or later, however, the site will be excavated, and Montezuma's treasure will be recovered.

10 : Panama's Treasures

During the summer of 1954 I made my first visit to Panama. Representing the Marine Corps in the International Spearfishing Tournament, I won four of the six first prizes. I stayed another week after the contest ended and found the beautiful country to be a treasure-hunter's dream. There is more treasure to be found there, both on land and in the water, than any other comparable area of the world. Over the centuries, incredible amounts of treasure were transported across this land bridge which separates two oceans, and a substantial portion of it never reached its destination. It lies waiting to be found. Between 1519 and 1821 the Spaniards shipped more than $5 billion dollars in treasure—gold, silver, precious stones, and pearls—and the forty-niners from California followed in their wake with millions more in gold.

Panama has a rich and fascinating history. In 1501 the Spaniard, Rodrigo de Bastidas, explored the Caribbean side of the isthmus and returned to Spain with exciting tales of having seen Indians wearing valuable ornaments made of gold. The following year, Columbus continued the explorations. In 1510 the Spaniards founded the settlements of Nombre de Dios and Santa Maria de la Antigua, but Santa Maria was destroyed by Indians and abandoned by the Spaniards 14 years later.

In 1513 the explorer, Vasco Núñez de Balboa, crossed the isthmus —the first European in the Western Hemisphere to set eyes on the Pacific—and six years later, the town of Old Panama was founded on the Pacific side of the isthmus. It first served as a base for expeditions engaged in the conquest of South America and later as the terminus for the treasures from Peru which were off-loaded from ships and taken via overland caravans to the Caribbean side. Because the harbor was unusually shallow, as well as being exposed to the open sea, the galleons often had to anchor six miles west of the town, in the lee of three small islands which today are joined to the mainland by a causeway. Several treasure galleons were wrecked near the Perico Islands, and an unknown amount of treasure was lost from the lighters that plied between the ships and the town, often in rough seas.

Overcoming formidable obstacles, the Spaniards built the Camino Real, a paved road 48 miles long, connecting Panama with Nombre de Dios, the Caribbean terminus where the treasures were reloaded on galleons for the transatlantic crossing to Spain. At times it took the mule trains—some numbering over 200 mules, each carrying a 300-pound load—a month to cover this short distance. The trail was rugged, leading up and down steep hills, and the mules, known for their recalcitrance, were sometimes the cause of lost treasure when they stumbled off the road, which in places was only two feet wide and bordered by precipices 500 feet high, falling into impenetrable jungle below. Many mule skinners suffered a similar fate. In 1970 an American treasure hunter discovered a skeleton in a valley off the trail; with it was a rotted leather pouch containing nearly a hundred silver coins. Even greater danger lay in the frequent attacks by the Cimarrones—bands of runaway slaves who attacked the mule trains and made off with a good deal of plunder, most of which they buried in jungle hideouts.

After several decades the Spaniards found a faster and safer way to get treasure across the isthmus. They built another road, known as the Las Cruces Trail, 15 miles long and leading from Old Panama to Las Cruces, a town at the head of the 50-mile-long Chagres River. The treasure was then taken downriver in barges and at the mouth was transferred to larger vessels for the trip down the coast to Nombre de Dios. Over the years many of the barges overturned in the river, particularly at the mouth, and treasure was lost. Frequently, due to floods or drought, the river route was impossible and the treasure had to be transported over the old Camino Real, which was used until late in the last century.

Freebooters from many nations were attracted to the great wealth of gold, silver, emeralds, and other gems, and exotic luxury goods from the Orient being funnelled across the isthmus. Some weren't content with attacking the coastal settlements but went far inland to the mountains, sacking the towns near the gold mines. By the end of the sixteenth century most of the gold-mining operations had been closed down; the Spanish crown couldn't provide protection from the pirates. Each year when the galleons arrived at Nombre de Dios and the treasure from Panama City, a great fair was held, with hundreds of merchants exchanging treasure for trade goods from Spain.

In 1572 Sir Francis Drake attacked the town and saw what he described as "a most wonderous sight." In the cellar of the governor's house Drake's men found a stack of silver bars, each weighing between 35 and 70 pounds, which was 70 feet long, 10 feet wide, and 12 feet high —in all, 360 tons of silver, worth more than a million pounds sterling in those days. Drake's pinnaces were unable to carry such a prodigious amount of silver, but the otherwise frustrated English did manage to carry off several dozen chests of gold and precious stones and leave the town in flames before the Spaniards arrived in force. In 1596 Drake returned but found only a deserted town which he again burned to the ground. The inhabitants had been forewarned, however, and escaped with their valuables. Discouraged and sick with fever, Drake died a few weeks later. His lead coffin was lowered into the sea off the entrance to Porto Bello Bay, near a small island now named for him.

The Spaniards finally faced up to the vulnerability of Nombre de Dios and moved their Caribbean terminus port to Porto Bello, which was easier to defend and therefore safer. Five forts and several batteries were built, and a town of considerable size sprang up. A road connecting it with the Camino Real was also built. In spite of its natural protection and fortifications, Porto Bello was captured by pirates six times and once by the British Navy. The most famous attack took place in 1668 and was led by Henry Morgan who held the town for two weeks before being paid a ransom of 250,000 pieces of eight. The notorious Morgan returned three years later with more than 1,000 men under his command and after a bloody battle captured Fort Lorenzo, which commanded the entrance to the Chagres. Then he crossed the isthmus and laid seige to Old Panama, which had become a town of moderate size, containing more than 2,500 buildings and homes. The buccaneers captured the town after both sides had suffered heavy casualties and seized 195 muleloads of treasure before retreating to the other side of the isthmus. (But Morgan missed the biggest treasure of all—a solid-gold altar in the main cathedral. The Spanish friars had painted it to deceive him and his pirates.) Most of the town was then destroyed by fire. Historians aren't sure whether the Spaniards or the pirates were responsible for the destruction. The Spanish abandoned the site and built New Panama City about six miles to the west. According to numerous historical sources, the Spaniards buried great amounts of treasure before the attack, but subsequently, because of the fire, were unable to relocate much of it.

Today Porto Bello is a sleepy hamlet of some 500 people. Only the moss-covered ruins give a hint of its historical importance. Until four years ago it could be reached only by water, but there is now a road connecting it with the outside world, and the Panamanian government is planning a complete restoration of the site.

During the week I spent in Panama in 1954, I not only found my first piece of gold underwater but, in fact, more treasure than I had ever found anywhere. This was no doubt one of the main things that convinced me to follow a treasure-seeking life. After spending the first day in a library, brushing up on the history of the area, I was ready for bear. I spent the next two days diving around the Perico Islands where the galleons bringing treasure up from Peru and Chile had anchored. Although I was only free-diving with snorkeling gear and picking things up off the surface, my finds were quite impressive: four gold coins dated from the 1780s; more than 200 silver coins dating from 1624 to 1812; a large silver candlestick weighing over 40 pounds; and hundreds of artifacts such as pewter tankards, bottles, cannonballs, and a gold pocket watch from the California gold rush period. The third day was spent using a World War II army mine detector I had borrowed from a U.S. military base near Old Panama City. I doubt if anyone had used a detector there before then. No matter where I searched, I found coins and other objects. By the time the detector's batteries were exhausted and my hands were covered with blisters from digging, I had found a total of 43 gold, 457 silver, and 23 copper coins—not a bad haul for a Marine making $100 a month. Today however, the government prohibits such searches.

I spent the next couple of days diving around Fort Lorenzo at the

Gold and silver artifacts that the author found by using a metal detector around the Spanish colonial settlements and forts of Panama

Pre-Colombian gold artifacts dug up in Panama

mouth of the Chagres River, on the Caribbean side of Panama. It was more remote than the Perico Islands or Old Panama City areas. On the second day of diving around those islands, a crowd of more than a hundred people was waiting on the beach when I came ashore, and by the time I had finished working the ruins of Old Panama City, I had an audience nearly as large.

Fort Lorenzo is American property and is located on the Fort Sherman army base. From my reading in the library, I knew that the Spaniards had lost a lot of treasure in this area. Also, as a result of the California gold rush of 1849, a small town of shacks had sprung up in near the fort. Like the early towns of the American West, the six-gun was the only law, and the men with the fastest draw ran the rough-and-tumble community of saloons, cheap hotels, and bawdy houses. Due to changes in the river's course, the vestiges of this town are now underwater. Snorkeling in depths ranging from only a few feet up to 20 or so, and using my hand to fan away the river mud, I found an impressive amount of artifacts dating from the middle of the sixteenth century to present times, including seven small gold nuggets and a handful of silver coins.

A map I had once seen indicated that on a shallow reef about a quarter of a mile offshore from the river mouth, Henry Morgan had lost his flagship and four others during his attack on Fort Lorenzo in 1671, so I devoted the last day of my stay in Panama to exploring the area. Although I located more than a hundred iron cannon and about 20 anchors, I was unaware that I had found the wrecks I was seeking. In those days I expected to find wooden hulls of shipwrecks. I had no idea what a shipwreck site actually looked like. Finding only cannon and anchors, I foolishly assumed that they had been jettisoned by ships that had run aground on the reef. If I had dug into the coral growth, I might have found many seventeenth-century artifacts.

Eighteen years were to pass before I got back to Panama. At the invitation of the Panama Tourist Board, I spent six exciting weeks there early in 1972. By this time I knew what a shipwreck looked like. My first expedition was to the reef where Morgan's shipwrecks lay. Unfortunately, someone had beat me to it. Two years earlier, a major expedition had been conducted in the area, and the wrecks were salvaged. Even the cannon and anchors were recovered. All I saw now was deep holes in the reef where the salvors had used explosives to excavate—

a reprehensible method of excavation, because so many objects are destroyed. In a small cove east of Fort Lorenzo, however, amateur divers from one of the nearby U.S. military bases had recently found a seventeenth-century shipwreck and had salvaged an undisclosed amount of treasure and artifacts. With several divers from the Panamanian National Guard, I spent several days recovering a large number of interesting artifacts—but not a single piece of treasure.

My next stop was up the coast a ways, to the sixteenth-century seaport of Nombre de Dios where, I knew from documents I had seen in Seville, there were several valuable treasure wrecks. I drew a complete blank there, at least in the sea. For nearly 10 days, the wind blew continuously at over 20 knots, making it impossible to dive in the open roadstead. During this time, I used a metal detector on land and found hundreds of artifacts for the government.

Our next stop was the famous port of Porto Bello. Although the wind was still blowing to beat hell, diving was possible there because the port is protected by high mountains. The government of Panama was planning to resurrect the past by rebuilding many of the town's old ruins à la Williamsburg, Virginia, as a tourist attraction. I was asked to make a feasibility study and try to determine whether there were any shipwrecks in the area that would produce enough historical artifacts to display in a museum the government hoped to build there. Without a magnetometer for the underwater survey, I had to use a thousand-year-old method of locating wrecks: towing a weighted line with grappling hooks attached to it. During the week I spent there, we located 16 old shipwrecks this way, dating from the early part of the seventeenth century to the late nineteenth. After collecting a sampling of artifacts from each one for identification and dating, I gathered other pertinent archaeological data for future use.

On his fourth voyage of exploration in 1502, Columbus founded a settlement at the mouth of the Belem River, located about halfway between Porto Bello and the Costa Rican border, but due to the hostility of the Indians, was forced to abandoned it four months later. Before leaving, however, he had one of his caravels, *Gallega*, scuttled because she was leaking badly. An American living in the Canal Zone told me that three years earlier, while diving for placer gold deposits, he had found an anchor at the mouth of this river. I convinced him to go with me, and within minutes of jumping in that alligator-infested river, I was looking at an anchor dating from the time of Columbus. In the same area we found ship's ballast stones and ceramic shards dating from the same period.

Thrilled by this find, I decided to spend a little more time following in the wake of Columbus. Farther to the west, and close to the Costa Rican border, are the 50 or so islands of the Archipiélago de Bocas del Toro. The main town on Columbus Island is Bocas Town. The island was so named because Columbus spent a month there to careen his ships during the same voyage. I didn't know until I arrived that the site of his encampment had already been found and plundered by natives and tourists. Nevertheless, I did discover a number of artifacts, mainly ceramic shards and animal bones from meals Columbus and his men consumed. Over the centuries, Columbus Island also served as a base for pirates, and several treasures are reported to be buried there. I spent a few days, searching with my metal detector, with negative results.

Perhaps the most fascinating indigenous peoples of Panama are the Cuna Indians who inhabit 30 of the 360 islands in the San Blas archipelago. They have maintained their culture in almost total ignorance of and disinterest in modern civilization. The lovely San Blas Islands are sprinkled over 200 miles of the Caribbean coastline between the Panama Canal and the Columbian border. The land on the islands of the Cuna is communally owned, and they govern themselves in a virtually autonomous society, passionately guarding their property and rights. Until recently few Americans were aware of these islands, and fewer still had been able to visit them. They have been free of developers, prospectors, speculators, and would-be settlers. Only since 1973 or so have the Cuna relented and allowed four carefully controlled small tourist developments to be set up on the islands.

Women's lib will not win any converts among the Cuna—they have a matriarchal society. Women already run the show and control the wealth. The women and girls are striking in their intricately made, brightly colored dresses. They bedeck themselves with as much gold jewelry as they have and sport a rather fetching gold ring in their noses. When she dies, a woman is buried with all her jewelry. . . . Forget about grave-robbing. Most of those who have tried have met with horrible deaths. Finding the *source* of their gold (which they speak of mystically as being "somewhere in the mountains") might be safer.

The same American who had shown me Columbus' anchor told me

that the year before, some amateur American divers had stumbled on a shipwreck in the San Blas Islands. Strewn among cannon and anchors lying on the wreck's ballast pile were hundreds of what appeared to be iron ingots. The divers took several home as souvenirs, and upon cleaning them, discovered that they were 70-pound silver bars! They had relocated the wreck, and though they tried to be secretive when I met them, I got enough information to enable me to search on my own. After several days of diving in those remarkable, crystal-clear waters, I gave up, though. I had too many other things I wanted to do in Panama.

Back in Panama City, I met an Air Force sergeant (who wishes to remain anonymous). Working on weekends over a period of five years, he had located more than $50,000 worth of treasure along the Camino Real and Las Cruces trails. His most notable find was a beautiful gold toothpick shaped like a sword. Engraved on it was the name Roderigo de Rebolledo who was an officer with Pizarro in the conquest of Peru. Shortly before I had arrived, he and a friend had discovered the campsite of a regiment commanded by General U.S. Grant. Grant and his men had been on their way to California but were stranded for a month along the Las Cruces Trail when the mules they had rented mysteriously disappeared. Before other mules could be arranged for, more than 200 of his soldiers had succumbed to disease. The two treasure hunters found hundreds of artifacts, including weapons, bottles, crockery, regimental buttons and buckles, and coins—besides the bones of the soldiers buried there.

My newfound friend spent a week with me exploring both trails. It was no picnic. The narrow trails wend their way over tortuous, steep terrain that abounds with snakes of many types and sizes, including eight-foot bushmasters and even larger boa constrictors. We were also plagued by nasty fire ants, ticks, and a particularly resistant breed of mosquitos. The expedition was well worth it, however, as we discovered quite a lot of treasure and artifacts.

As a result of the building of the Panama Canal, two large, manmade lakes—Gatun and Madden—covered a large section of the Camino Real Trail, and more than 30 towns and settlements could be located, using old maps. During the dry season, the level of the lakes drops and small islands rear out of the water, exposing sections of the trail and settlements. In was in these areas, and by diving near them, that we made our best finds, as the dry sections of both trails has been combed for years by treasure hunters.

Using a helicopter, I made two other important discoveries along the desolate section of coast between the San Blas Islands and the Columbian border: Acla and New Caledonia. Although both sites are mentioned in history books, their exact locations were unknown. Armed with old charts from European archives, showing their locations, I found them, however. Acla was a Spanish settlement from 1515 to 1532 and then was abandoned because of hostile Indians. In 1698 New Caledonia was settled by some 3,500 Scotsmen who were expelled the following year by the Spanish. Due to the limited time in which I had the use of the helicopter, I could spend only an hour at each site, but this was long enough for me to gather sufficient evidence of their identities. Sometime in the near future, I hope to conduct a proper exploration of both sites.

In conversation with a leading scholar in Panama City, I was dismayed to hear him defend the plundering of his country's unique and irreplaceable archeological sites. He argued that, unlike the aborigines of Peru and Mexico, those of Panama did not construct any monumental temples or buildings, so ancient ruins are not further destroyed in the search for relics. He went on to say that the National Museum is already so full of pre-Columbian pieces that the staff refuses to accept donations of more unless they are in some way unique. However, the government now has regulations protecting their precious historical patrimony.

Panama is a beautiful country of varied terrain, but with the exception of a small number of stone statues and rocks covered with petroglyphs, there is little for visitors to see of the pre-Columbian cultures that once thrived there. Most of Panama's archeological past lies buried in tens of thousands of grave sites scattered throughout the country, from the northern mountains bordering on Costa Rica to the southern jungles near Colombia. Only a little work has been done by qualified archaeologists. Most of the notable discoveries have been made by dedicated American amateurs from the Canal Zone. On the fringes of Lake Gatun, these zealous, amateur archaeologists have discovered projectile points dating back to 6500 B.C. and ceramic vessels from 2300 B.C.

My government guide in Panama was a 340-pound archeologist

whose chief qualifications were his uncanny skill in locating grave sites and his relationship with Panama's leader, General Omar Torrijos—his uncle. For years Fernando had worked as a successful *guaquero,* or gravedigger, until his uncle became chief of state. He had made a tidy fortune and had found, among other things, two solid-gold figurines of a king and queen eight inches high, which brought him $50,000 from a New York collector. He was assigned to take me on a tour.

First stop was the small town of El Real in Darien Province where, Fernando claimed, every grave held magnificent gold jewelry and ornaments. Our visit there, however, was brief. Upon arriving, we learned that the day before, a team of four surveyors had been massacred by Choco Indians, and the local police refuse to allow us to go into the jungle.

Returning to Panama City, we heard that, while plowing up a field for pineapples near Puerto Armuelles on the Pacific coast, a farmer had turned up more than 800 small, gold figurines of animals, birds, and insects buried only a few inches deep in the soil. I could see that Fernando had gold fever. We drove at breakneck speed to the site, reducing the normal eight-hour journey to less than five—only to find that we were too late. The field was swarming with some 250 *guaqueros* and about 30 American tourists. Fernando, sure that there would be little left for us to discover, pressed on to the town of David, capital of Chiriqui Province and the center of *guaquero* activity.

The next morning, after providing ourselves with the tools of the trade—pick, shovel, trowel, machete, rope, paint brushes, snakebite kit, and an ample supply of insect repellent—we headed for a high hill overlooking a nearby river. Fernando wielded the most important tool of all: a five-foot-long metal rod with a wooden handle called a "chuzo." He explained that most ancient graves were located on high terrain, near a river and with a good view of the setting sun. At the site we were confronted by a number of recently dug holes, but Fernando was undeterred. He quickly set to work with his chuzo. Most of the graves were only four or five feet deep, covered by flat stones usually found about a foot beneath the surface. After locating a small area of buried stones, the *guaquero* pushes his chuzo into the soil at a 45-degree angle around the perimeter of the stones, to determine whether the soil is compact or loose. If it is loose, a burial is usually found.

In less than an hour Fernando had covered an area about the size of a football field and reported finding nearly 30 graves. We spent the next six days excavating 11 of them—no easy task, with the temperature hovering above a very humid 80 degrees most of the time. But the back-breaking labor paid off handsomely. We found more than 50 ceramic vessels and figurines, 22 stone figurines, a stone metate (for grinding corn), and a large number of axe heads and projectile points —all more than a thousand years old. Because of the damp soil, we found no bones, but Fernando said he had found many skeletons in other regions. Once he found a skull with the brain intact, still covered with hair.

Unhappy that he hadn't found any gold, Fernando suggested that we head for the mountain resort town of Boquete, in the shadow of El Volcán, an extinct, 11,000-foot volcano. There he was sure we would find gold relics. In the local cantina we heard many rumors of gold being found, but Fernando attributed them to local *guaqueros* who were merely spreading false leads to keep the competition away from their good areas. Before sunrise the next morning, he and I were hiding on the outskirts of town near a trail leading up to El Volcán. Soon four men with picks and shovels passed us, and we followed them at a discreet distance until they arrived at a place where many holes had recently been dug, and set to work. When we made our presence known, one of the *guaqueros* pulled a pistol. Were it not for the fact that Fernando convinced them that General Torrijos was his uncle, no doubt we would have been buried alongside the pre-Columbians. After heated negotiations, the men reluctantly agreed to let us dig in the area —with the stipulation that we give them half of what we found and not tell anyone about the location. In less than two hours I had unearthed a magnificent gold figurine resembling a jaguar. By the end of the day, the six of us had found 28 gold figurines and 60 ceramic vessels, which we turned over to the government authorities in Panama City for display in the museum.

While descending El Volcán, one of the *guaqueros* told us of an enormous cavern which, he insisted, was a manmade tunnel leading to a room containing great treasure. In town that evening, I learned more about it. It was generally believed to be an unlucky place. Many had gone in after the treasure, but none had come out alive. My hands were covered with painful blisters after more than a week of digging, so I suggested to Fernando that we explore the cavern the next day.

The cavern was close to the nearby village of Potrerillo. We were told it would be only a 15-minute walk to it, but it turned out to be a four-hour trek that involved fording three rivers. The entrance to the cavern was impressive. There was a small stream running into it and numberless bats hanging amid dripping stalactites. As our eyes became accustomed to the gloom, we saw that we weren't alone: a 10-foot boa constrictor was napping. In the course of chasing it away by throwing rocks, Fernando hit a hornets' nest, and we were stung unmercifully. He announced that it was a bad omen and refused to explore the cavern with me.

I pressed on. The massive entrance quickly dwindled to a passage about six feet high and five feet wide. Wading in the chill waters of the spring-fed stream, I walked for nearly an hour, when suddenly the passage became so small that I had to crawl in order to continue. After crawling 30 feet or so, I was able once again to stand and make good time. About 10 minutes later I noticed that the stream was rapidly rising, due to a torrential downpour outside which I was unaware of at the time. I gave up further penetration and started back for the entrance as fast as I could go. By the time I reached the section where I had crawled earlier, the water was three feet deep—right up to the roof—which meant I would have to swim underwater to get through. After reluctantly abandoning my camera equipment, flashlight, and boots, I hyperventilated for a few minutes and then dived underwater, battling my way against the strong current, clawing along the bottom until I finally emerged on higher ground. It took me four more hours of alternately wading and swimming in the stream to reach the entrance. When I was back outside, I found that Fernando had left; he had returned to the town, convinced that I wouldn't come out alive.

Jenifer, my new wife, who had been visiting friends in Panama City, joined me in Boquete the next day. By then I had had my fill of digging and spelunking, and we decided to do something I was much better qualified for—diving for relics. We had heard stories about the lake in the crater of El Volcán being sacred to the pre-Columbians, similar to lakes I had explored in Mexico and Guatemala, and we wanted to make a brief survey of the crater before heading home. Unable to obtain SCUBA equipment or the rubber suits essential in the freezing waters of the mountain lake, however, we were restricted to exploring a shal-

Jenifer Marx with pre-Colombian human skull and ceramic figurine found in a lake in Panama

low section with snorkels. Still, this brief foray confirmed my belief that the lake contains a wealth of artifacts, for we found several ceramic figurines and vessels and a human skull.

As a result of these six treasure-filled weeks in Panama, I decided to return and spend several years working the area; so I applied to the government for permission. After a wait of over three years, I finally got permission to search for and excavate shipwrecks for a period of 10 years on both sides of the isthmus. As soon as I have finished writing this book, I'll be heading for Panama.

11: Expedition Holy Book

As preposterous as it may sound, there are still people around who believe that Queen Victoria of England is alive and reigning. During an expedition in 1971 to the jungles of Quintana Roo, a federal territory located on the eastern part of the Yucatán peninsula, writer Milt Machlin and I met Mayan Indians in remote villages who not only believe the old queen is still alive but that she will eventually help them to secede from Mexico and become a part of Great Britain.

Although the rest of Mexico was conquered fairly rapidly by the Spaniards, Yucatán wasn't defeated until 1546 and then only after 19 years of brutal conflict. During the next 300 years there were several minor revolts in Yucatán which were quickly supressed. Catholicism was forced on the Indians by the Spanish missionaries, but a large percentage of the indigenous population clung to their ancient pagan religion. Even today, many Indians still practice a synthesis of the two religions. As was the practice in the places conquered by the Spaniards, the Mayan Indians were treated little better than animals by their white masters and *mestizo* cohorts. After Mexico gained its independence from Spain in 1821, the condition of the Indians worsened. Exorbitant taxes were imposed by the civil and church authorities, and many priests charged so much for administering the sacraments of baptism and marriage that the Indians were kept destitute.

After three centuries of white domination, the Indians revolted in 1847, and the brutal, little-known Caste War began. During the early years of the war, it seemed that the non-Indians would be annihilated or at least driven from the peninsula. The Mexican government sent in large numbers of troops, and even American mercenaries were used. Then the Indians resorted to guerrilla warfare. The vast amount of plunder they had obtained from the towns they captured bought guns and supplies from the English in nearby British Honduras.

During the first eight years of the war, more than 300,000 lives were lost on both sides. The Mexicans were in control of the northwest section of the peninsula around Merida, but the rest of the peninsula was in the hands of the rebel Indians. Realizing that they weren't making any headway, fighting an offensive war against the Indians, the Mexicans went on the defensive. Throughout the remainder of the century, the Indians continued making raids against the settlements held by the Mexicans, usually for alcohol, food, and prisoners (who lived out the rest of their lives as slaves in Indian villages).

Several years after the war began, a band of Indian warriors were being pursued by a superior force of Mexican soldiers. Taking refuge one night in a cave, they discovered a large crudely made wooden cross. Their leader, who was a good ventriloquist, impersonated "God's voice," and his men believed that God was speaking to them through the cross. The voice convinced them to stop their flight and turn and attack. The next morning they ambushed the Mexican soldiers and massacred them.

This was the foundation of the Speaking Cross cult which became an element of their syncretic religion. Soon after this, a town named Chan Santa Cruz was founded near the cave. It became the religious and military center of the rebel Indians. A massive stone church was constructed, which still stands today, and the cross was placed over the altar. Beneath the altar, there was a hidden chamber with excellent acoustics. During religious services, a priest impersonated "God's voice." The entire war effort was directed through the voice of the Speaking Cross.

The church was lavishly decorated with statues and other religious items which the Indians had stripped from churches and cathedrals on the peninsula. Many of their leaders became the priests of the new cult, wearing sumptuous religious vestments also obtained in their raids. They developed their own society and maintained a more or less independent nation. A strong trade in chicle and mahogany was maintained with British Honduras, and repeated, abortive attempts were made to have the area they controlled annexed to British Honduras. At the time that the Mexicans discontinued their offensive war, there were more than 100,000 Indians living in the 20,000-square-mile area, but by 1900 repeated epidemics of smallpox, cholera, and whooping cough decimated their numbers to less than 10,000.

The Mexican government, which had been biding its time for half a century, decided to go on the offensive again and obliterate the Indian stronghold, and an army under the command of General Bravo was sent to accomplish this. After winning a series of minor skirmishes with the Indians, the army entered and took possession of Chan Santa Cruz on May 5, 1901, without any resistance. The population had already fled. Mexican soldiers were then dispatched throughout the captured territory—then called Quintana Roo—and hundreds of the Indians were slaughtered. Even today the Mexicans are so violently hated by the Indians, that it is suicide for a Mexican to enter many of the remote jungle villages.

Some of the survivors of the war with General Bravo are still living. They and their descendants number about 5,000. They shun all contact with the outside world, especially with Mexicans. Before escaping from Chan Santa Cruz, they stripped their church of all religious items, including the Speaking Cross. Fearing that the Mexicans would discover and destroy any new religious center they might create, the Indians decided to build three separate centers, on the premise that at least one would survive. The three places selected were Champon, Chancah, and Tixcacal Guardia. Their locations were kept so secret that it was not until a few years ago that their existence became known to outsiders. A church was built at each place. The Speaking Cross was converted into three smaller crosses, one for each church, and the statues and other religious items rescued from their church in Chan Santa Cruz were divided up among them.

The old religion is still practiced by some five to eight thousand faithful. During times of religious festivals, some Indians come from as far as a hundred miles away to attend ceremonies at each of the villages. Men from the various villages in the territory are sent for a week at a time to stand around-the-clock guard duty at the churches.

Very few outsiders have ever been in any of the three villages, and none has been permitted to even approach their churches. A few American Maryknoll missionaries have visited the villages, but they made little progress in trying to convert the Indians to Catholicism.

Quite by accident, I was one of the first outsiders to enter one of the villages. In 1958, while living on Cozumel Island, I was alone on a week-long hunting and exploring trip in the Quintana Roo jungle, and as I had done before, got lost. Sighting smoke from a tree top, I made my way into the settlement of Champon, nearly crazed with thirst. I was relieved of my rifle and pistol by a welcoming committee of six armed Indians and tied to a tree. I attempted to explain in Spanish that I was lost, but no one understood me. They spoke only Mayan.

Soon afterward, I was approached by a very old, distinguished-looking man. He ordered me untied and took me to his thatched hut where he gave me food and water. Speaking fluent Spanish, he told me that he was the chief of a large number of Indians and that I had entered one of their important religious centers where no outsiders had ever been permitted. He said that the high priest of the church wanted me killed but that he had interceded in my behalf. The chief said he was called "Tatich" by his subjects. But his real name was Juan Baptista Vega. He had been born on Cozumel Island in 1888. In 1897 he went on a boat trip with his father and two other men, one of whom was a Spaniard, to search for a buried treasure on the coast of Quintana Roo. Shortly after landing on the coast near the ruins of Tulum, the party was attacked by Indians and the three adults were hacked to pieces with machetes. His life was spared because of his youth and because the Indians discovered he could read and write (making him an asset in questioning prisoners). Within a few years he was named secretary to Florentino Quituk, who was the "Tatich" of the Indians. After the deaths of Quituk and several of his successors, Vega became "Tatich" in 1955.

We talked for several hours, and I learned a great deal about his life and the people he led. What really aroused my interest was the mention of two "holy books" which he said were kept in the church there. The oldest book was written shortly after the Conquest. It was made from tree bark coated with chalk. Half of the pages consisted of Mayan hieroglyphics and the other half of Maya written in Latin characters, which he said was very difficult to read because much of the writing was faded and the language hard to understand. The second book he called "The Book of God." It was written in a language resembling modern

Maya and dealt with religion and prophecies. During the two masses said each day in his church, he read parts of the book to the congregation—claiming that he was the only one capable of reading in the village.

After our talk he recommended that I leave the village, because the high priest was very unhappy about my presence, and the Tatich feared for my life. Giving me food and water, he had two armed guards escort me. They stayed with me for the three days it took to reach the coast where my boat was anchored.

During the Conquest the Spaniards destroyed nearly all of the ancient Maya books. Three of these codices, manuscript books in hieroglyphics, have survived. One is in Madrid, one in Paris, and the third Moscow. With the exception of the hieroglyphics denoting some of the ancient Gods, dates, and numerals, none of the codices has been deciphered.

There also exists another type of old books, called *Chilam Balam,* but these postdate the Conquest and are written in Maya with Latin characters. They contain various segments of the history of the ancient Maya of Yucatán, which were preserved over the years by oral tradition and were compiled during the second half of the fifteenth century by literate Indians, possibly at the instigation of Spanish scholars. Both of the books in the church at Champon would be of great historical and anthropological interest, as they are probably *Chilam Balams,* but the one with both Latin characters and hieroglyphics might be of immense importance in deciphering the ancient hieroglyphics of the Maya, which not only exist in the three codices but are on thousands of other archeological artifacts such as stela, wall frescoes, ceramic objects, and various semiprecious stones.

I mentioned my discovery to several archeologists but was unable to convince them to follow up on attempting to see and photograph these books. Some of the Maryknoll missionaries showed more interest than did the archeologists. In 1960 Father Bernard Nagle went to Champon but failed to accomplish any more than I had—other than discovering that the only outsiders welcome there must be of British nationality. He passed this information on to Pablo Bush Romero, who decided to send an expedition into Champon to find out whether they would have any better luck in seeing the books. Under the auspices of CEDAM, an archeological group run by Romero, several Americans made the rough trip to Champon, taking a picture of Queen Victoria with them for the villagers. They convinced Vega to let them see the books, but when they approached the church, they were stopped by the high priest and armed guards who threatened to shoot them. The Americans made several major mistakes which Milt and I later discovered. Otherwise, they might have gotten to see the books. Coming to the village with a large group, naturally they frightened the villagers who weren't accustomed to seeing outsiders. Identifying themselves as Americans instead of British was another mistake.

The Americans found Vega dying from a stomach hernia and a tumor in his mouth. Upon learning of this, Romero decided to try to get medical help for him and quickly arranged for a helicopter to airlift Vega to civilization and a hospital. It took a great deal of persuasion to convince the old man to leave his people and village, but he finally agreed. He was treated in a hospital in Mexico City and returned, cured, to his village where he died in 1969.

For several years I had been contemplating making another attempt to see the ancient books in Champon, but everyone I talked to about it thought I was nuts and would probably end up getting killed. I mentioned my plan to Milt, who is a man that loves to tackle the impossible. He jumped at the idea and offered to go with me. Our goal was not only to see the old books but to visit all three religious centers, get into each church if possible, attend their religious ceremonies, and come out alive with a photographic record of everything we saw.

Thoroughly researching every aspect of our planned expedition, we waited six months for the end of the rainy season. Arriving in Mérida, Yucatán, we were met by Pablo Romero who spent several days filling us in on everything about the area that he had learned from the Americans he had sent into Champon in 1962. We also obtained valuable information from the Maryknoll missionaries who knew the area. One of them, Father Walter Winrich, had recently been to Champon. He reported that our chance of seeing the books now was even less than when Vega had been alive. The high priest totally controlled the villagers; his orders were to shoot anyone even approaching the church. Father Winrich suggested that we forget about Champon and visit Chancah and Tixcacal instead, where we might receive a better reception. He further suggested that we take gifts such as small bells, mirrors, combs, and brightly colored cloth. (The gifts were eagerly received in each of the villages we visited.) We received another valuable piece of advice from Dr. Victor Segovia, the government archaeologist in charge of the Yucatán peninsula. His suggestion was to take a Polaroid camera and plenty of film to help win the favor of the Indians.

Our plan entailed going into each place with only one guide who could speak both Maya and Spanish fluently, carrying no firearms, and posing as Englishmen. Milt had gotten an assignment from an English newspaper to cover our expedition for them, so we figured it would not be amiss if we wore small British flags on our jungle jackets.

We made Carrillo Puerto (the new name for Chan Santa Cruz) our base of operations, where we were fortunate in obtaining the services of an excellent guide and translator named Julian Xix (pronounced *Shish*). Julian was the sexton of the Catholic Church in Carrillo Puerto and was widely known and respected throughout the territory. Several people told us that if he hadn't taken up with the Catholic missionaries, he might have been the person to succeed Vega as the Tatich of the Maya. He had been to all three of the Mayan religious centers but not inside the churches.

Our first objective was Chancah, which was about 20 miles from our base. The night before we started out, the governor's representative in Carrillo Puerto came to us and begged us to forget about the expedition and go home. It would save him a lot of worry and us, our lives.

The following morning after a breakfast of cold tortillas and beans washed down with warm Pepsi-Cola, we left before sunrise, reaching Chancah just as the sun appeared over the high trees surrounding the village. We had explained in detail to Julian that we must let the people know we meant no harm, that we merely wished to photograph the holy books. Since many unsophisticated peoples are afraid that the camera will steal their soul, we knew it would be difficult to get permission to photograph the books. But Julian, we quickly discovered, was a born diplomat.

The village consisted of 36 thatched huts clustered around the church, which was the focus of community life. The church was about 120 feet long and 55 feet wide, with stucco walls and a thatched roof. Adjacent to it was the guard shack with three armed guards on duty. Julian took us directly to the guard shack. He knew one of the guards and, without our understanding what he was saying, convinced them that we were ambassadors sent by the Queen of England and that the queen was eager for news about their church. The guards decided to unlock the church and let us in to see and photograph it. But just as one of them was unlocking the massive church door, an old woman with bright blue eyes and wearing several gold necklaces, one of which contained two large rubies, ran up and pushed the guard aside and started screaming at him. She was the wife of the high priest and would not allow anyone to enter the church without her husband's permission. She said her husband was away working in a corn field and that we would have to await his return.

We had heard that a few miles away there was a lake, and decided to go there and skin dive, rather than sit around in the village all day waiting for the high priest. Several of the village men acted as guides, including the son of the priest. After spending several hours exploring the lake and discovering the remains of an ancient Mayan temple that had fallen into it, we came out to find Julian very excited. While we were diving, it seems, the Indians had told him that vicious alligators as large as 18 feet long had recently been captured in the lake. During our dive we *had* run into several baby gators, and I was damn glad we hadn't met any of their parents.

We hiked back to the village. Remembering that this was the day the Apollo 14 astronauts were landing on the moon, I told Julian to mention this fact to the high priest's son. He suddenly became enraged and said that surely I was trying to make a fool out of him in trying to tell him such a lie. Neither he, nor for that matter, any of the other villagers, had heard of the flights to the moon.

Back in the village, we found the people very suspicious of us. Julian soon discovered that they suspected us of being spies of the Mexican government. To break the ice, he went into great detail about our being representatives of the English queen, and we began passing out our gifts. They were afraid of our cameras, and it was difficult getting the first Polaroid picture; but after it was taken and shown to the people, everyone wanted one of his own. Milt went through several rolls of film. On the last roll, he encountered problems. The emulsion on the film had been affected by the intense heat of the jungle. He used up all but the last photograph on the roll. All were duds, so he stopped, saving the last one for an emergency.

Late in the afternoon the high priest returned after a long debate. He finally agreed to let us inside of the church, providing that we took a

Polaroid photograph of him and his wife. Milt explained through Julian that we only had one photograph left and that it might not work. The priest was adamant, saying that if the photograph did not come out well, it must be a sign from God that we should not be permitted inside the church. By a miracle (or just plain fool's luck), the photograph came out, and for the first time we saw his face break into a broad smile. We then gave him the small bells and candles we had brought and said we wanted him to officiate at a mass for the Queen of England. He agreed and we headed for the church.

Passing the guard shack, we were halted by a command from an old man inside. He was introduced as the chief of the village. He said he was 107 years old and had fought in the Caste War. Julian spent another hour convincing him of our good intentions. The hardest part was making him believe that Queen Victoria had died in 1901 and that a new queen ruled Great Britain. He told us of many injustices inflicted on his people by the Mexicans and begged us to convince the new queen to send his people arms so they could wage war against the Mexicans and become an independent nation or a part of Great Britain. We heard this same request in the other villages when we visited them. Finally he said we could have our mass for the queen if we promised to send him a photograph of the Queen Elizabeth and tell her everything he had told us.

Our candles were lit. We knelt for the mass in front of a large stage with a closed drape on it. When the drape was opened, we could scarcely believe our eyes. There were 28 statues of various saints, ranging from six to ten feet high. All were between 200 and 400 years old, and many were ornamented with elaborate gold crowns and other gold and gem-set jewelry of great beauty. Several of the saints wore no crowns. In their place they sported modern Panama hats. In the center of the stage was a wooden cross about 20 feet high and around the outside of the stage were about 30 small wooden crosses, all nearly identical, partially covered with brightly colored cloth. (Later we were told that one of them was the one made from the original Speaking Cross and that no one except the high priest really knew which was the real one.) There were also seven tabernacles, several of which were richly ornamented with gold leaf. Scattered about between the statues were many time-worn, but still gorgeous, church vestments of silk and brocade. It was like being in a church museum, like stepping back into history. These items had been taken from various churches during the Caste War.

The mass lasted about half an hour, by which time our knees were really aching. It didn't even remotely resemble a Catholic mass. The priest and several of his assistants prayed continually in Mayan and occasionally sang a few lines in high-pitched voices.

They refused to permit us to photograph the interior of the church, for fear that the saints would punish them. After the mass was over we saw that at the rear of the church there were three old bronze church bells, one dating from 1578, as well as a large drum they had captured from the Mexican Army.

Soon after we left the church, we saw many of the men carrying buckets of water into the church and asked what they were doing. We were told that the high priest was conducting a purification ceremony in the church. We were the first outsiders ever to enter the church, and he didn't want to be punished by God or the saints.

After resting for a day, we decided to tackle Tixcacal Guardia. Julian suggested that we go to the town of Senor first and ask an old man there, who had much influence with the high priest in Tixcacal, to go there with us. The old man in Senor turned out to be a 97-year-old Chinese who had been captured as a boy by the rebel Indians while working with some Englishmen who were selling guns to the Indians. He was one of the most skilled *curanderos,* or healers, in the area and was widely respected. As soon as he saw the British flag on my shirt, he came up to me, pointing at the flag and pulling my hair. He called us "Englishmen" and agreed to go with us.

Tixcacal Guardia was similar to Chancah. As soon as we entered the place, Julian went to work, telling the people that the queen had sent us and that we had come in peace. This information was quickly relayed to the high priest who sent word that we must wait for a formal escort into the village, as befitted representatives of the queen. After about half an hour the high priest and two other priests, as well as the captain of the guard, appeared with seven armed guards. The high priest was one of the grimmest-looking men I had ever seen. We weren't sure just what kind of reception awaited us. After the long speeches, which were demanded by protocol, we were given oral messages for the Queen of England. We then gave the high priest three small bells. He took them in his hand, testing each one. Then, satisfied with their tone, he broke out into a friendly grin and passed them on to the other two priests who went through the same ritual. The high priest apologized for not giving us a proper salute with firearms; his people, he said, might soon have to make war with the Mexicans, and they would need every bullet they had.

Then we were marched to the church between the guards. We stopped at the door to remove our shoes, which was the custom at all of their churches. The church was smaller than the one at Chancah. At the rear were three old bronze bells and two drums. Each of us gave 13 candles for the mass (a lucky number to these people). We knelt before a large table of burning candles placed in front of a small altar. The inside of the church wasn't as richly decorated as the one at Chancah, but the mass was the same, although twice as long. These men permitted us to take all the pictures we wished, even during the mass.

After the mass we asked if they had any ancient books. To our astonishment, they said they did and that they would show it to us. The high priest opened the door of the only tabernacle on the altar and took out the book, which was wrapped in a yellow cloth. He placed it on a table that was covered with an old religious vestment and gave us permission to inspect and photograph it. The book, written in 1848, was copied from a much older document which Julian had difficulty reading, since it was in archaic Maya. However, he was able to determine that it pertained to religious matters and predictions about the future of the people.

The high priest invited us to a good lunch of boiled chicken, tortillas, and hot peppers. Then we headed back to Carrillo Puerto, after expressing thanks for the hospitality we had been shown.

We next went to Champon, the third religious center. Originally we had expected a two- or three-day walk to the village, but recently a road had been cut through the jungle, which passed fairly close to the village. The road-builders had originally planned the road to cut right through the village, but the high priest and other leaders, quite naturally, refused to let them. When they persisted in building the road through Champon, several engineers who were surveying the terrain were fired on by villagers from Champon, and the route was changed. The 14-kilometer hike over rugged rocky terrain took about four hours. We saw plenty of interesting animals—snakes, deer, armadillos, and wild boar—but luckily no jaguar, which was just as well, since we only carried machetes. I had made a little better time than Milt and Julian, and when I was about a kilometer from the village, I was stopped by four armed guards who escorted me into the village. Fortunately, I was unarmed, as I later learned that they had orders to shoot any armed person approaching the village.

Milt and Julian soon arrived and we gave our usual speech, passed out the gifts, and took Polaroid pictures. Several of the older villagers remembered me, mentioning the fact that I was now quite a bit heavier. The same high priest I had crossed swords with years before was still there, but after hearing that we had come from the Queen of England, he was friendly. He explained about his people shooting at the road surveyors saying that this had probably precipitated a war between his people and the Mexican government. A week earlier, the government had sent word that every firearm in the Indian villages must be turned in to army or police officials no later than the very day we were there, that if this was not done, the army would be sent in and take them by force if necessary. He explained that their firearms were an essential part of their life. Not only were they used to guard their church, but also to acquire wild game and fowl and protect themselves against wild animals such as jaguars which were plentiful in the area. Milt and I quickly realized that this was no place for us to be if the army arrived. We might be shot as spies or foreign agitators, since we were wearing the British flag and posing as ambassadors from the queen. We had originally planned to spend the night there but decided instead to get out before dark.

The church was encircled by a barricade about six feet high, made of rocks. The high priest said that they would fight to the death before letting any Mexican soldiers inside the holy building. Not surprisingly, the interior of the church was almost an exact duplicate of the one at Tixcacal Guardia. In the rear there were the drums and bronze church bells, but in addition there were two old bugles, a violin, and a small iron cannon with part of its muzzle missing.

Although the mass was supposed to be offered in honor of the queen, it must also have been to ask God for victory against the Mexican Army, because it lasted about two hours, and every male in the village —about 50 men and boys—took part. (Women, it seems, are never permitted in the churches.) This mass differed somewhat from the other two we had witnessed, in that there was a great deal of bell ringing, wailing, and singing. Again, we were permitted to photograph anything we wished.

At the end of the mass we inquired about the two old books. At first they claimed that none existed but then said that they wanted to have a discussion in private. Waiting outside of the church, we could hear plenty of arguing going on inside. After about an hour we were summoned inside again and the high priest said that we could see the books —providing that we have the queen first send them two cases of rifles and shotguns. We argued that this wasn't possible because England and Mexico were at peace and we had to remain neutral. The high priest then became so agitated, that, to calm him down and before our welcome was withdrawn, we agreed to go to the queen and request the weapons and bring them to the village as soon as possible.

There were two trails from Champon back to the road. We decided to split up, so that if we met soldiers, we wouldn't all be taken. Milt and Julian took one trail and I took off alone on the other. On the way, I almost stepped on a four-foot rattlesnake. Startled, I fell, and my left foot got caught in some rocks. I ended up flat on my back, unable to move. I can't remember ever being so scared. I remained motionless, scarcely breathing, as the snake crawled across my knees, hissing, flicking its tongue, and rattling its tail. It's a miracle it didn't strike. Despite the fact that I had twisted my ankle and was in pain, I made the rest of the hike out in record time. Milt and Julian had a rough time getting out themselves. In most places the trail was overgrown and they got lost several times. Milt's boots were full of blood from various blisters that had burst.

As soon as we reached Carrillo Puerto we rushed to see the two missionaries and tell them about the impending war and asked if they could do anything to stop it and help the Indians. That night they convinced the army commander not to move until they had talked to the governor the next day down in Chetumal. The governor was sympathetic and ordered the army to forget about the shooting incident and let the Indians keep their weapons. I like to think we were instrumental in preventing bloodshed among the Indians, who only wanted to be left in peace.

From several sources we had heard that a man in the village of Yaxley had some ancient documents and maps written on animal skin and decided that they would be worth seeing. Milt was barely able to walk because of his swollen feet and blisters, so Julian and I went.

Reaching Yaxley after a four-hour hike, we discovered that the man we had come to see was at his corn patch several hours' walk away. The village was keeping watch over a 10-year-old girl who had been bitten by a fer-de-lance snake and was dying. So Julian and I took off after the man who, the villagers said, had the documents and maps we hoped to see. At the corn patch his wife told us that her husband was somewhere deeper in the jungle, collecting chicle. We scoured the area and finally had to call it quits because of darkness and trek out to the road. By the time we reached our car, we had covered over 30 miles and had been walking for over 11 hours.

By this time we had already accomplished a great deal more than we had hoped for, and urgent commitments back in the States dictated our return to the rat race. We planned a return trip and felt certain that next time we would get to photograph the two ancient books at Champon.

Milt and I were to deeply regret publicizing the existence of the two books at Champon, because someone else, not content with photographing them, somehow got one of the manuscripts. Three months after returning to the United States, just as we were making plans to return to Yucatán, an 11-page fragment of a Mayan code turned up in an exhibition in New York City, causing a lot of excitement among scholars. This segment of the code dealt with the religious and astrological philosophy of the Mayan culture. Secrecy surrounded the manuscript. The *New York Times* article said that those in charge of the exhibition "declined any comment on the name of the owner, his nationality, or even the exact year or location of the discovery." Fearing the worst, I caught the first plane for Mérida, Yucatán—a move that almost put me in jail. A friend who met me at the airport warned me that the Mexican authorities believed that Milt and I had found the codex, smuggled it out of the country, and sold it for two million dollars.

I rented a car and rushed to Carrillo Puerto. There I contacted Julian and found that matters were even worse than I had thought. Not only were the Mexican authorities after me, but the Mayans of the three religious centers, as well. About a month after we left, someone had gotten into the church and stolen both books undetected. Unfortunately, but not surprisingly, the Indians thought Milt and I were behind the theft. Heeding Julian's advice, I left town, but very angry at whoever had robbed the Indians of the thing most sacred to them and sad that I couldn't tell the villagers that we did not commit the theft.

The identity of the culprit or culprits has never been discovered, but Milt and I were eventually cleared of any involvement by the Mexican authorities. Months of investigation yielded only the information that the code had been cut up in many parts and that the 11-page fragment that ended up in New York had been purchased by a rich Texan for two million dollars.

12: *Discovery of the Richest Wreck in the World*

On the morning of February 13, 1654 the Consejo de las Indias held a special meeting in Madrid at the order of King Philip IV. The night before, news from England had reached the royal court that Oliver Cromwell, the Lord Protector of England, had ordered a large fleet of ships readied for a voyage to the West Indies. Although England was then officially at peace with Spain, the members of the Consejo realized that such a fleet could be sent out only to cause Spain serious harm, either to attack and capture one or more of the Spanish colonies or to make an attempt on the returning treasure galleons sailing later that year. To prevent the latter, the Consejo decided that an armada should be sent as quickly as possible to the Indies to bring the treasure back to Spain.

As soon as officials in Seville received orders to dispatch the armada, preparations got under way, and the ports of Cádiz and Sanlucar de Barrameda became scenes of frenzied activity. Finally, on May 16, 1654, the Real Armada de la Carrera de las Indias—consisting of eight large galleons, four merchant ships, and two smaller vessels under the command of Captain General the Marques de Montealegre—set sail from Cádiz for the Indies with orders from the king to pick up the treasure and return immediately to Spain before the English reached the West Indies.

After an uneventful crossing the armada reached Cartagena de las Indias on August 22, and word was immediately sent overland to the viceroy of Peru to have the vast treasure of gold, gems, and silver shipped to Panama. On October 18, 1654, the Armadilla de Mar Del Sur, consisting of two galleons—*Capitana* and *Almiranta*—sailed from the port of Callao groaning under the weight of the more than 10 million pesos in treasure stowed in their holds. During the night of October 26-27 the two ships suddenly found themselves in treacherous shallow water off the coast of Guayaquil, Ecuador. After hitting some rocks several times, *Almiranta* escaped and made it to Panama. But *Capitana* wrecked on Chanduy Reef and was lost. Meanwhile, the Real Armada of the Marques de Montealegre was anxiously waiting in Cartagena for news of the treasure's arrival.

The president of Panama dispatched salvage vessels and trained divers to Chanduy, and by the middle of March 1655, the salvors had recovered more than 2,800,000 of the 5,000,000 pesos from the wrecked *Capitana,* including a large solid-gold statue of the Virgin Mary holding the Christ Child. Then the treasure from both galleons was shipped overland to Porto Bello, Panama on the Atlantic side. After the arrival of the armada of Montealegre, a grand fair lasting for days was held in celebration.

On May 13, just as the armada was preparing to sail for Havana and Spain from Cartagena, word reached the Spaniards that an English fleet of 56 warships had laid seige to Santo Domingo. Montealegre decided it was too dangerous to sail. By this time, unknown to the marques, the English had been repelled from Santo Domingo and had gone on to attack and capture the island of Jamaica. On July 1 an advance boat reached Cartagena from Spain with orders from Philip IV that the treasure must reach Spain with all haste, regardless of the dangers involved. Spain was in dire straits. The country faced bankruptcy if the Spanish treasure were lost. Two days later, the armada sailed. As the fleet approached Cabo San Antonio on the western tip of Cuba, a small boat appeared to advise them that 27 English warships had been sighted in the vicinity several days earlier. Accordingly, Montealegre changed course for Veracruz on the Mexican coast, to keep the ships and their precious cargo out of English hands. On August 25 word reached Veracruz that the English fleet had abandoned their blockade of Havana and had sailed for England. The armada again set sail for Havana, after embarking more treasure and luxury trade goods from Mexico and the Philippines. They reached Havana on October 10.

Bandito diving on the Pedro Serrano shipwreck sunk in 1526 on Serrana Bank in the Caribbean

Several of the ships were in need of repair, and more time was lost. Although Montealegre had eight galleons capable of carrying the treasure, he decided to transport most of it aboard only two—his own *Capitana* and *Almiranta,* commanded by Admiral Mathias de Orellana. Each ship carried more than five million pesos in treasure—gold, silver, jewelry, precious stones, and pearls, plus some cochineal, indigo, sugar, and dyewood.

After those who were sailing had heard mass in Havana's great cathedral, the ships left port at noon on January 1, 1656. Around midnight on January 4, the lookout on *Almiranta,* which was the lead ship of the armada, discovered that they were in shallow water on a sand bank. A cannon was fired to warn the other ships away from the danger. Confusion ensued, mainly because the ships' captains thought they had already passed through the dreaded Bahama Channel and were in the open ocean. In addition, they were unsure why *Almiranta* had fired a cannon. Several of the ships continued on their original heading, and one collided with *Almiranta.* A large hole was knocked in her bow below the waterline and she began to fill rapidly. All four of the ship's pumps were manned. Everyone aboard the stricken galleon bailed desperately with whatever was at hand, but to no avail. Seeing that there was no chance of saving the ship, Admiral Orellana decided to run her aground to keep from sinking in deep water, so that as many lives and as much of the treasure as possible could be saved.

Less than 30 minutes after the collision, the galleon struck a coral reef violently and slid off, sinking in about 50 feet of water. No sooner had *Almiranta* settled to the bottom than a strong northerly wind began to blow, churning up huge waves which dashed her to pieces. Most of the 650 men aboard the galleon grabbed hold of floating pieces of debris and drifted away in the dark sea, never to be seen again. About 150 of them clung to pieces of the galleon that were sticking above the water, but many died from exposure during the night. As they lost their hold and fell into the water, waiting sharks devoured them. By sunrise there were only 45 survivors, and many of them were in grave condition. Another galleon of the armada had also struck a reef but miraculously had lost only her rudder. She anchored about a league (at that time, four nautical miles) north of the lost *Almiranta,* while the rest of the armada had escaped danger and were continuing on their way to Spain. Despite the storm which was still raging, the 45 survivors were rescued and carried to the anchored galleon which was commanded by Captain Juan de Hoyos. A new rudder was constructed and buoys were placed on the site of the wreck, although no longer was any part of it visible. Then Hoyo's galleon left for Spain. Very little of the treasure ever reached Philip IV, however. An English squadron was waiting for the ill-fated armada off Cádiz. The English captured or sunk all of the ships except two small vessels which weren't carrying valuable cargo.

Meanwhile, after enduring another great storm south of Bermuda, in which his galleon was further damaged, Hoyos headed for Puerto Rico to make vital repairs. But as he approached the island, contrary winds kept him from entering any port there, and he was forced to continue on to Cartagena de las Indias, arriving March 10, 1656. After learning of the loss of *Almiranta,* the governor-general of Cartagena dispatched six frigates with 40 divers and a large number of soldiers under the command of Captain Juan de Somovilla Texada, a military engineer then in charge of building fortifications in Cartagena, to find and salvage her. The salvage vessels reached the site of the wreck on the Little Bahama Bank in mid-June 1656 and found that *Almiranta* had been broken into small pieces that were now scattered over a large area. In 13 days they recovered 480,000 pesos. Then a bad storm struck, and they had to head for a safe port. Four of the ships carrying the salvaged treasure were lost, two on the coast of Santo Domingo and two on a reef off Cayo Gordo in the Bahamas. The two remaining vessels managed to reach San Juan de Puerto Rico and were later used to salvage most of the treasure off the other four.

During the next three years other salvage vessels recovered about a fourth of *Almiranta's* treasure, but when they returned for the fifth season of salvaging, they couldn't find any trace of the shipwreck. It had been completely covered by sand. For more than 20 years there were repeated attempts to find the wreck, which not only contained the greatest treasure ever lost on a single ship, but also the gold statue of the Virgin Mary and Christ Child which had been sent from Lima. It appeared that *Almiranta* was lost forever, but such was not the case; I was to find her more than 300 years later.

I first became interested in the story of *Almiranta* in 1960 while doing research in the Archivo de las Indias in Seville. After locating more than 12,000 pages of documents dealing with this ship—including a copy of her original cargo manifest, which listed and described every item she was carrying when lost—I came across a 144-page book published in Madrid in 1657 by one of the survivors of the wreck, a Dr. Diego Portichuelo de Ribadeneyra, who was once the "Procurador General del Tribunal de la Inquisicion de Lima." This gentleman wrote an exciting and vivid account of everything he observed from the time he boarded *Almiranta* until he reached Spain more than a year later. I also found three nautical charts showing the precise location of the shipwrecked *Almiranta* and knew then that she could be located with the right equipment.

Up till now, many treasure hunters had spent a lot of money and time searching for her in the Florida Keys, using erroneous information given in various "nonfiction" books on sunken treasures. Unable to go after her myself, since I was then living in Europe, I gave this new information to a group of American treasure hunters in return for a percentage of the find. They failed to locate her, however, and, in turn, passed on my information to others. This resulted in a stampede reminiscent of the California gold rush. At one time or another, practically everyone in the treasure-hunting field searched for *Almiranta,* using the information I had found.

Early in 1972, with the help of oceanographer Willard Bascom, we raised a substantial amount of money and formed a corporation— Seafinders, Inc.—to search for and salvage *Almiranta.* After obtaining a salvage lease from the Bahamian government and carefully putting together the best in equipment and personnel, we began a systematic search, using a proton magnetometer which detects the presence of ferrous metals. Unlike most shipwrecks, which contain large masses of ferrous metal in the form of iron cannons, *Almiranta* carried 58 bronze cannons, which made her a difficult target to locate. In addition, we were searching in a section of the notorious "Bermuda Triangle" where electronic equipment seems to function properly only sporadically. There were periods of days at a time when we were unable to use the marine radio, and on two occasions we were almost zapped by hurricanes before we heard of their approach by radio and retreated to port.

From the start I was convinced that we would eventually find the wreck, but as the long grueling days of searching dragged into months, the rest of my crew lost heart and began to wonder if they weren't on a wild goose chase. By the middle of August we had covered more than

35 square miles of the bank, finding about 20 other shipwrecks in the search—but no sign of *Almiranta*. Bascom, who controlled the purse strings of the operation, repeatedly tried to talk me into giving up the search and head for Colombia where we had several other good wreck locations; but I refused to admit defeat.

Although we were using the most advanced search methods, we finally found *Almiranta,* not with the help of technology, but through a piece of good luck. On August 20 we were about to head for port to get supplies. As David Edgell, one of the divers, and I pulled up the anchor of our main vessel, the *Grifon,* we found two Spanish-type ballast stones stuck in its flukes. I quickly threw a buoy overboard to mark the spot, and we headed for port. We had been finding wrecks all summer with similar ballast stones, but this time, for some strange but compelling reason, I knew we had found *Almiranta*.

Three days later we were again over the spot where I had dropped the buoy. Diving down, I found a small coral reef which was covered with ballast stones and pottery shards from the period of *Almiranta*. The reef was surrounded by deep sand. I was positive the wreck was buried beneath it, so we positioned *Grifon* and began excavating with the "blaster," a tubular metal device that fits over the ship's propeller and deflects a steady stream of water downward to blow away the sand. David and I were on the bottom when the blaster cut through about 25 feet of sand and laid bare the hard limestone bottom which was covered with more ballast stones, ceramic shards, and coral-encrusted iron objects. David found a clay smoking pipe and seconds later I found a piece of eight dated 1655. I was jubilant, thinking we had found *Almiranta* for sure.

An hour or so later, a rival group of treasure hunters that had been shadowing us all summer long appeared in their vessel. I went aboard and convinced them that we were excavating a Civil War shipwreck. The leader of the group told me I would never find *Almiranta,* that she was 10 miles north of where we were. At that moment we were right on top of the site, and our divers were bringing up treasure. By sundown we had recovered a beautiful gold dish in the shape of a scallop shell, with two silver spoons, one silver fork, a silver inkwell, a silver snuff box, and two pairs of brass navigational dividers attached to it by coral growth, as well as a number of other valuable artifacts.

The next day we found four of the ship's iron anchors, ranging from

Diver Dave Edgell inspecting one of the bronze cannon near the *Almiranta* shipwreck

5 to 22 feet in length. The smallest was probably used aboard one of the ship's longboats *(chalupas)* and the others for *Almiranta* herself. Nearby we discovered two ornately decorated bronze cannon of 18-pound shot. Both were identical—11 feet long and weighing about two tons—and bore the coats of arms of Philip IV and of the Marques de Leganes and an inscription stating that the Marques de Leganes had donated the money for these cannon to be used by the ships of his most sovereign king, Philip IV. Near the bore of the cannons was the date 1653 and inscribed at the other end of the cannon was the name of the founder, or man who had cast the cannon, Johannes von Horst. The dolphins, or lifting rings of the cannon, were beautifully made. I have seen cannons in museums and forts all over the world, but none as magnificent as these. Unfortunately, they were too heavy to be raised with the equipment we had at the time.

Under one of the cannon, which was resting on some loose ballast stones, I spotted an intact ceramic jar about four feet tall. Throughout the period of navigation between Spain and her New World colonies, these "olive jars," as they were called, were used to carry everything from wine to gunpowder and even, at times, coins. It was a mystery how such a fragile container could have survived intact under the weight of that enormous cannon. Working as cautiously as a surgeon, I extracted the jar. When I reached the surface with it, I discovered that it was still sealed with a cork and was filled with wine. The wine, however, had turned to bitter vinegar.

In the small area where we found the anchors and cannons, we also found 600 silver coins, several small silver bars, four silver plates, two silver cups, a silver pitcher, a brass apothecary mortar and pestle, and hundreds of other artifacts. The silver coins we were recovering were mostly pieces of eight *(reales de ocho),* but there were also a small number of four- and two-real pieces minted at the three main Spanish-American mints, Lima, Potosi, and Mexico City. The small silver bars were assayed and made into bars in the refinery at Potosi, as revealed by the markings on them. One of the silver plates had "J.M.D." on it, probably the initials of the owner.

We continued to work on the wreck and were off to a fine start the morning of the fifth day. The first hour's diving yielded more than 2,000 silver coins, five large clumps of coins weighing over 150 pounds which were held together by coral growth, dozens of silver items, and a complete sword. Then, as the blaster was gently blowing the pale sand away and enlarging the hole, David found the first of many gold coins we were to find, and I suddenly spotted five silver bars being uncovered as I filmed the entire scene. After pointing to the bars, David stuck the gold coin he had found in his mouth and with great effort carried each of the five bars, which weighed about 90 pounds apiece, directly under the stern of *Grifon* and put three of them in the "goodies basket," a wire basket we had rigged to haul up artifacts. Just as the basket reached the surface, the rope parted and the basket, with its precious load, came falling down through the water, almost landing on top of us. Finally, after all five bars were safely on the deck of *Grifon,* I cleaned the coral encrustation and a thin coating of silver sulphate off them and found that they all bore beautiful markings—the mint, assayer, and tally marks, plus the mark indicating that the "royal fifth" (the king's duty) had been paid, the "bit" taken out by the assayer to show that he had taken a small part of the bar to pay him for his labor. Even more interesting were the special markings on each bar, in the form of initials denoting the bars' owners. From my copy of *Almiranta's* manifest I was able to determine that two of the bars belonged to a merchant named Juan Fernandez de Orozco, another to a man named Antonio Peralta, and the last two to none other than Dr. Diego Portichuelo de Ribadeneyra, the survivor who wrote the account of the disaster. Having read his book so many times, I had come to feel that I knew the man. Finding the two large silver bars which had once been his, made me feel even closer to him.

By the time it became too dark to continue diving that day, we had recovered more than an estimated $200,000 in treasure. It broke my heart to have to head for home port in Florida. Bascom had gone to Nassau to meet with government authorities to establish our ownership of the wreck, and I needed to hire more divers because David and I had been spending 10 to 12 hours each day on the bottom and couldn't continue at that exhausting pace any longer.

Treasure has an insidious way of warping men's minds and values, and this time was no exception. Upon reaching port, our cook disappeared, taking several sacks of silver coins and was never heard from again. Our captain—a former shrimper captain who had declared from the outset that he wasn't the least bit interested in treasure and who, I thought, was a nice fellow—suddenly decided that his share of the treasure wasn't enough and demanded a percentage 10 times greater than he had signed an agreement to accept before we began the search. When we couldn't meet his demands, he quit and in revenge, telephoned many treasure hunters throughout the country, attempting to sell the precise location of the wreck to the highest bidder. Fortunately for us, the wreck lay in the area for which we already had a salvage lease with the Bahamian government, so it didn't really matter who else knew the location. This didn't preclude future problems, however, because once the secret was out, every pirate diver around wanted a piece of the action, and we had to drive more than a dozen salvage vessels away from the site.

With three new, experienced divers—John Hollister, Michael Daniels, and Neal Watson—and a captain named Charles Sherman, we returned to *Almiranta* and worked her for six weeks before being forced to stop. Our first two days back on the site were like the last day before we had returned to port. At times, treasure was being uncovered so fast that we had to have all five divers on the bottom at the same time. Sherman almost broke his back pulling up the goodie baskets filled with treasure and artifacts.

Our finds included more than 2,000 silver coins, two silver bars, and many other silver items such as plates, bowls, cups, pitchers, spoons, forks, knives, riding spurs, buttons, sword handles, and candlesticks. We also found 12 more gold coins which were of great value, as I later discovered, because they turned out to have been minted in Bogotá and are the oldest known gold coins minted in the New World. Not all our finds were gold and silver, though. We recovered thousands of items of copper, brass, pewter, lead, wood, ivory, horn, ceramic, glass, and stone. Among some of the more interesting were beautifully decorated shards of Chinese porcelain, a Mayan Indian jade axe head, a large three-legged stone metate, a number of human bones, fragments of cotton and wool clothing, and part of a wig of human hair. During these same two fruitful days we also recovered more than three tons of coral-encrusted iron objects, the majority of which were ship's fittings and spikes. We were also delighted to find among the many iron objects, seventeenth-century hammers, axes, chisels, keys, padlocks, swords, knives, cannonballs, kettles, pots, pans, serving ladles, and a wheel off one of the cannon carriages. These objects, attesting to the routine of life aboard ship, brought home to us more than the items of gold and silver a feeling for *Almiranta,* her crew, and passengers, and their ill-starred voyage.

Although diving conditions in the Bahamas are quite good, we were all diving 10 to 12 hours a day. In spite of the warm water, the strain was beginning to show. We had all lost weight despite the bountiful meals prepared by Captain Sherman, and were beginning to suffer bleeding gums, earaches, and other annoying minor pains. A major problem was badly lacerated fingers and hands, caused by small fish and crabs which were attracted to us by the various types of minute marine life uncovered as the blaster removed the sand over the wreck.

As long as we were raising large amounts of treasure and artifacts, I had the happiest crew in the world; but when we had an occasional off day, each diver took it personally and became gloomy. After the first two incredibly exciting days back on the wreck, we had a three-day slump in which we found only 79 silver coins, and little else. The problem wasn't that we had uncovered a nonproductive area of the wreck, but that we had found an area where the ballast rocks were about five feet deep and all of them—each probably weighing 10 to 15 tons—had to be moved by hand to another area before we could continue the excavation. I insisted on doing it in a logical, thorough manner. Moving large ballast stones underwater is perhaps the most exhausting work in the world. It caused us all to suffer aching backs, in addition to our other sores and injuries.

The slump was followed by another two-day frenzy during which we salvaged more than a ton of silver in bars and large clumps of coins (in the shape of the canvas bags which had once held them), plus several thousand loose silver coins, a five-pound gold disk, dozens of other silver items, many emeralds and amethysts, a large ivory elephant's tusk, and scores of other valuable and interesting artifacts.

We were never without unwelcome visitors. Barely a day went by that a plane didn't buzz low overhead or vessels weren't on the horizon, waiting for us to leave so they could move in. And several times we had problems with hungry sharks and barracudas. Usually we were able to chase them away by swimming toward them and shouting underwater, but several times we had to resort to using powerful explosive spears.

We maintained our frantic pace, after awhile becoming so accustomed to treasure that we didn't consider a day especially good unless

The author holding a small silver bar near the *Almiranta* wreck. Stacks of pieces of eight and silver bars can be seen in the foreground

we had brought up more than $100,000 worth. All this time we had been working on the bow section of the wreck. According to the documents, the bulk of the ship's treasure was in the main hull which had broken away from the bow and was lying in another area. On October 6, by which time we had recovered more than $2 million in treasure, I left the rest of my team hard at work on the bow and went in search of the rest of the wreck. Less than three hours later, I got a strong magnetometer reading and discovered the fluke of a large anchor protruding from the sandy bottom. Using a small metal detector, I surveyed the area and discovered that I had found the rest of *Almiranta*. Digging down only a few feet, I clutched silver coins, all dated from the period of the wreck. My spirits soared; I had found the mother lode!

Returning to *Grifon* with the intention of moving her to the new area which was about two miles to the east, I found everyone waiting for me with downcast faces. Captain Sherman had overheard a radio message from the commissioner of police in Nassau, ordering a police launch to bring us in. Realizing that we would have to leave at once or be arrested without explanation, I rushed back to where I had found the bulk of the wreck and cut loose the marking buoys I had tied over the site, and dragged the anchor away with our small boat and dumped it in another area. I then went over the area once again with the magnetometer and got no readings (the ferrous anchor had given me the previous reading). Convinced that only I could find the site again, I went back to port.

Bascom had stayed ashore after the first few days of working the wreck to deal with the government officials. All went well at first. He had gotten permission for us to keep the treasure and artifacts in Florida banks until we divided it with the Bahamian government. However, the person he had been dealing with directly, Dr. Doris Johnson, was replaced as minister of transport, and problems mounted as we were caught in an internecine government squabble. The new minister, Darrel Rolle, refused to honor most of the arrangements that Bascom had worked out with Dr. Johnson, the most serious of which concerned our keeping the treasure and artifacts in Florida. On October 5, 1972, Bascom, who refused to take the treasure and artifacts back to the Bahamas, met with the prime minister of the Bahamas. The prime minister decided that the best way to get the treasure to Nassau, where it rightfully belonged, was to suspend the lease.

After seven weeks, during which we could not return to the wreck for fear of being arrested, Bascom agreed and reluctantly took all of the treasure and artifacts to Nassau. Naturally, I was furious to learn that our salvage lease had been suspended and the division date postponed. I then publicly accused the Bahamian government of illegally seizing the wreck and the treasure, which didn't make me too popular in the Bahamas. Unbeknownst to me, several other treasure hunters had gone to Nassau, claiming to have discovered the wreck before us, and there were rumors around that we hadn't returned all of the treasure. Consequently, the Bahamians had to investigate before permitting us to continue working the site or giving us our 75 percent share of the find.

In February 1973 Jack Kelley, a diving friend from Tulsa, replaced Bascom as president of Seafinders, Inc. and immediately began trying to improve relations between Seafinders and the Bahamian government. Although it took more than a year to accomplish, Kelley was eventually successful, and our salvage lease was reinstated. We received our full share of the treasure. I was as happy as a kid at Christmas, but my happiness was short-lived.

We spent two months during the summer of 1974 getting our salvage vessel ready and finding a good crew, but just two days before we were to sail for the wreck, the Bahamian government told Kelley that I was forbidden to work on the wreck because of the remarks I had made in the press two years before. Dick Anderson, a treasure hunter from California, replaced me as the expedition leader and did a very good job. During the two-month diving season, he and his crew recovered over a half-million dollars in treasure, which included a 15-foot solid-gold chain.

Because I had been forbidden to work on the shipwreck, however, I refused to reveal the location of the mother lode. Kelley and others thought me stubborn in not telling them where the rest of the treasure lay. For years I had searched for *Almiranta*. I had found the wreck, and it was only right that I should be the one to supervise the recovery of probably the richest treasure ever found. During the summer of 1975 Kelley and his team did all they could to find the rest of the wreck, but without success. Eventually, I feel, the Bahamian government will have a change of heart, and I will be permitted to salvage my fabulous treasure galleon.

13: The Phoenicians in the New World

The greatest seafarers and traders of antiquity were the Semitic Phoenicians, a skillful and enterprising people who lived along the narrow coastal plain of Lebanon and Syria. For 2,000 years before the birth of Christ, these practical men set out from their centers at Byblos, Tyre, and Sidon on both Mediterranean coastal trading ventures and amazing long-range voyages that took them to Africa and Arabia, Spain and other distant parts of the ancient world, in search of gold, ivory, tin, and copper (the last two essential for making bronze and other goods which they traded for). They flourished—exporting timber and carved furniture from the legendary cedars of Lebanon; purple dye from the murex shell, which was so highly prized by the ancients; as well as cloth, silk, glass, and other items. It was from these Phoenician ports that many ideas, both in writing and in art, reached the Western World via Greece. Tradition has it that the alphabet which, along with the abacus, was developed by the Phoenicians to aid in their commercial enterprise, came to Greece with the Phoenician prince, Cadmus, who founded Thebes.

The Phoenicians were great middlemen, consumate merchants. During their golden age under King Hyram of Tyre, Phoenician craftsmen, architects, and materials were used to build Solomon's great golden temple at Jerusalem. They founded colonies at Carthage in the ninth century B.C. and in Sicily, Tunisia, Cyprus, and Malta. Their descendants in Carthage went on to establish settlements in Algeria, Spain's

Balearic Islands and southern coast, and along the Moroccan coast. It was from these sites that the intrepid Phoenician mariners embarked on their search for raw materials, reaching such distant places in that long-ago world as the Azores, West Africa, and the coast of England, at Cornwall. Some think they ranged even farther afield.

During the past 20 years I have amassed a great deal of documentary and archaeological evidence, which has convinced me that these unsurpassed sea-traders made transatlantic crossings to the New World as early as 1500 B.C. If we consider that they may have been accidently blown across the Atlantic during one of their frequent voyages along the western coast of Africa or out to the Azores, we can better understand the references of so many ancient authors to the oceanic lands far out in the Atlantic. They had developed nautical science to a high degree, but owing to their policy of keeping sea routes and navigation methods secret, much of their knowledge was lost when their power faded and they were eclipsed by the Roman Empire.

My initial interest in the Phoenicians was kindled by a number of discoveries I made in Yucatán during the three years I lived there, from 1956 to 1959. During the summer of 1957 I was leading a group of Americans on a hunting safari about 20 miles into the jungle when we stumbled on several overgrown Mayan ruins. On the walls of one of the buildings were beautifully colored frescos depicting three vessels which looked like Greek or Phoenician galleys, each with dozens of men standing with shields, spears, and long-handled swords in their hands. I was amazed and fascinated. I knew that the Maya were supposed to have made very large dugouts in which they traveled all over the Caribbean, but these ships were obviously not dugouts. The men had light-red hair and beards. They certainly didn't look like the Maya or any other indigenous Latin Americans. They were similar in appearance to the hooked-nosed bearded men I had seen in frescos at Chicen Itza, the important Mayan site in central Yucatán, which many scholars say depicts Europeans who came to the New World long before Columbus.

Nearby, in another ruin, we found two more walls covered with frescos, this time of horses: horses grazing, frolicking and running, some mounted by riders. Again, I was amazed. According to scholars, there were no horses in America (except the small ancestor of the horse, which became extinct before man appeared) until the Spaniards arrived. Archeologists later confirmed, from architectural drawings I made of the two buildings and from pottery samples, that both predated the arrival of the Spaniards by many centuries.

Not long after this, I made another discovery. I had taken a group of tourists to the coastal Mayan ruins of Tulum. I noticed that one of the walls of the largest temple had fallen since my previous visit. On inspecting the damage, I saw that the plaster covering the wall next to it had also crumbled, revealing a large bas-relief carving of a bull. Like horses, cattle were supposedly unknown in America until imported by the Spaniards. The ruin on which the bull was carved dated from before the tenth century. Worship of sacred bulls, such as Apis of the Egyptians or the Minotaur of Crete, was well known in early Mediterranean cultures.

While carrying out research in various European archives and libraries, I also found a wealth of documentary evidence to substantiate early contact between the Old World and the New World. The most interesting documentation was an account by a bishop who visited Yucatán around 1550. He reported that while visiting the village of Mani, near Mérida, he saw a number of strange buildings unlike any he had seen in his travels on the peninsula. These closely resembled the ruins of many stone structures he had seen on a visit to the Holy Land. In describing their construction, he said that the stone roofs of the buildings were held in place by iron rods. (Iron was unknown in the New World before the Spaniards arrived.) From the village elders, the bishop learned that legend attributed these centuries-old buildings to white men who had come from a place called Carthage. Carthage, the last Phoenician stronghold in the Mediterranean, was destroyed by the Romans in 146 B.C. Possibly some of the survivors of the famous seaport sailed to the New World to avoid enslavement, and set up a colony in Yucatán.

There has recently been new evidence that the Phoenicians actually reached the New World. In 1872, near Paraiba, Brazil, a stone bearing a Phoenician inscription was discovered. But for many years it was thought to be a forgery. Then in 1968, Dr. Cyrus Gordon, then chairman of the Department of Mediterranean Studies of Brandeis University, announced that after careful study of the inscription's text, he was convinced of its authenticity. It said that when 10 Phoenician trading ships were sailing around Africa in 531 B.C., one ship, carrying 12 men and three women, was separated from the others in a storm and blown across to Brazil.

Although a great deal of archeological evidence has been found in this hemisphere, indicating Phoenician contact with the New World, the largest amount has turned up on the Yucatán peninsula. During a recent excavation by Dr. Victor Segovia, at Comalcalco, another example came to light. Unlike other ruins found in Mexico, those he excavated were constructed of clay bricks and are architecturally different from all others known in the Western Hemisphere. During the course of the excavation, Dr. Segovia discovered a life-size stone head of a bearded man with definite Semitic features which looks Phoenician in origin. Nearby, in another set of ruins, he discovered two stone friezes that are identical to those found in some ruins in Cambodia. When I first met Dr. Segovia about 15 years ago, he was very skeptical of my theory of Old World contact with America, but he has since become a believer. In addition to his own discoveries, he has inspected several interesting artifacts uncovered by outlaw diggers. These include several Japanese clay figurines, a copper disk with three Egyptian-type pyramids and a Sphinx engraved on it, an Egyptian-looking statue of a man, and countless pieces of ceramic ware of definite European pre-Columbian manufacture.

During the past few years I have made four trips to Yucatán to gather more evidence to support my theory that the Phoenicians came to Yucatán and have met with greater success than anticipated. During the first two trips I saw a number of ceramic figurines of bearded men (the American Indians never grew beards) with Phoenician facial characteristics, which had been dug out of various ruins by antiquity plunderers. Elsewhere, from Guatemala to Peru, I located more than 200 others, which indicate that the Phoenicians may have reached widespread areas throughout the hemisphere.

Then in the spring of 1971, on an expedition with Milt Machlin, I made a fabulous discovery. While exploring the ruins of a sixteenth-century cathedral in the village of Tihosuco, we noticed that a large stone lintel over a doorway in the church had an inscription carved in it. Expecting the inscription to be in Spanish or Latin, I was amazed to find to find that it was in some strange writing which was not Mayan hieroglyphics. I knew we were onto something important. Dr. Cyrus Gordon has identified the script from photographs as belonging to an

248 • STILL MORE ADVENTURES

ancient form of Mediterranean writing—probably Phoenician. Apparently the stone was found by a Spaniard or Indian and incorporated in the building of the church.

A year later, I found still more proof of Phoenician contact with Yucatán. On the island of Cozumel, with some friends I began exploring ruins where I had earlier found pottery possibly of pre-Columbian, European origin. Unfortunately, we were a bit late: a bulldozer building a new road across the island had just cut through the largest ruin on the site. Ceramic shards were scattered over a wide area. We began searching through the debris. Willard Bascon called me over after an hour of searching and pointed to an object embedded in one side of the ruin where the bulldozer had cut through. Gingerly we extracted what turned out to be a bronze axe head. This was a rare find, since bronze was a metal which, although used by several other Indian cultures in America, was never used by the Mayans. Chemical analysis has shown that the copper used in the axe head came from somewhere in the western Mediterranean—the ancient home of the Phoenicians. Identical axe heads have been recovered from Phoenician sites in Lebanon and Israel and can be seen on display in the national museums of both countries.

Shortly after my ill-fated voyage in the Viking ship replica in 1969, I decided to construct an authentic Phoenician vessel and sail to Yucatán. Realizing that icongraphical evidence wasn't sufficient to build a completely authentic ship, I decided that I must find and carefully excavate one or more Phoenician shipwrecks in order to obtain the necessary data for construction. At that time none had been discovered. During 1970 and 1971 I made several trips to the Mediterranean to uncover clues as to the possible existence of Phoenician shipwrecks. My travels took me to Spain, France, Italy, Greece, Israel, and Tunisia where I interviewed hundreds of divers and fishermen. I drew a complete blank and temporarily became discouraged.

Then in January 1973 I decided to try my luck in Lebanon. At the invitation of Emir Maurice Chehab, the director general of antiquities of Lebanon, I was able to explore the ancient ports of Byblos, Sidon, and Tyre to determine whether there is sufficient sediment on the seafloor of these ports to preserve the remains of Phoenician shipwrecks. When ships were lost on rocky or coral-covered bottoms, very little if any of their wooden hulls survived over the centuries because of exposure and the devastations of the wood-boring shipworms. What I needed to find was a Phoenician wreck that had been buried and preserved under deep sediment.

Interestingly, just a few days before I was to fly to Lebanon with Milt Machlin and Jack Kelley, the *New York Times* carried a story about a Phoenician wreck dating around the fifth century B.C. The wreck had been found off the coast of Israel near the port of Shavei Zion, which is quite close to the Lebanese border. This find excited the archaeological world, not only because it was the first Phoenician wreck to be found, but because part of the cargo it carried was clay figurines of Tanit, the goddess of fertility and a major female deity of the Phoenician world. These ranged in size from 6 to 15 inches. Previously, archaeologists had found only drawings and symbols of the goddess, as well as impressions on bronze coins, all discovered during excavations at Carthage. A phone call to Dr. Elisha Linder, Israel's leading underwater archaeologist and the archaeologist in charge of the newly discovered site, revealed that the cargo was found on a hard rocky bottom and that no traces of the ship had survived. I headed for Lebanon, hoping for better luck.

Our first stop was at Byblos, which, according to tradition is the oldest continuously inhabited city in the world. Recent excavations have shown the existence of a Neolithic culture dating back to 5000 B.C. Long before the Greeks and Romans arrived, Byblos was a powerful, independent city-state with its own king, culture, and trade. During the third millenium B.C., it was the most important seaport in the Mediterranean, finally being eclipsed by Tyre and Sidon. (It was here that the alphabet we use today was developed.)

Although the coast here is rocky, earthquakes over the centuries have toppled many of the ancient buildings into the sea and caused soil to slide into the water. Underneath the debris there is a chance that remains of wrecks can be found. Emir Chehab arranged for us to meet Pepe Abed, who has the most impressive private museum in the country. He has discovered priceless artifacts underwater at Byblos, including many Greek and Roman statues. An important discovery in recent years was a golden ring with a reversible setting, showing a Phoenician king and his son on one side and the queen and her daughter on the other. Along the beach local boys find coins—copper, bronze, sometimes silver and gold—which they sell to tourists.

The water was cold—45 degrees—but the excitement of diving in such a place kept us from minding the temperature. I'll never forget my first look at the seafloor off Byblos. It was like an underwater museum. Scattered over the bottom were large numbers of immense marble columns and hand-worked building stones, many with beautiful designs carved into them and covering thousands of years of history. Even more exciting was our discovery of the cargo of a Phoenician shipwreck dating to the eight century B.C. and consisting of amphorae and other ceramic objects. We found no wood of the ship's hull, however. During the four days we spent surveying the site, we recovered eight Phoenician stone anchors, many ceramic artifacts and shards covering a span of 3,000 years, and the lower torso of a Roman terra-cotta man.

We then went to Sidon, founded around 1400 B.C. and second only to Tyre in the heyday of the Phoenicians. This city was destroyed many times by earthquakes and invaders, and very little of it can be seen today. The most impressive building still standing, a sea fortress built by the Crusaders at the port entrance, dates back only to the twelfth century. After diving at Byblos, we found Sidon a bit of a letdown, since the seafloor was covered with tons of modern trash. It was almost impossible to find any remains from antiquity without first removing the layers of debris. In addition, a large portion of the seabed was covered with thousands of projectiles and bombs—all of them still armed. During World War II, before a fleet of Vichy French warships surrendered to the British, they dumped their munitions overboard at their anchorage off Sidon. Nevertheless, we were fortunate in finding the cargo of a second Phoenician ship, a cargo of amphorae. But no traces of the ship itself.

Tyre, founded by the Phoenicians in 2750 B.C., was one of the most celebrated cities in the ancient world. Her flourishing maritime trade, colonies all over the Mediterranean and Atlantic coast, and famous purple dye and glass industries made her the most important commercial center in the eastern Mediterranean.

Originally Tyre consisted of a mainland settlement and an island city a short distance offshore. In 332 B.C. Alexander the Great stopped with his army at Tyre's mainland settlement and was offered the hospitality of the inhabitants. However, those living on the island, believing themselves invincible because of a 150-foot wall that surrounded the city and a large fleet of galleys which formed a barrier to the entrance of her two harbors, refused entrance to Alexander and his men. Incensed by this breach of courtesy, Alexander besieged the island for seven months. A fleet of 250 vessels was assembled to blockade the city by sea, and during a number of encounters, ships were lost by both sides.

This is the first recorded time that divers were used in warfare. Both sides used them. After reducing the fighting spirit of the defenders, the Macedonians gave their divers the task of destroying the boom defenses of the harbors, and the Tyrian divers rebuilt them. According to legend, Alexander himself descended in a diving bell to inspect the destruction of the defenses. After failing to capture the city by sea, the Macedonians built a causeway connecting the island to the mainland, which they made use of to breach the city walls. Once inside, Alexander's men massacred more than 11,000 inhabitants and sold 30,000 others into slavery. Before departing they set the city afire and razed it to the ground.

Although Tyre was rebuilt, it never regained its former glory. Carthage, on the African coast, soon replaced it as the most important Phoenician seaport in the Mediterranean. Many believe that some portion of the island-city is now sunk under the sea and covered by sand. As at Byblos, the seafloor around the island is littered with hundreds of columns and massive building stones. The ancient jetties and moles of the two harbors are also visible underwater at an average depth of six fathoms. Excavations on land during the past 30 years have uncovered remains of Crusader, Arab, Byzantine and Graeco-Roman cities; but archeologists haven't yet reached the level of the Phoenician city. One of the largest hippodromes of the Roman period has recently been uncovered. Built during the second century, it lay buried under 20 feet of windswept sand.

Arriving at Tyre, we were shocked to see a clam-shell dredge being used to deepen the modern harbor on the north side of the town. This harbor was one of two harbors in use in ancient times. As bucket after bucket of mud was brought up, we spotted many artifacts, including a couple of Roman amphorae, miraculously intact. When one of the Lebanese archeologists who had been assigned to work with us tried to take possession of several important objects, a number of the workmen launched into a furious argument. Violence was averted only by the well-timed arrival of several police officers.

We were soon to discover that the modern inhabitants of Tyre feel that anything coming out of the sea belongs to *them* and not to the government. The illegal sale of ancient artifacts is one of the town's main businesses. Several dozen sponge divers work out of the port and are known to make more from the sale of antiquities than from the sponges they recover. They took great offense at our coming there to find anything that might deprive them of a source of income. Most of the fishermen felt the same way and it was with difficulty, that we were finally able to rent a small boat.

Only after plying the fisherman whose boat we rented with a staggering amount of the local brandy did we got him to take us to an area where he had snagged and raised several amphorae in his nets. He put us right on top of a Roman amphora wreck dating from the first century. Unfortunately, he had also shown others the site—probably the sponge divers. Where once there were thousands of intact amphorae, there are now only thousands of shards because of dynamiting by someone trying to dislodge the amphorae from the coral growth holding them. After mapping the site for the government archaeologists, we dug into the mass of broken amphorae and managed to find two that were still whole. Nearby we found another area containing a large number of Roman ceramic oil lamps, plates, small jars and ointment bottles, all of which appear to have been lost when a small boat capsized.

Half the town's inhabitants were waiting as we came ashore with our find that day, and our poor fisherman bore the brunt of angry remarks for having shown us a good area and helping us find artifacts. We spent the next three days with the same fisherman, who professed to know many other sites with ancient objects; but all we found were several Phoenician stone anchors which have no value to the local people. We realized that he had been deliberately taking us to areas where he was sure nothing would be found, in order to keep his good standing in the community.

When we reported this to Emir Chehab, he arranged for one of the men on his excavation team, who had a small boat, to work with us. Our first goal was to survey a large area near the southern harbor where Chehab believed a number of vessels had been lost during the siege by Alexander the Great. After a visual search, which produced only a few pieces of pottery and one large lead Roman anchor stock, Kelley and I used metal probes to locate solid objects buried under the deep sand.

In four areas we found what we were sure are shipwrecks, but lack of excavation equipment prevented us from verifying the find.

We then began searching visually again, this time closer to shore, inside the southern harbor, and made one exciting find after another. The bottom was almost completely paved with artifacts which we recovered samples of for study by Chehab and his staff. When the local seadogs learned that we were recovering more important objects without their help, they resorted to drastic action. Many of the fishermen use dynamite to kill fish, and we soon found that some of them were always nearby whenever we were on the bottom. They were soon dropping dynamite to discourage us. When we moved on to a new site, so did they.

To cover larger areas, we hung on lines and were towed behind our boat, always with at least two fishing boats following. In two days we found four more shipwreck sites: a Phoenician wreck from the fourth century, two Greek wrecks from the third and second centuries B.C., and a Byzantine wreck dating from about 600 A.D. The Phoenician and Greek wrecks were on rocky bottoms with no surviving traces of the ships that carried cargoes of amphorae. Like the Roman wreck we had found our first day at Tyre, all three of these had been dynamited and plundered, but we still brought up an interesting collection of artifacts from them. The Byzantine wreck was on a sandy bottom. Only by digging in the sandy bottom and in the sand were we able to recover part of her cargo of brightly colored plates and bowls, ceramic jugs, and several mortars of basalt.

We began our last day at Tyre, using the probes to determine the depth of sand and mud in the center of the southern part of the harbor. The day began badly, but ended happily. After about two hours on the numbingly cold bottom, I accidentally touched a poison scorpion fish. I had to surface immediately because of the severe nausea. While recuperating in the boat, I saw Kelley surface. He reported that his probe had struck something solid six feet beneath the sand. By this time he was out of air and too cold to go back down, so I went back in, although I was still dizzy and on the verge of vomiting. I loosened Kelley's probe, which felt as if it had been stuck in wood. Digging by hand in loose, powdery sand is no easy task. After an hour, I had been able to dig only a small hole about three feet deep.

Kelley then rejoined me and we finally reached a depth of four feet

Terracotta figurines found at Tyre

The author holding three terracotta Phoenician figurines he found on a shipwreck off Tyre in Lebanon

where we uncovered several Phoenician amphorae which our archaeologist quickly dated to the fifth century B.C. While widening the whole and uncovering more amphorae, I suddenly spotted three clay figurines ranging from 5 to 13 inches long. Nearby I found two more and brought them to the surface. The two archaeologists were ecstatic, their excitement was boundless when Kelley came up with two more. Our air was almost depleted and the sun was already fading on the horizon, so I made one last brief dive. Forcing my hand as far down in the deepest part of the hole we had dug as if it were a drill, I felt hard wood which to me was far more important than anything else we had found during our stay in Lebanon. Only a complete excavation of this site will reveal whether we found only a small section of the hull or a greater part of the wooden remains of a Phoenician ship that once plied the Mediterranean.

The statuettes we found are identical to those found at Shavei Zion in Israel (the two sites are only about 15 miles apart). The figurines present the goddess Tanit with her right hand raised in a gesture of blessing and her left hand either over her breast or holding a baby, and two of them show her pregnant.

Our trip was more than we had bargained for. We had come to Lebanon to study the feasibility of locating ancient shipwrecks, never thinking that we would find as much as we had in such a short time.

Immediately upon my return to the States, I began making plans to return to Tyre to excavate the Phoenician shipwreck, but my initial joy over the discovery soon died as frustration mounted. I had applied for an excavation permit, and Emir Chehab had indicated that it would be forthcoming shortly. Weeks dragged on to months and a year and a half passed before it was finally granted.

Upon arriving in Beirut in July 1974 to begin a two- to three-month excavation of the site, we learned that earlier that day, Israeli commandos had attacked and destroyed more than 40 fishing vessels at Tyre which were suspected of carrying terrorists into Israel. The Lebanese government placed the area off-limits to foreigners, and it remained off-limits for the three weeks while I waited in Beirut. Again in September and December that year, I attempted to get back to Tyre; but each time I was thwarted by the activities of the P.L.O. terrorists who use Tyre as their main base in southern Lebanon.

During the first eight months of 1975 matters got worse instead of better. I finally concluded that it might be years before I would be permitted to work at Tyre. Hearing of my dilemna, Dr. Elisha Linder invited me to search for Phoenician shipwrecks in his country's waters.

During September and October 1975 I spent five fascinating weeks working with Dr. Linder and his marvelous team of divers and archaeologists. It was almost a repeat of Tyre. We found two Roman, two Hellenistic, and four Phoenician shipwrecks in the general area of Acre, a port once used by the Phoenicians and later by the Crusaders. Unfortunately, all of the Phoenician wrecks lay on rocky bottoms, and none of the ship's wooden remains have survived. The Israelis proved to be so cooperative and enthusiastic about the construction of the Phoenician ship replica and voyage that I plan to return there and remain for as long as necessary to achieve my goal of sailing a Phoenician ship replica to the New World.